SPENSER STUDIES

XXI

SPENSER STUDIES

A Renaissance Poetry Annual
XXI

EDITED BY
William A. Oram
Anne Lake Prescott
Thomas P. Roche, Jr.

AMS PRESS
NEW YORK

SPENSER STUDIES
A RENAISSANCE POETRY ANNUAL

edited by Anne Lake Prescott, William A. Oram, and Thomas P. Roche, Jr.

is published annually by AMS Press, Inc. as a forum for Spenser scholarship and criticism and related Renaissance subjects. Manuscripts must be double-spaced, including notes, which should be grouped at the end and should be prepared according to *The Chicago Manual of Style.* Authors of essay-length manuscripts should include an abstract of 100–150 words and provide a disk version of the article, preferably in a Windows-compatible format. One copy of each manuscript should be sent to Thomas P. Roche, Jr., Department of English, Princeton University, Princeton, NJ 08544, one copy to Anne Lake Prescott, Department of English, Barnard College, Columbia University, 3009 Broadway, New York, NY 10027–6598, and one copy to William A. Oram, Department of English, Smith College, Northampton, MA 01063.

Please send inquiries concerning subscriptions or the availability of earlier volumes to AMS Press, Inc., Brooklyn Navy Yard, 63 Flushing Ave.—Unit 221, Bldg. 292, Suite 417, Brooklyn, NY 11205–1005, USA.

ISSN 0195–9468
Volume XXI, ISBN–10: 0–404–19221–1
ISBN–13: 978–0–404–19221–1

Contents

THERESA KRIER

Time Lords: Rhythm and Interval in Spenser's Stanzaic Narrative

This paper, the Kathleen Williams Lecture for 2006, uses the *katabasis* motif of *The Faerie Queene* I to formulate functions of the stanzaic interval and its alternation with stanzas, arguing that this form, best understood as the temporal phenomenon of the sojourn, shapes readerly experience, and that it has implications for genre and literary history. The paper examines the Night episode in *Faerie Queene* I.v; it examines the kind of reader proposed by Jonathan Goldberg in his 1981 book *Endlesse Worke*; it moves to the tradition of neoplatonically-inflected allegorical fiction with its journeys among multiple regions of the cosmos; it concludes with an analysis of George Saintsbury's famous remarks about the Spenserian rhythm.

> the lowering and sudden softening of all betweens [of which
> every few minutes one] out of which the first crash
> yet again can rise. Also the momentary lull: which now lets in
> the sound of distance in itself:
>
> —Jorie Graham[1]

*H*ARRY BERGER HAS RECENTLY REMINDED us that in the career of the Redcrosse Knight, Spenser makes much of the topos of the *katabasis*, "an infernal journey in quest of truth, prophecy, power, demonic assistance, or rehabilitation."[2] He mentions the journey to the house of Morpheus, Duessa's visitation to Night, Despair's dark cave, Despair's pictorial representation of the damned, Redcrosse's brief "descent" in the House of Holiness, even Error's cave. We might add Orgoglio's dungeon and Redcrosse's evening and morning

---

descents and risings during his battle with the Dragon.[3] For Berger, not surprisingly, the Spenserian *katabasis* deploys its massive literary history "to question, criticize, and parody . . . in short, to disestablish" the very tradition. Thus when Berger thinks of the temporality of *katabasis*, he is attracted to a Virgilian notion that such a descent is "a backward-looking discourse of nostalgia and pathos," a retreat from the political costs and complexities of an implied or represented Present, a retreat into a "dream-world produced by a spell-binding illusion" (Berger, "Archimago," 48–49). These are of course productive terms in which to think about the relation between a *katabasis* like the journey to Morpheus that's engineered by Archimago, and that episode's exposure of masculinist fantasy and illusion. But Redcrosse isn't the only focus of *katabasis* in this first book of Spenser's poem, and the *katabasis* has more hopeful temporal functions.

These functions emerge to view when we realize the frequency with which the *katabases* and *anabases* or ascents of *The Faerie Queene* Book I are linked to mythico-natural personages who figure daily temporal intervals, like Morpheus or Night, and to the many chronographiae of dawn and sunset. Again and again, in miniature *katabases*, Phoebus descends into the cool waters of the western ocean, lunar Cynthia floats upward and shines through the night, Aurora rises the next morning.[4] The constellating of these temporal figures, and the fluidity with which brief chronographiae ease into major set-pieces like the domains of Night or Morpheus, make me wonder what Spenser's up to. They serve, of course, as formulaic punctuation to episodes, as bows to an epic topos of descent, as conventional linkages of death with sleep—but they must surely be doing more. With more leisure we could survey the dozens of stanzas that bring us into the company of charismatic time-lords like Phoebus, Aurora, Tithonus, and Cynthia. Such personages establish, border, and shape various temporal intervals within the narrative and so help to establish the very sense of given world—and time—in the poem. But these temporal figures serve here as markers of rhythm: diurnal rhythm, stanzaic rhythm, the rhythms of the readerly process. And each of those rhythms relies on an underlying model of the sojourn: a lingering in a place, a lingering associated by its etymology both with the sense of a journey and with the turning of a day. The sojourn as formal, narrative time-unit constitutes one of Spenser's major contributions to later narrative and contemplative poetry. So here I turn first to the most spacious *katabasis* of Book I, Duessa's descent to Night in *The Faerie Queene* I.v, and its the rhythm of stanza and stanzaic interval, in order to think about the precise kind of sojourn provided by the interval. Then I consider the implications of this rhythm for a reader in our scholarly tradition, namely, for Jonathan Goldberg in 1981; then I offer a thread in the history of allegorical fictions, before closing with a return to epic and the Spenserian stanza rhythm.[5]

To think of Spenser's chronographiae, his descents and ascents, and his stanzaic intervals alike as sojourns has the virtue of making salient a number of odd and lovely Spenserian features. Spenser loves just marking how time passes as characters visit places.[6] We usually speak of episodes in a shorthand of their locales: the House of Holiness, the Bower of Bliss, the Cave of Mammon, the Garden of Adonis. But we could equally, perhaps better, speak of the characters' and readers' time spent there, the distances they traverse, the nature of their movements and of time passing: their sojourns. A rhythmically complex sojourn like Redcrosse's in the House of Holiness has elements in common with simpler sojourns like the chronographia of the sun's journey across the sky and its nightly immersion in the western sea. The rhythms of both these kinds of sojourns have implications for stanzaic form and for major traditions of narrative and allegorical poetry, as I will eventually suggest. First I demonstrate with the specific sojourn of Duessa's visit to Night and their journey to rescue Sansjoy in Book I, Canto v. The Redcrosse Knight has been visiting the House of Pride, where he prepares for combat with Sansjoy, whose two brothers Redcrosse has killed. The canto opens with an heroic and energetic dawn, and the emergence of the hero confident in his own solar, masculine strength. But the combat is long and tiring; the two warriors come to seem less and less distinguishable from each other; energy drains away from their increasingly heavy and cumbersome battle; the day passes. When Sansjoy is wounded and lies unconscious, Duessa arranges for a magical cloud to enfold him and make him invisible; at the same time Redcrosse has been seriously wounded and is borne off the battlefield. Both warriors are insentient and passive. Duessa, who has all along assumed the guise of Redcrosse's lady, weeps at his bedside but plans to visit the Underworld, and Night, in order to marshal a rescue for her true love Sansjoy, who still lies invisible on the battlefield.

The Night episode is of course a *katabasis*, a descent to an underworld, a critique of pride and Redcrosse's share in pride, an examination of coming near to death, and so on. But it's also a chronographia on a grand scale. It marks the onset of night-time on the day of Redcrosse's great battle with Sansjoy; it bears us through a long Underworld episode; at its end, the formidable grand-dame Night is morphing back into the diurnal phenomenon of night-time. This chronographia doesn't simply picture temporal phenomena; it shapes our readerly experience of the fictive world's temporality. The narrative treatment of Redcrosse's yielding consciousness after he's wounded merges into the reader's periodic yielding to stanza breaks. For the purposes of our subject here, the readerly experience of movement across stanzas and intervals is more germane than any interpretive activity about pride or heroism or gender. (Of course, the story itself is reflexive on this matter: it's about movement to a place that is also a temporal interval, night-time. Spenser likes episodes of movement, and they tend to carry metaphysical implications for metrics and form.) My point is that, in traversing Spenserian stanzaic intervals, we are all the time both drifting into latency and coming into consciousness.

Here's how that happens.

Night's episode is notable, broadly speaking, for its slide away from Redcrosse's story and down to an Underworld episode, in which the heroic topos of the underworld journey is surprisingly transferred to female characters; notable for its surprising alliance of Night with Duessa and the transformation of Night's hateful character. In this narrative moment Redcrosse and Sansjoy are wounded, asleep, insentient. The alert solar focus and assured will that drove the canto's opening yield altogether as heroic agency drifts to the mysterious powers and passages of Duessa and Night.

Narrative events happen to Redcrosse and Sansjoy, Duessa and Night in the first instance, but events, sensations, and affects are transferred to us readers also, to borrow William Empson's brilliant description of reading the Spenserian stanza, as we "yield to the verse movement very completely" (Empson, 34). On the level of plot and theme, Redcrosse and Sansjoy come to yield focus and agency because of the physical vulnerabilities of the fighters, the incoherencies of the chivalric system, and Redcrosse's erratic relationship to his spiritual values. On the level of form, the obscuring of heroic agency and the transfer of agency from characters to readers happen through the management of verb tenses, adverbs, and especially verb aspect, all of which shape the movements of stanzas into intervals. Verb aspect is the grammatical category indicating onset, duration, and completion of an action; in Spenser it works in conjunction with verb tenses and adverbs that reinforce a sense of duration in ongoing actions. Linguists tell us that imperfective verb aspect ("Jane was walking home") makes a character and an event more available to readers than perfective aspect ("Jane walked home"); with verbs of open duration we have greater access to the internal structure of an event than we do with perfective verbs.[7] Verb aspect keeps many actions of the Night episode open and ongoing, to create an effect of continuing or steady-state conditions; it alerts us to the salience of process and movement.

The stanzas describing the flurry of events that overtakes both wounded warriors as their battle is aborted repeatedly shift from a conventional past tense to the abrupt immediacy of present tense. At first this is a matter of events befalling, bewildering, or gathering into cloudy oblivion the warriors and their sense of heroic agency with a shift into present tense and into verb aspects of ongoing states. In just one instance of many, Redcrosse casts about for Sansjoy who is now magically shielded by an encompassing cloud:

> Not all so satisfied, with greedy eye
>   He sought all round about, his thirsty blade
>   To bathe in blood of faithlesse enimy;
>   Who all that while lay hid in secret shade:
>   He standes amazed, how he thence should fade.
>
> (I.v.15)[8]

Once the two knights have drifted into oblivion, the present tense shifts its attachment from the warriors to the grand, uncanny figures of Duessa and Night. Duessa begins these actions of duration in her semblance as Redcrosse's lady: at the bedside of the wounded warrior she "all the while . . . wept full bitterly" (I.v.17), and "So wept . . . vntill euentyde" (I.v.19). With darkfall, the verbs carry the ongoing action of her passage through and to Night, where she finds herself met by Night's own durative and present-tense actions: "But to the Easterne coast of heauen [Duessa] makes speedy way" (I.v.19); "Where griesly *Night*, with visage deadly sad, / . . . / She findes forth coming from her darksome mew" (I.v.20). It is by means of these open-ended actions of passage that Spenser carries the reader into stanzaic intervals, allowing brief moments of readerly drift, relinquishment of alert cognitive agency, while also keeping active our engagement with the story insofar as we continue to desire access to the internal structures of these events. In the stanza breaks, a reader experiences suspension, that great Spenserian-romance condition, but this is an active condition of change and novelty and surprise, not a static or somnolent condition.[9] It's a sojourn.

For Night and Duessa, narrative time fills with vigorous and heroic action. It also fills with the emotional grandeur of their verbal exchanges; this content of heightened action and affect is how Spenser gives us that access to the internal structure of an event of which

linguists speak. The surprising emotions that Night and Duessa express fashion a complication and expansion of readerly affect, perhaps
most notably when Night reverts to imperfect and present verb tenses
at the end of her stanza recognizing Duessa as her kin: "O welcome
child, whom I haue longed to see,/And now haue seene vnwares.
Lo now I goe with thee" (I.v.27). Night's concluding sentence, the
second half of the alexandrine concluding the stanza, might be expected to be future tense: "I *will go* with you as you ask." Her choice
of present tense adds gravity and force: the future is already in the
present. The alexandrine's verb aspect, initiated by the grandeur of
"Lo now," opens immediately into the subsequent stanza break and
therefore holds us in a sustained interim with Night's remarkable
sentiment. The apparent warmth and dignity of this new alliance,
and the duration of its surprise to the characters as well as to the
reader, are sustained by the continuing elevation of the journey's
often present-tense movements right through the stanzaic intervals:

> O welcome child, whom I haue longd to see,
> And now haue seene vnwares. Lo now I goe with thee.
>
> Then to her yron wagon she betakes,
>   And with her beares the fowle welfauourd witch:
>   Through mirkesome aire her ready way she makes.
>   (I.v.27–28)[10]

Such stanzaic intervals carry readers across a duration in which complex linguistic details of the present and preceding stanzas unfold,
disseminate, reconstellate within the reader, aside from any overt
interpretive and cognitive actions of reading. The interval invites
the reader to register a gathering volume (not necessarily conscious)
of the increasing density of the reading processes just past, whether
these move toward interpretive clarity and concepts, or toward
clouding, latency, drift.

   Many actions of the reader within stanzaic intervals are precon-
scious, sheer registrations of resonances among passages rather than
explicit interpretive questions, and these actions eddy back in reading
time as well as forward. We may *eventually* wonder: What is the
significance of having Redcrosse and Sansjoy double each other in
their oblivion, and in their new status of being tangential to the
narrative line? We'll wonder: Why and how do both Duessa and
Night seem to become figures of sympathy and gravitas? How does
Duessa's lament convert Night, who is essentially hateful, to a capacity for gestures of affection? What does it mean that Duessa and

Night turn out to be granddaughter and grandmother? What's the relationship between a fancy Nile simile occurring here and the unforgettable Nile simile of the first canto, in the Errour episode? and so on. But the experience of the stanzaic intervals permits, even fashions, a reading process in which cognitive engagements with such questions have not yet become explicit; they have not been fully posed as questions. We ride out the passage, encouraged to abandon cognitive focus by verb aspect, tense, and what Paul Alpers has beautifully analyzed as the independence of line (Alpers, 1967). This happens whether we have read the poem once or a hundred times; whether we have already written tomes analyzing these poetico-narrative events or not.

Spenser's stanzaic intervals invite breathing space for discontinuity, not to solve or interpret, nor solely to do the precognitive work that will make renewed conscious thought possible, but to hold open for the reader a brief sojourn in which unconscious representations and states can multiply. They multiply regardless of their future fates as material of consciousness, and it is this that gives Spenserian stanzaic intervals their characteristic sense of being variously buoyant and full, restfully spacious or alive with the rumble of potential action. Time has volume as well as duration, whether the tempo of any particular interval is swift or slow, smooth or rough, whether we're aware of pausing or reading swiftly for what comes next in the story. In Spenser, time has amplitude.

At the end of this excursus, Night is in the process of returning from a character to a power, thence to an entirely natural temporal process; the verbs accordingly return to imperfective and continuing actions. Night observes Hippolytus healing Sansjoy;

> Which hauing seene, from thence arose away
> The mother of dredd darkenesse, and let stay
> *Aueugles* sonne [i.e., Sansjoy] there in the leaches cure,
> And backe retourning tooke her wonted way,
> To ronne her timely race, whilst *Phoebus* pure
> In westerne waues his weary wagon did recure.

                                                            (I.v.44)

This fluency of a numinous being's multiple ontological states is, of course, another signature Spenserian gesture, and here serves as a cadence, releasing us from narrative episode altogether for as long a pause as one wishes before returning to the main narrative line. The

paired movements of Night and Phoebus form a glide between narrative and natural world, or between the stresses of following the Underworld descent and the rest of returning to diurnal process, in the
descent of Phoebus. It becomes a voluminous and even peaceful
stanza interval because we are in no hurry to rush across to the next
event, but to sojourn in the capacious, no longer grotesque environ-
ing of night, and into a space between Night and night that's poetic
(tropological and topical) and diurnal. This matter of the diurnal is
one that I return to when considering the literary-historical implications of Spenser's stanzaic intervals.

Spenser is, like any competent stanzaic poet, alert to the interval's
potential to refresh the reader's cognitive processes, to sharpen up
interpretive focus in its launch of the reader toward the brightening
consciousness of a new stanza or a cognitive return to an earlier
stanza. But my argument is rather the reverse: that Spenser particularly values the virtues of *lessened* consciousness, on an utterly regular
basis, in the interest of further *unconscious* representation and affect,
including the slowly dawning readiness for a new stanza. The rhythm
of stanza-interval-stanza-interval provides, to borrow Christopher
Bollas's words, an experience that feels psychically dense "because,
saturated with simultaneously evoked planes of unconscious ideation
occurring at the same time, they provoke a kind of not unpleasant
turbulence."[11]

Any stanza and interval by any poet could provide this experience,
but Spenser's stanzas are nearly unique in his period, I think, in
marking themselves *as* moments, temporal events, of intensity that
give way to dissemination or diffusion. It is the dawns, dusks, night,
moon, constellations, glimmering stars of *The Faerie Queene*, Night,
Aurora, Phoebus, Cynthia, and other time-lords whose arrivals frequently announce this oscillation. But even when they don't, the
process fashions readerly activity and tempo in this way. The complex, relatively conscious activity of reading a stanza with its many
threads of verbal structure, affect, and cognition gives way, in stanzaic
intervals, to an *evenly hovering inattentiveness*: unbinding, release, drift
into unconscious scatterings or destructions or renucleating of those
intensities. These disseminations in turn provoke new psychic intensities, new bindings of significance, in the reader about to meet the
next stanza.

In the temporal interval after stanza A, one becomes a rather different person from the one who will read stanza B. This is not an
entirely novel point but bears rehearsing here because it turns out
to have implications for form and genre. The familiar Spenserian
wandering takes place not only in the poem's unending green world

but also in untrackable, aleatory processes in the reader. Form, even the reliable Spenserian stanza form, is always unpredictable in its reading effects, or more precisely becomes activated by reading.[12] In the unbinding of the stanza break, the reader is released from the relative explicitness of the stanza into the sub fusc self-state one was in just a few minutes earlier, before having read the stanza. That earlier self already includes all the latent, sometimes far-ranging traces that had already arisen in reading earlier stanzas and cantos of the poem, which must have made the reader dense with submerged impulses toward further temporal waves of extension and retrogression. Of course, a reader may come to the poem ill at ease with or incapable of the mobility already guaranteed by the stanzaic interval. But the poem implies or fashions a more supple reader, a reader startlingly willing to drift or even to lose track of details. Nor is willingness to drift always a pleasant thing; it entails a capacity to yield to gaps, failures of meaning, repeated experiences of that death-like oblivion which is never far from Spenser's mind. A trust in drift is perforce a trust in vacancies.

This may be the reason that Jonathan Goldberg runs so hard from it, in his brilliant and influential 1981 book *Endlesse Worke*.[13] Goldberg makes much of the productivity of ruptures, discontinuities, and unanswerables in Spenserian narrative. Deeply informed by structuralism and the Barthes of *S/Z*, Goldberg makes these ruptures produce a compelling account of the frustrated reader. It's the feeling-tone of being such a reader that interests me about Goldberg's book. The Spenserian phrase "endless work," in Goldberg's title, carries for him a tone not of pleasure or exuberance, but of fatigue and entrapment. Thus "the poem is not merely finally unfinished, but frustratingly incomplete and inconclusive throughout, even when it encourages its readers to expect conclusions" (1); "the 1596 ending . . . refuses us even the partial and displaced satisfaction of the first reading and draws all the characters, and the reader too, into a situation of general frustration" (2). On every page, Goldberg's reader is a man alarmed, not to say panicked, by "the endless flood of signifiers" (25), by his own proliferation of interpretive questions, and by the apparent tease of the text; questions are not only undecidable but undecipherable:

The sentence [at *Faerie Queene* IV.vii.10.9] is quintessentially Spenserian, and the voice . . . produces a piece of text that appears to be capable of endless reading, yet is and remains finally

undecipherable. This line about the self undoes the voice speaking—it is no self speaking—and it undoes the reader reading—we will never come to the end of this line. Overloaded
with meaning, the words hover on the margins of meaning-
lessness. . . . We are overcome, as those in the text are overcome, by a demand the text makes and we cannot meet.

(109)

The notion of a reader confronting a poem that continually makes
excessive demands on him is a recurrent leitmotif: "the new ending
makes demands upon the reader to revaluate notions of narrative
satisfaction" (2); "the reader is being asked to take as the pleasure of
the text this moment of doubled loss . . . a paradox that nonetheless
satisfies continuing structural demands in the text's language" (3);
"The text is not a product or an object; it is a demanding production,
demanding both on the reader, and on the writer" (25) both a character and the narrator "act under equally stern commands. Even the
compassionate response that appeared to locate the narrator outside
the story is dictated: 'I must rue,' the narrator reports. *Must*" (18).
Moreover Goldberg's reader is continually disappointed; the very
insistence with which Goldberg promotes a Barthesian erotics of
reading and the idea of frustration's pleasure is built upon a deep
nostalgia or desire for a teleological clarity, which makes him surprisingly similar to nineteenth—and early-twentieth-century readers
who complained about Spenser's incoherence and who longed for
narrative clarity. It is startling, now, to register the notes of disappointed masculinist voyeurism in a passage that Goldberg quotes sympathetically in his preface, by Frank Kermode. "We are all fulfillment
men, *pleromatists*," Kermode says;

World and book, it may be, are hopelessly plural, endlessly
disappointing; we stand alone before them, aware of their arbi-
trariness and impenetrability. . . . Hot for secrets, our only conversation may be with guardians who know less and see less
than we can; and our sole hope and pleasure is in the perception
of a momentary radiance, before the door of disappointment is
finally shut on us.[14]

Goldberg's reader is always already overwhelmed, exhausted, fearful,
hoping against hope that pained subjection to the desire of an authoritative Other will come to be felt as a pleasure. Why is this reader,

flayed by what he experiences as relentlessly painful diminishments, incoherencies, and vertiginous losses of character and identity, continuing to read *The Faerie Queene*?

Goldberg recognizes that "the text undergoes continuous reconstitution in the empty spaces between stanzas" (21), but his description of the reader's experience is the nightmare inverse of that I offer here. One reason for this is that the tormented Goldbergian reader pays no attention to what might be taking place in those apparently blank voids; he seems to have no temporal experience of the poem and its formal oscillations of stanza and interval. He is like the kind of reader whom Umberto Eco remarks, one who does not know how to cooperate with the speed or pace of a narrative.[15] Nor does Goldberg's reader change with time or with the reading of the poem, except to become more irritable with frustration. To my mind this is the gravest difficulty of Goldberg's account of the reader of such a long poem. The regularity of stanza and interval over a large arc of time, and the variousness of its local effects, surely modulate the mind of the reader in unpredictable ways. Everything that occurs to such a reader in the accumulation and drift of stanzas and the amplitude of intervals structures an unrushed release or distancing of the reader from any interpretive urgencies of the narrative. The capacity for the kind of distancing that scholars perceive these days between the poet and his materials is made possible in large part by the rhythm of alternating stanza and interval.

We don't speak of such internal distantiation in terms of tempo or release or drift, however. Rather, insofar as distancing and tempo are both critical topoi, it is salutary to realize that most instances of such analysis—always instances of vigorous interpretation—are, like Goldberg's book, subtended by a logic about *a struggle for mastery* between text and person. This is an issue always at stake in attempts to describe the experience of reading *The Faerie Queene*. Thus, for instance, Goldberg's tense peppering of the text with interpretive questions and challenges implies a struggle for mastery between reader and text; Harry Berger continually stages a contest between poet or narrator and the stuff of his stories. Neither Goldberg nor Berger is going to allow himself or his proxy (reader or poet) to lose that struggle.[16] Or again, older critical accounts of reading the poem evince unhappiness or anxiety with a poem that, as it seemed to readers at the turn of the twentieth century, encourages enervation and passivity in the reader. This is also a struggle for mastery; here the reader is losing the game, and furthermore losing his manliness to the indolence of the poem. Perhaps we can simply step outside this logic underlying discussions of distancing and of tempo by positing a

readerly experience that doesn't involve a struggle for mastery, and
this by taking into account the idea that stanzaic intervals, like stanzas
with their more evident mental actions, have duration; they are sojourns. One might say to a Goldbergian reader: This moment is a
sojourn, not an imprisonment. The combination of utter reliability
through thousands of stanzas and intervals, along with their open
textures of syntax and space, creates a deliberateness and temporal ease
that permits but does not demand interpretation and interrogation,
critique and parody, or any other intellectual intensities within the
reader. But the experience of reading is more than interpretation.
This, too, isn't entirely a novel idea; only we don't link it to genres
and literary traditions very often

Jeff Dolven addresses in gentler vein a problem similar to that
experienced by the Goldbergian reader, and uses the word "para-
noid" to describe this kind of reading. "Spenser may not be the only
inexhaustible Renaissance poet, but there is something distinctively
exhausting about reading his romance, a sense peculiar to him of
wandering in a vast, interinanimated landscape within the bounds of
which nothing can be understood without understanding everything."[17] His notion of Spenser's alternative to the nightmare of
ceaseless interpretation is that the poem itself "entertains the idea that
what may save us—characters and readers—is a kind of metaphorical
putting down the book" (35), by means of an idea of "ordinariness"
adapted from Stanley Cavell. For Dolven, the poem blessedly provides us, occasionally, with "the inarticulate detail and its consequences, the apparent lapse out of allegory altogether into the
everyday" (37). This is a fine response to the Goldbergian panic of
reading, and his mentioning of allegory is entirely to the point. I
want to turn now to allegory, thinking of it less as a generalized
interpretive demand arousing anxiety than as a poetic and narrative
tradition, the stories of which we might desire to read.

My present thought about allegorical fiction runs counter to a
current and vivid sense, perhaps most influentially crystallized by
Gordon Teskey, of the *violence* of allegory. Too bright a focus on the
violence of allegory as interpretive practice might dim the particulars
of specific allegorical fictions, especially when this focus on violence
turns out to encourage an overestimation of the stranglehold that the
very idea of "allegory" has within allegorical fictions

Because I had been thinking about *katabases* and chronographiae
and allegorical personages like Night and Duessa in *The Faerie Queene*,
I'd also been thinking about such descents, ascents, dawns, dusks,
and nights in earlier allegorical fictions, chiefly those by Macrobius,
Martianus Cappella, Boethius, Bernardus Silvestris, Alan of Lille,

Chaucer. These are scopey poets, who freely range the resources of allegorized epic and cosmogony, in order to represent regions and residences of allegorical personages and deities, and to represent journeys among those regions. A sense of mobility among regions of the cosmos has always been a feature of allegorized epic and philosophical poetry. In late antiquity the converging traditions of Stoic, Neoplatonic, and Gnostic allegorizing make possible not only a narrative complexity in allegorical fictions, but also great sophistication in their representations of time that marks movement among cosmic regions, and the implications of temporality in allegorical *katabases*.[18] The early Chaucer is an especially important figure in the tradition of allegorical temporality that Spenser takes up. Chaucer's reading and dreaming protagonists assimilate allegorical descents and ascents among regions of the universe to *diurnal* rhythms in this world: dawn and dusk, reading late into the night, drifting into sleep and awakening. It's from Chaucer's dream visions that Spenser takes his cue to link the great regions and journeys of allegorical fiction with figures of diurnal temporality, the sunrises and sunsets and night-times with which we began.

But why? Why that link, and why should it matter? I go into this Chaucerian connection more fully in another essay, but here I'll say this. The Chaucerian dreamer's immediate, first-person experiences—of pain, of the romance of reading, of sleepiness, of eagerness, and so on—put the tropes of allegorical fictions, including ascents, descents, and dreams, to work in the service of opening us readers to the immediacies of creaturely existence: being embodied, having feelings of one's own and sympathy about others' creaturely condition. Joseph Campana argues that Spenser's is a project that seeks narrative and poetic routes to sympathy, openness to the corporeal and affective experiences of other creatures. It seeks to counter alienation from the lived experience of corporeality, to keep us close to acknowledgment of the pains, pleasures, processes of embodiment: "Spenserian poetics makes available a vitality of material experience otherwise occluded by the clarity and truth that violence comes to be known as. . . . Spenser's poetry asks us to participate in the painful experience of animation and in the vitality that inheres in the opacity of living flesh."[19]

It may seem paradoxical that Spenser uses resources grounded in a tradition of allegorical fictions to make his argument against what we take as a constraining fiat to read allegorically, resources like the descents and ascents, minor deities and their houses, a fictive universe comprised of many cosmic planes. I suggest that he uses such resources *because* their narrative multiplicity of cosmic domains immerses the reader in many kinds of matter, and sojourns in many kinds of time; and further, that this multiplicity of time and cosmic region is what allows for latitude in the degrees of reader enrollment that any one sojourn might claim. The journeys, descents, and ascents of allegorical fictions elicit a reader who remains mobile rather than one who seeks the violence of fixity, one who opens up to temporal experience, its adventures and its pathos, rather than straining to live up to the presumed demandingness of a text. The journey from the stanzas into the stanzaic intervals, then through them and on into another stanza, creates a rhythm of identification and disidentification allowing for complex ironies, combinations of sympathy and detachment, narrative suspicion and narrative trust. This would imply, perhaps, that the poem is less invested in control over a reading community whose wayward reading causes its author anxiety, but more in the temporal process by which it can fashion an audience of readers who move to its tempo.

I've spoken about the poem's shaping of a reader's trust. To conclude I turn to the question of *Spenser's* trust. It happens that one of the great commonplaces of Spenser scholarship is that very issue of trust, in the Spenserian narrator. Does he trust? What does he trust? Does he trust his materials? his readers? the given resources of his language? some external set of values? Paul Alpers argues that Spenser demonstrates "confidence that he speaks for realities genuinely external to him. . . . [H]is mode of narration . . . derives its authority . . . from theological, cosmic, moral, and historical truths and the literary traditions which record them."[20] Alternatively, Harry Berger finds a relentlessly ironic narrator, interrogating, sending up, parodying discourses. Thus, the text "develops a critique of the storytelling mode and of its picture-making narrative and of its moral allegory; it represents them as elements of a prime-time pacifier."[21] From Berger's point of view, critics as various as Northrop Frye, Stephen Greenblatt, and Paul Alpers too easily take straight the poet's commitment to discourses in his world; instead, he argues, what Greenblatt calls "reality as given by ideology" "is continually posed, deposed, and exposed as a countertext."[22] A Bergerish poet would trust nothing at all but his own struggle for mastery over his discourses.

But all these readers cleave to the images, words, syntax, assertions, and propositions of *The Faerie Queene*, as do most of us most of the time. We might otherwise imagine that what Spenser and his narrator trust is rhythm itself, worked out in the sequence of stanza and interval. Kenneth Gross gestures toward this idea of trust in rhythm when he says, "we need to reflect on what it meant for the poet to have a thing like this [the stanza form] on which he could depend, a form to which he could commit himself and his writing day after day, year after year."[23]

Gross's remark implies that something large and urgent about life is at stake in Spenser's stanza form, when taken over the decades of Spenser's writing life; here I turn the point slightly to think about trust in the duration of an interval. Spenser's thousands of oscillations between stanza and interval elicit a sense from readers that even when events in a stanza, or an episode, or a life seem to be at an end, *something* does continue. Sansjoy and Redcrosse both return to the realm of the living. Night returns to her diurnal role as a reliable temporal process, linked with sunrise. New possibilities catch the Spenserian characters who so regularly venture into some realm of death. One of the ways that the momentary drift or oblivion of the interval sustains the poem and its readers is by making room for that radical of oblivion, death itself. The letting go of a stanza's interpretive relevance, one kind of descent into oblivion, is countered when a wave of new stanzaic narrative rises to catch the reader: the ascent of an inventive *anabasis,* and new constellations of energy in interpretive action.

The rhythm of stanza and interval, with its surprising relation to death, therefore has its heroic, even epic aspect. In the most unrestrained description of Spenserian stanza breaks, George Saintsbury says this: "the long Alexandrine at the close seems to launch [the stanza] on towards its successor *ripae ulterioris amore,* or rather with the desire of fresh striking out in the unbroken though wave-swept sea of poetry. Each is a great stroke by a mighty swimmer."[24] Saintsbury's prose, we may think, is nothing if not impressionistic. But it poses a strong argument, for he is staunchly holding a line about "the *untiring* character" of Spenser's poem against readers of the late nineteenth and early twentieth centuries who condemn the indolence of Spenserian versification. Saintsbury insists: "I know of course that it has been the fashion to deny this [untiring] quality. But I say boldly that anybody who finds the *Faerie Queene* wearisome either has not given it a fair trial . . . or else has no real and vital love for poetry as poetry—" (Saintsbury 367).

Saintsbury has already, triumphantly fueled this argument with a double epic allusion. He begins with the great Virgilian line from the *Aeneid,* where souls of the dead waiting to cross over into the underworld stretch their hands "in yearning for the farther shore" (*Aeneid* III.314). But Saintsbury's *correctio* surprisingly shifts to the Homeric vigor of Odysseus' swim in *Odyssey* V, when Saintsbury speaks of a new stanza as "the desire of fresh striking-out in the unbroken though wave-swept sea of poetry." Odysseus, who early in Book V has had to decide whether to rejoin his mortal life with Penelope, has left Kalypso who dwells on the isle of Ogygia or Oblivion, been shipwrecked, nearly descends to death and the fatal oblivion of the sea. But at the prompting of the sea-nymph Ino he awakens to his desire to live, and strikes off through the waves, toward life. After an interval with the Phaiakians who rescue him and convey him home, he wakens from sleep to find himself in the Cave of the Nymphs. Not accidentally, it is a great ancient allegorist, Porphyry, who understands this Cave as the site of another *katabasis*: this one the whole region below the Milky Way into which the starry soul falls to begin its sojourn as an embodied and temporal creature.

Macalester University

NOTES

1. Jorie Graham, "The Complex Mechanism of the Break," in *Never: Poems* (New York: HarperCollins, 2003), 35. Copyright © 2002 by Jorie Graham. Reprinted by permission of HarperCollins Publishers.

2. Harry Berger, Jr., "Archimago: Between Text and Countertext," *Studies in English Literature 1500–1900* 43.1 (2003): 19–64, at 63.

3. For the history of the topos, see pages 228–38 of the Variorum edition, *The Works of Edmund Spenser: Faerie Queene, Book One*, ed. Edwin Greenlaw, Charles Osgood, and Frederick Padelford (Baltimore: Johns Hopkins University Press, 1932); A. C. Hamilton's notes in *The Faerie Queene,* 2nd ed. (New York: Longman, 2001). Hamilton's edition is the one cited in this essay.

Jon Whitman provides an excellent discussion of passages of ascent and descent in the context of allegorical fictions and allegorized epic, in *Allegory: The Dynamics of an Ancient and Medieval Technique* (Cambridge: Harvard University Press, 1987), chapter 3.

4. See, e.g., 1.1.22, 1.1.32–33, 1.2.1, 1.2.29, 1.3.15–16, 1.4.44, 1.5.2, 1.11.31, 1.11.33, 1.11.51–52, 1.12.2, 1.12.21, besides the set-pieces on Morpheus and Night. The great chronographiae of sunrise and sunset continue throughout the 1590 *Faerie Queene*, but most thickly populate Book I. Geoffrey Hiller has useful remarks on this alternation of night and day in his entry "Night" in *The Spenser Encyclopedia*, ed. A. C. Hamilton, et al. (Toronto: University of Toronto Press, 1990). Jon Quitslund, in discussion, raises the relevance of Orpheus to Spenser's understanding of Night; in my view it is Orpheus and Hesiod together who interest Spenser for their primal means of establishing time and space as spreading out within a poetico-fictive world. To borrow Angus Fletcher's concept, Orpheus and Hesiod are in this sense *configurative* (Hugh Haughton, "Progress and Rhyme: 'The Nightingale's Nest' and Romantic Poetry," in *John Clare in Context*, ed. Adam Phillips, Haughton and Geoffrey Summerfield [Cambridge: Cambridge University Press, 1994], 53, cited by

Angus Fletcher in *A New Theory for American Poetry* [Cambridge: Harvard University Press, 2004]).

5.   The most formative remarks are those of William Empson, *Seven Types of Ambiguity* (1930; 2nd revised ed. London: Chatto and Windus and New Directions, 1947; New Directions paperback 1966), 33–34. See also George Saintsbury, *A History of English Prosody from the Twelfth Century to the Present Day* (London: Macmillan, 1923), 3 volumes; vol. 1, pages 363–69; Paul Alpers, *The Poetry of* The Faerie Queene (Princeton: Princeton University Press, 1967); Kenneth Gross, " 'Each Heav'nly Close': Mythologies and Metrics in Spenser and the Early Poetry of Milton," *PMLA* 78. 1 (January 1983): 21–36; Gross, "Shapes of Time: On the Spenserian Stanza," *Spenser Studies: A Renaissance Poetry Annual* XIX (2004): 27–35; Jeff Dolven, "The Method of Spenser's Stanza," *Spenser Studies* XIX (2004): 17–25; Donald Cheney, *Spenser's Image of Nature: Wild Man and Shepherd in "The Faerie Queene"* (New Haven: Yale University Press, 1966), 97–98; John Hollander, "The Footing of His Feet: A Long Line Leads to Another," in *Melodious Guile: Fictive Pattern in Poetic Language* (New Haven: Yale University Press, 1988), 164–79, and "Spenser's Undersong," ibid., 148–63. Among the collections reprinting excerpts from readers of four centuries, including crucial and sometimes hostile passages by Hazlitt, Lowell, Walter Raleigh, Yeats, G. Wilson Knight on Spenserian versification, see *Edmund Spenser*, ed. Paul Alpers, Penguin Critical Anthologies (Harmondsworth, England: Penguin, 1969). The present essay extends some aims of Paul Alpers's 1971 study of the temporality of the Spenserian line, as Andrew Escobedo points out in conversation. Roger Kuin writes powerfully about gaps in sonnet sequences in "The Gaps and the Whites: Indeterminacy and Undecideability in the Sonnet Sequences of Sidney, Spenser, and Shakespeare," *Spenser Studies* VIII (1987): 251–85.

6.   Thus Richard McCabe, *The Pillars of Eternity: Time and Providence in* The Faerie Queene (Dublin: Irish Academic Press, 1989): "The extent of any given quest . . . is generally measured in terms of its duration in time. . . . At the moment we meet them, the present identity of any knight is virtually determined by the space he has travelled and the places he has stopped" (30).

7.   Carol J. Madden and Rolf A. Zwaan, "How Does Verb Aspect Constrain Event Representations?" in *Memory and Cognition* 31.5 (2003): 663–72.

8.   See also I.v.13, 16, 17.

9.   On dilation and suspension see Patricia Parker, *Inescapable Romance: Studies in the Poetics of a Mode* (Princeton: Princeton University Press, 1979).

10.   See also the transition between I.v.28 and 29.

11.   Bollas, *Cracking Up: The Work of Unconscious Experience* (New York: Hill and Wang, 1995), 56–57.

12.   Ellen Rooney, "Form and Contentment," *Modern Language Quarterly* 61.1 (March 2000): 17–40: "The work of form is revealed only in the act of reading, and just as no theory is ever fully adequate to a textual instance, no subjectivity ever fully realized in an individual, no formal feature stands as the full expression of a text *before* reading has set it in motion" (38).

Carol Kaske makes the wonderful proposal, in discussion, that perhaps the solution to the riddle of why Spenserian stanzas set the first, iambic line flush with the hexameter line, as if to imply that they are both long lines, is that the poet wants to create a visual frame for the interval. Theodore Steinberg points out that readers see on the page not only stanzas and intervals, but numbers heading each stanza; in terms of their effects on readers, one might imagine that the numbers provide stable points of orientation.

13.   Goldberg, *Endlesse Worke: Spenser and the Structures of Discourse* (Baltimore: Johns Hopkins University Press, 1981). Goldberg is not alone in his anxious sense of the pressures on the reader; see Maureen Quilligan's entry "reader in *The Faerie Queene*" in *The Spenser Encyclopedia*. As Anne Lake Prescott made clear in discussion, anxiety itself became a critical commonplace in the latter third of the twentieth century, a partner to the issue of struggles for mastery.

14.   Goldberg, xii, citing Frank Kermode, *The Genesis of Secrecy* (Cambridge: Harvard University Press, 1979), 72 and 145.

15.   Eco, *Six Walks in the Fictional Woods* (Cambridge: Harvard University Press, 1994), 5.

16.   Berger's rhetoric tells the tale: "the written text may represent, supplement, reinforce, and extend the author's presence, or the presence of authority; on the other hand, written discourse escapes the author's intention, is appropriated by readerships, and confronts the author with the problem of trying to anticipate, control, and outmaneuver invisible readers." "Narrative as Rhetoric in *The Faerie Queene*," *English Literary Renaissance* 21.1 (1991): 9. David Lee Miller provides a useful survey of the history of readers' interest in distancing, under the rubric of the large scholarly project of working out the text's ways of "staging and exploring the disjunctions between . . . conventions" (163) in "*The Faerie Queene* (1590)," in *A Critical Companion to Spenser Studies*, ed. Bat van Es (Houndmills: Palgrave Macmillan, 2006), 116–38, at 161–64.

17.   Dolven, "When to Stop Reading *The Faerie Queene*," in *Never Again Would Birds' Song Be the Same: Essays on Early Modern and Modern Poetry in Honor of John Hollander*, ed. Jennifer Lewin (New Haven: Beinecke Library, Yale University, 2002): 35–54.

18.   See Jon Whitman, *Allegory: The Dynamics of an Ancient and Medieval Technique* (Cambridge: Harvard University Press, 1999): "With the coalescence of Jewish, Platonic, and Gnostic elements in early Christian exegesis, the different senses of a divine text come to imply different orders of the cosmos, which in turn imply different stages in time, as an individual or a civilization converts from flesh to spirit" (68–69).

19.   Joseph Campana, "On Not Defending Poetry: Spenser, Suffering, and the Energy of Affect," *PMLA* 120.1 (January 2005): 33–48 at 46. On Spenser's opposition to a hardening of the heart associated with allegorical interpretation, see also Theresa Krier, "Psychic Deadness in Allegory: Spenser's House of Mammon and Attacks on Linking" in *Imagining Death in Spenser and Milton*, ed. Elizabeth Jane Bellamy, Patrick Cheney, and Michael Schoenfeldt (New York: Palgrave Macmillan 2003), 46–64.

20.   Alpers, "Narration in *The Faerie Queene*," *English Literary History* 44. 1 (Spring 1977): 19–39, at 28.

21.   Berger, "Archimago," 28.

22.   Berger, 30. Greenblatt's phrase comes from *Renaissance Self-Fashioning: From More to Shakespeare* (Chicago: University of Chicago Press, 1980), 192.

23.   Gross, 2004, 31.

24.   Saintsbury, *History of English Prosody*, I: 366–67. Kenneth Gross describes the effect of the alexandrine in diction that summons a romance mode: "the hexameter acts as a minimal conceptual refrain, gathering half-remembered gestures from earlier stanzas, prophesying the energies of those which come later. The hexameter always holds us with a slight breathlessness, leads us to that silence which follows the close of each stanza—for we must always remember that it is a temporal space and silence between the stanzas, as this is continually recharged and made strange by the recurrent hexameter, that . . . keeps the poem alive, lends the unfolding cantos their particular lightness and confidence in confronting shifted possibilities, unexpected contingencies of order and change" (Gross 2004, 30).

For Porphyry's middle-Platonic allegorical interpretation of Homer's Cave of the Nymphs, see *On the Cave of the Nymphs*, trans. Thomas Taylor (Grand Rapids, MI: Phanes Press, 1991).

I am grateful to the organizers of Spenser at Kalamazoo for the invitation to speak, and to the audience for the suggestions that emerged from discussion after the lecture. Thanks also to Elizabeth Jane Bellamy and Elizabeth Harvey, who read drafts of this essay.

STEVEN K. GALBRAITH

Spenser's First Folio: The Build-It-Yourself Edition

The first folio of Spenser's works appears to play the traditional role of the literary folio and serve as a monument to its author. A thorough examination, however, reveals a cheaply produced and bibliographically unstable folio, which was printed in sections over the course of more than a decade. Further investigation of the folio's print history suggests that its instability was a part of an intentional strategy by its publisher, Matthew Lownes, to create a publication that accommodated both bookseller and book buyer. The result was a "build-it-yourself" folio that was more cost-effective for the publisher and provided more buying options for consumers.

MONUMENTS—STONE AND OTHERWISE

*I*N 1620, ANNE CLIFFORD, Countess of Dorset, commissioned Nicholas Stone to erect the first monument to Edmund Spenser. It bore this inscription:

> HEARE LYES (EXPECTING THE SECOND
> COMMINGE OF OVR SAVIOVR CHRIST
> JESVS) THE BODY OF EDMOND SPENCER,
> THE PRINCE OF POETS IN HIS TYME;
> WHOSE DIVINE SPIRRIT NEEDS NOE
> OTHIR WITNESSE THEN THE WORKS

Spenser Studies: A Renaissance Poetry Annual, Volume XXI, Copyright © 2006 by AMS Press, Inc. All rights reserved.

WHICH HE LEFT BEHINDE HIM.
HE WAS BORNE IN LONDON IN
THE YEAR 1510, AND
DIED IN THE YEARE
1596.[1]

While the details of the inscription that first catch the eye are most likely the erroneous birth and death dates, more intriguing is the curious title given to Spenser, "The Prince of Poets in His Time." It is not the phrase "Prince of Poets," a fine title for Spenser, but rather the "in *his* time" (my emphasis). This wording is deceptive. What at first seems like high praise is, at a second glance, also restrictive, confining Spenser's literary title to the period in which he was alive.

As a point of comparison, take Ben Jonson's famous exaltation of Shakespeare, "He was not of an age, but for all time." Written for Shakespeare's first folio in 1623–roughly the same time as the inscription on Spenser's tomb—Shakespeare's literary reputation is said to be without bounds. His works are not simply relevant to "his time," but "for all time." Four centuries later, Jonson's observation has certainly come to fruition and has become the most frequently quoted description of Shakespeare. Spenser's title is often quoted as well, but when modern scholars cite it they usually amend the monument's inscription to the unrestricted and unambiguous "Prince of Poets."

Monuments are not always made of stone. Equally reverential and often equally enduring are the *printed* monuments to authors, the folios. As Fredson Bowers observed, "it is true that in general the Elizabethans printed works in folio that they considered to be of a superior merit or of some permanent value."[2] More recently, Peter W. M. Blayney has noted, "the folio format was usually reserved for works of reference (on subjects as theology, law, history, and heraldry) and for the collected writings of important authors, both ancient (Homer, Tacitus, Saint Augustine) and modern (Spenser, Sir Phillip Sidney, Bishop Joseph Hall)."[3] Blayney further cites Ben Jonson's folio *Workes* (1616)[4] and the first folio of Shakespeare (1623),[5] two editions that together have received the lion's share of scholarly discussion. In the case of both books, folio format constitutes an expression of authorship. As David Scott Kastan observes, "the ambition of the folio is to create Shakespeare as an author."[6] For Jonson's 1616 folio, Kastan's observation might be slightly altered to read "Jonson's ambition in producing his folio is to create *himself* as an author." In this way, folios can serve to monumentalize an author, or, for authors to monumentalize themselves.

Spenser's work first appeared in folio in 1609, when Matthew Lownes published a folio edition of *The Faerie Queene*, printed by his brother Humphrey Lownes.[7] Two years later, Matthew Lownes incorporated what was left of the original print run of the folio *Faerie Queene* into the first folio edition of Spenser's works: *The Faerie Queen: The Shepheards Calendar: Together with the Other Works of England's Arch-Poet, Edm. Spenser: Collected Into One Volume, And Carefully Corrected*, also printed by Humphrey Lownes.[8]

At first glance, the first folio of Spenser's works may appear to play the role of an apparently stable monument to the author. However, like Stone's 1620 monument to Spenser, appearances can be deceiving. A thorough examination reveals an economically produced and bibliographically unstable folio. Further examination of the folio's print history suggests that its instability was a part of an intentional strategy by its publisher, Matthew Lownes, to create a publication that accommodated both bookseller and book buyer. The result was a "build-it-yourself" folio that was more cost-effective for the publisher and provided more buying options for consumers. In short, Spenser's first folio was more a consumer's product than a printed monument to its author.

THE 1609 FOLIO *FAERIE QUEENE*

By the end of the sixteenth century, nearly the whole of Spenser's body of work had found its way into print, the exceptions being the *Two Cantos of Mutabilitie* and *A View of the Present State of Ireland*. William Ponsonby, who had been Spenser's chief publisher, produced the last of his Spenser editions in 1596 when he printed parts one and two of *The Faerie Queene, The Fowre Hymns* (with the second edition of *Daphnaïda)*, and *Prothalamion*. A year later, John Harrison II published the fifth edition of *The Shepheardes Calender*.[9] After this, twelve years would pass before any of Spenser's work would once again find its way into print

In the meantime, William Ponsonby died and the rights he held to Spenser's works were transferred to his brother-in-law, Simon Waterson, a London bookseller who ran a shop at the Sign of the Crown in St. Paul's Churchyard.[10] On September 3, 1604, shortly after Ponsonby's death, the *Stationers' Register* records:

Master Waterson Entered for his copies, certen copies which were Master Ponsonbies . . . 1 *The Arcadia* by Philip Sidney ij

The ffayrie quene both partes of Spencer 3 *The felicitie of man* by
Sir R[ichard] Barc[k]ley 4 Master Edmondes his *Discours vppon*
C[A]EASARs Comentaries both partes 5 *The Fflorentine History*
by Machiauel[li] 6 *MAMILLIA* the second parte 7 The Card of
ffantasie[11]8 Lipsius *politiques* Englishe 9 Mounsieur [Du] Plessis
[Mornay] *of life and Deathe* Englished by the Countesse of Pembroke.[12]

Although Ponsonby held the rights to all of Spenser's works save
The Shepheardes Calender and the Spenser-Harvey correspondence,
the only work that he officially transferred to Waterson was *The Faerie*
Queene. It does appear, however, that the rights to all of Ponsonby's
Spenser titles transferred along with *The Faerie Queene*.[13]

Two months after receiving Ponsonby's titles, Waterson transferred eight of the nine, including *The Faerie Queene*, to Matthew
Lownes.[14] Interestingly, Waterson retained part of his rights to Sidney's *Arcadia*, which he entered into the *Stationers' Register* with Matthew Lownes.[15] The two later co-published a folio edition in 1605.[16]
In the five years after receiving Ponsonby's catalog from Waterson
in 1604, Lownes published four of the eight titles: Sir Clement Edmondes's *Obseruations vpon Cæsars Commentaries* in 1604[17] and 1609;
Philippe de Mornay's *A Discourse of Life and Death* in 1606 and 1608;
Robert Greene's *Card of Fancy* or *Gwydonius* in 1608; and Spenser's
The Faerie Queene in 1609.

With the exception of the addition of the *Two Cantos of Mutabilitie*,
Lownes's 1609 *Faerie Queene* is, for the most part, a folio reprint of
Ponsonby's 1596 quarto. It omits the letter to Ralegh, the commendatory poems, and dedicatory sonnets, which had appeared in the
1590 edition.[18] Lownes's edition also omits the Saint George and the
Dragon woodcut, which appears at the end of Book I of *The Faerie*
Queene in both the 1590 and 1596 quarto editions. This woodcut
originally belonged to John Wolfe, the printer of the 1590 edition,
who lent it to Richard Field, the printer of the 1596 edition.[19]
Lownes evidently made no effort to acquire this woodcut or to commission a new woodcut to replace it. In fact, he commissioned no
new woodcuts for the folio. Instead, generic reuse woodcuts supplied
the decorative matter. There is nothing surprising about this practice.
Indeed, reusing generic woodcuts was a very common practice. Yet,
not all folio printings at this time exhibit such a no-frills approach.
The printers and publishers of other contemporary folios paid the
extra expense of commissioning new woodcuts that specifically cor-
responded to their projects. Lownes, however, stuck to the more

common, economical production style, a style that not only marked his 1609 *Faerie Queene*, but also his 1611 folio edition of Spenser's works.

SPENSER'S FOLIO WORKS 1611–c.1625

How well the 1609 folio *Faerie Queene* sold is difficult to assess. Bibliographic evidence, however, demonstrates that sometime around 1610 or early 1611 much of the original print run remained unsold. Matthew Lownes used copies in stock as the foundation for a folio of Spenser's works, to which he added folio editions of the following: *The Faerie Queene*'s dedication to Elizabeth, the letter to Ralegh, and the commendatory poems and dedicatory sonnets; *The Shepheardes Calender*; and *Colin Clouts Come Home Again* with Spenser's other minor poems.[20]

Before Lownes could publish the whole of Spenser's printed works, he had to secure permission to print Spenser's most popular work, *The Shepheardes Calender*.[21] He had acquired the rights to all of the works of Spenser owned by Ponsonby, but this did not include *The Shepheardes Calender*. The rights to this book belonged to John Harrison II, who had published all of the four editions that followed Hugh Singleton's first edition in 1579. How Lownes came to print *The Shepheardes Calender* is uncertain, because no record of any transfer of the rights from Harrison to Lownes exists in the *Stationers' Register*. There are two possibilities: "Lownes may have made some private arrangement with him [Harrison] for the publication of this edition"; or, Lownes published it "without securing Harrison's consent."[22] The former is the more likely explanation, because Lownes's 1611 folio edition included the twelve woodcut illustrations that had accompanied each month's eclogue in every preceding quarto edition of the book.

It is worthy of note that in the course of an economical production Matthew Lownes would go out of his way to acquire the use of these woodcuts. Unlike the Saint George and the Dragon woodcut, which Lownes chose not to include or reproduce in his folio *Faerie Queene*, *The Shepheardes Calender*'s twelve woodcuts are an intrinsic part of the book. Each illustration constitutes a more or less accurate visual representation of the story presented in its corresponding eclogue. Not only did Lownes find it essential to include these illustrations, his brother Humphrey Lownes had to devise a clever way to fit the quarto-sized woodcuts onto the larger folio page. He did so by buttressing each of the woodcuts with two layers of decorative borders, thus enhancing their size.[23]

Harrison surely retained ownership of these woodcuts. Their appearance in the folio therefore suggests that Harrison and Matthew Lownes had entered into an arrangement that included permission to print *The Shepheardes Calender* and the use of the woodcuts. Lownes was most definitely in contact with Harrison for the second printing of the folio *Shepheardes Calender* in 1617. The title page of this edition bears the following imprint: "Printed by Bar: Alsop *for* Iohn Harrison the elder, and are to bee solde at *his* shop at the signe of the golden Anker" (my emphases).[24] The "for" in this imprint indicates that Harrison was the publisher of this edition. He either discovered that Lownes was printing his work and asserted his rights to the text, or, more likely, retained his rights throughout and amended an earlier arrangement with Lownes to include more participation in its production and sale.

With all of Spenser's previously printed work accounted for, Lownes published *The Faerie Queen: The Shepheards Calendar: Together with the other Works of England's Arch-Poet, Edm. Spenser: Collected Into One Volume, And Carefully Corrected* in 1611. Rather than producing it in a single print run, he spread publication over a decade. ˎ

Each of the seven parts to the folio would go through two different printings from 1611 to sometime after 1620.[25] The parts are as follows:

1) Title page and dedication to Elizabeth, printed in 1611 and 1617.
2) *The Faerie Queene* part 1, printed in 1609 and sometime between 1613 and 1617.
3) *The Faerie Queene* part 2, printed in 1609 and 1612–13.
4) *The Shepheardes Calender,* printed in 1611 and 1617.
5) *Colin Clouts Come Home Again* and minor poems, printed in 1611 and 1617.
6) The letter to Ralegh, the commendatory poems, and dedicatory sonnets, printed in 1611 and 1617.[26]
7) *Prosopopoia or Mother Hubberds Tale*, printed in 1612–13 and after 1620, but no later than 1629.[27]

Using the different states of the first two parts of *The Faerie Queene* as his guide, Johnson defines four groups under which copies of the Spenser folio may be classified:

Group I: "Copies having the 1611 general title page, and the 1609 printing of both parts of *The Faerie Queene*." This group does not contain the 1612–13 printing of *Prosopopoia*.

Group II: "Copies having the 1611 general title-page, the 1609 printing of the first part of *The Faerie Queene* and the 1612–13 printing of the second part."

Group III: "Copies having the 1611 general title-page and the second printing of both parts of *The Faerie Queene*."

Group IV: "Copies having the 1617 general title-page and the second printing of *The Faerie Queene*."[28]

While these groups classify surviving copies that contain all seven parts of Spenser's first folio,[29] other copies survive in more varied states, including single issues.[30] When copies do contain all seven parts, the order in which they are bound consistently varies, as demonstrated by a sample of twelve copies from the Rare Books and Manuscripts Library at The Ohio State University and the Folger Library (see Appendices 1 and 2). Remarkably, these copies rarely contain the same contents bound in the same order. Some patterns of placement do emerge. For example, the folios usually begin with the title page and the two parts of *The Faerie Queene*, and tend to end with *Colin Clouts Come Home Again*. Often, *The Shepheardes Calender* immediately follows *The Faerie Queene*. On the whole, however, the placement order varies.[31] Ultimately, the only real stability in Spenser's first folio is its instability.

An Unstable Book

The instability of Spenser's first folio is immediately apparent from its obvious lack of preliminary materials such as dedications, epistles, and tables of contents. Linking to either pagination or foliation as their system of reference, tables of contents are bibliographic controlling devices that organize a book's contents into a strict order. The Spenser folio has no table of contents.[32] Rather, surviving copies tend to move from the title page, with the dedication to Elizabeth on its verso side, directly into part 1 of *The Faerie Queene*. As a consequence, no fixed order in which the contents should appear exists

Adding further instability to the Spenser folio is its inconsistency in pagination. *The Faerie Queene, The Shepheardes Calender,* and *Proso-popoia* each has its own discrete pagination, yet no pagination exists for the letter to Ralegh, or for the section containing *Colin Clouts Come Home Again* and the minor poems. The lack of any sequential pagination is mirrored by the lack of one continuous signature run.[33] Instead, each section of the folio (with the exception of the two parts of *The Faerie Queen*) has its own signature run. Discontinuous signing is not uncommon, but it normally does not result in this kind of bibliographic instability. Shakespeare's first folio, for example, is divided into three sections—Comedies, Histories, and Tragedies—each with its own pagination and signature collation. Yet, each section is not independent, because the book's "Catalogue" maintains control over its contents. The Spenser folio, however, has no overarching bibliographic control. Each section is self-contained and independent of the others.

Adding to this independence is the inclusion of a title page for each section and, at times, for individual works. For example, in the section that includes *Colin Clouts Come Home Again* and the minor poems there are a total of nine title pages. Providing title pages for each work within a collected works was not an unusual printing practice. For instance, each play in Ben Jonson's 1616 folio has its own title page; yet the order of the plays remains fixed under the control of the book's "Catalogue" and continuous pagination. This is obviously not the case with the first folio of Spenser's works, which survives in many states, including single sections that survive as freestanding editions.

Why is there such a lack of bibliographic control in the Spenser folio? If several different printers were contributing to its production, its instability might make sense. However, the same printer, Humphrey Lownes, printed all the sections, save the 1617 printing of *The Shepheardes Calender*.[34] The fact that a single printer was responsible for nearly all the sections raises the question of whether the folio's instability could have been purposeful. Despite its instability, many copies survive bound together as a complete folio. Thus, the folio does, for the most part, remain stable as a complete collection. If this stability is not owed to bibliographic control, what is stabilizing the folio as a complete collection?

CONSUMER CONTROL, OR BUILD YOUR OWN SPENSER FOLIO

Labeling Spenser's first folio "unstable," as I have done thus far, may be to impose an anachronistic bibliographic point of view and overlook an intentional methodology. What modern bibliographers might find to be bibliographic *instability* may have been to the early seventeenth-century book trade a desirable *flexibility*. Constructing an unstable folio created more options for both publisher and book buyers.

Book Buyers

Rather than ask *what* was maintaining bibliographic control, might it be more appropriate to ask *who*? I argue that the printing of the folio created a flexibility over which the consumer exerted control. Because of the independence of the folio's sections, book buyers had more options. They could buy the whole folio at once, or in sections over a period of time. Or, if they had no interest in owning the complete works, book buyers could simply purchase any single part or parts of the folio.[35] The survival of freestanding editions of *The Shepheardes Calender* seems appropriate, because those who had already bought Lownes's folio edition of *The Faerie Queene* in 1609 may have wanted only to buy Spenser's other major work when it was produced in 1611 and 1617.[36]

Once customers had bought one or all of the sections of Spenser's folio, they could arrange the contents however they saw fit. The varied states of surviving examples clearly indicate that consumers were choosing the order in which their folios were bound. Bibliographers have long recognized that, for the most part, early booksellers did not bind books; rather, book buyers would bring the unbound gatherings of the book, which may have been sewn together, to bookbinders. Bibliographic evidence demonstrates that the sections of Spenser's first folio were sold in sheets and did not even come sewn together. That the folio exists in so many variant states of assembly implies that book buyers were not purchasing the folio pre-assembled in any fashion.

Publisher

The flexibility afforded by a book printed in parts also provided advantages for the publisher, who assumed financial risk in order to print a book. Matthew Lownes appears to have purposefully constructed a bibliographically flexible folio with the help of his brother

Humphrey Lownes. Selling the folio as a whole would have been the most profitable option, but just in case the folio as a whole might not sell well, Matthew Lownes could sell parts of the folio and recoup some of his investment. In order to do this, Lownes had to produce a book that was bibliographically flexible by omitting a table of contents; by not having continual signatures, pagination or foliation; and by not sewing any of the parts together.[37] What's more, he had to keep production costs down. The print history of the first Spenser folio demonstrates a no-frills publication. As was the case in his 1609 *Faerie Queene*, Lownes commissioned no woodcuts, nor did he write nor solicit any new preliminary epistles or dedications. There was also no significant editorial investment. Lownes's editing of the 1611 editions of *The Shepheardes Calender* and the minor poems was limited and, on the whole, "distinctively sloppy."[38] Not only was Lownes's folio a minimally adorned, flexible product, it was a fairly economical book to produce. Oddly enough, the use of the folio format kept the cost of production down.

An Economical Folio?

Modern bibliographers do not normally consider folios affordable publications. One of the most common assumptions about early modern printing is that folios were more expensive to produce than smaller formats because of the amount of paper needed for printing. Hence, when scholars discuss the format of the first edition of *The Faerie Queene* published by William Ponsonby in 1590, they assume that Ponsonby chose the quarto format because it was a less risky venture than a folio. Contrary to this traditional line of reasoning, *The Faerie Queene* was less costly to produce in folio than in quarto. William Ponsonby's 1596 edition of both parts of *The Faerie Queene* was a quarto in eights printed in single columns of english roman type. In this format, the book required 139 unfolded sheets of paper per book. When Lownes published *The Faerie Queene* in folio in 1609, he made good use of the large folio page. Setting the text in double columns of the smaller long primer roman type, he required only ninety-two sheets per book (fig. 1). Because Lownes's folio actually required less of an investment of paper, the chief determinant of the cost of the book, it was less of a financial risk than printing a quarto.

Lownes continued to economize in this way when he set the rest of Spenser's works to the folio page in 1611. Most of Spenser's work

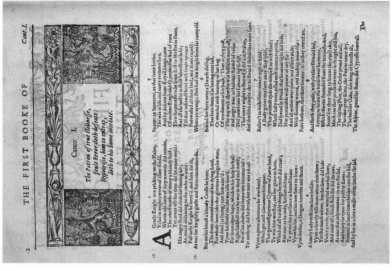

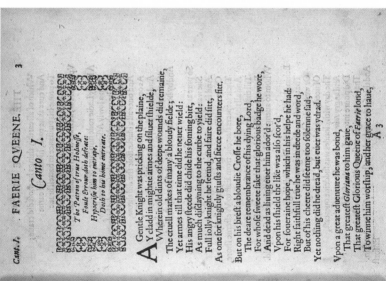

Fig. 1. A comparison of pages from the quarto and folio editions of *The Faerie Queene*. By using smaller type on the larger folio page, Lownes's folio edition required less paper and was therefore less expensive to produce. Courtesy of The Ohio State University Libraries.

previously appeared in quarto and in single columns of english roman type. Shifting to the folio page, Lownes again set the vast majority of text in double columns of long primer roman type. Adding the new sections required only an additional sixty sheets of paper. In total, the 1611 folio, including *Prosopopoia* required 152 sheets per book. On the whole, this is still quite a large production. But Lownes did not publish all of the parts of the folio at the same time. He began in 1609 with *The Faerie Queene* and added the rest of Spenser's works in 1611, therefore spreading out the production costs. After 1611, Lownes proceeded to print on an as-needed basis. Spreading out the production continued to help keep costs low, particularly because he never printed the two parts of *The Faerie Queene* during the same year that he printed *The Shepheardes Calender* and the minor poems.

The Folio and Notions of Authorship

The notion of an intentionally unstable folio should give a modern bibliographer pause. Bibliographic instability and a lack of editorial concern are at odds with traditional perceptions of folio books. So, too, is the notion of a barebones, economical folio. From a modern, bibliographic point of view, literary folios are thought to transcend their commercial roles and remain, in some degree, author-centered. Yet, this notion derives from the reputation of the two most frequently studied early modern English literary folios, Ben Jonson's 1616 folio *Workes* and Shakespeare's 1623 first folio. In these two examples, the folio undoubtedly functions as a monument to its author.

From the title page onward, the overall tenor of Shakespeare's first folio is a celebration of the Bard. Shakespeare's name not only begins the text of the title page, it appears in capital letters that are by far the largest on the page. Even more striking is the large engraved portrait of Shakespeare by Droeshout that fills most of the page. Ultimately, the whole of the preliminaries with its iconographic portrait of Shakespeare, its author-promoting title-page, and its words of high praise provided by Jonson, John Heminge, Henry Condell, and Hugh Holland, construct the pedestal on which sits the monument of Shakespeare's works. Similarly, the preliminaries to Jonson's 1616 folio also work to monumentalize their author. The book's title page is the most immediate and obvious example of this. A Roman theater, an amphitheater, and figures representing comedy and tragicomedy surround the title, *The Workes of Beniamin Jonson*, all of which are framed by an elaborate, classically influenced architectural design. Jonson is consciously placing himself in the milieu of classical literature, thus positioning himself within the neoclassical literary tradition.[39] Further asserting his role as an author committed to his art, Jonson quotes from Horace's *Sermones*: "neque, me, vt miretur turbo laboro: Contentus paucis lectoribus," that is, "I do not work so that the crowd may admire me, I am contented with a few readers."[40] Beyond the title page, the preliminaries contain poems supplied by contemporaries such as Francis Beaumont and George Chapman that praise Jonson and his works.

In comparison, the first folio edition of Spenser's verse is decidedly not a monument to its author. This is clear from the onset. The folio's ornate title-page border is not only a reuse, but its details signify the life and works of Philip Sidney, having been first commissioned and used for Ponsonby's publication of the 1593 folio edition of *Arcadia*. In the top center of the woodcut border is Sidney's crest; on its two sides are a shepherd and an Amazon, representing the characters Musidorus and Pyrocles from Sidney's *Arcadia* (fig. 2). The choice of this woodcut border could be a question of availability. Ponsonby surely owned it and handed it down to Waterson, who then gave it to Matthew Lownes. Yet it could also be a reflection of Spenser's continued association with Sidney. Indeed, from its first use in 1593 through 1624, the border only adorned one other book outside of editions of Sidney's *Arcadia* and Spenser's *Faerie Queene*, when it appeared on the cover of Ponsonby's edition of Machiavelli's *The Florentine Historie* (1595).

The text of the title page also suggests that Lownes's folio was not dedicated to monumentalizing Spenser. The title of "THE FAERIE QVEEN," which appears first on the page in all capital letters, is clearly the selling point of the collection. Second to it is "The Shepheards Calendar," which, while not set in capital letters, appears in the second largest type. In contrast, "EDM. SPENSER," though set in capital letters, appears in the second smallest type on the page; only the words "carefully corrected" are smaller. The size of Spenser's name is also noticeably smaller than the names of the producers of the book, the printer "H.L." (for Humphrey Lownes) and publisher "Matthew Lownes." What's more, their names appear in an italic type; a typographical move that, much like in today's books, places special emphasis on text. The closest Lownes comes to promoting Spenser is dubbing him "England's Arch-Poet."

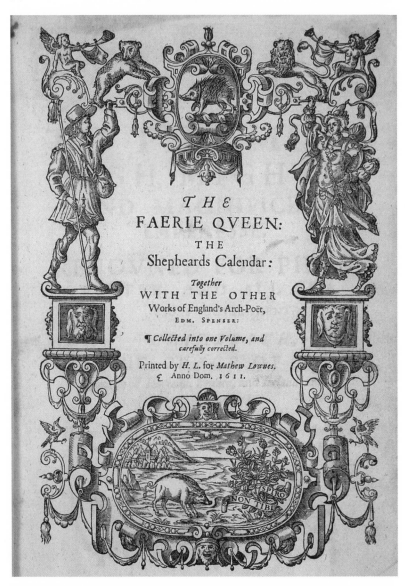

Fig. 2. The title page border used for Spenser's first folio originally appeared in the early folio of Sidney's *Arcadia*. Thus, its images correspond with Sidney and his text. The Sidney family crest is in the top-center, the lion and the bear from the *Arcadia* are in the upper corners, and the characters Musidorus and Pyrocles stand on pedestals on each side. Courtesy of The Ohio State University Libraries.

The absence of any homage to Spenser continues in the folio's preliminaries. More to the point, the folio has a conspicuous lack of preliminaries. While the folios of Jonson and Shakespeare feature verse and prose that shower praise upon their authors, the Spenser folio contains only a reprint of *The Faerie Queene's* dedication to Elizabeth. Furthermore, Spenser's first folio includes no portrait of the author, as found in Shakespeare's first folio and contemporary folio works of Geoffrey Chaucer.[41]

All of this bibliographic evidence confirms that Spenser's first folio was chiefly a consumer-based product rather than a monument to the author. This becomes even more evident when we think about who was responsible for the publication of the folio. Unlike the folios of William Shakespeare and Ben Jonson, which were initiated and constructed by company colleagues or the author himself, Spenser's first folio was the product of a collection of stationers collaborating in a business venture initiated by Matthew Lownes. Unlike the men behind the folios of Shakespeare and Jonson, Lownes demonstrates no interest in monumentalizing Spenser. The materiality of his folio editions neither celebrates nor enhances Spenser's literary reputation. He did not commission a new title page border, he did not commission a portrait of the author, nor did he add any new preliminary text or end matter.

Compared to the folios of Shakespeare and Jonson, Spenser's first folio may come across as an inferior book, a cheap imitation of a proper literary folio. But rather than viewing the Spenser folio as an inferior anomaly, we should recognize that literary folios were not always intended to be monuments to their authors. Nor did folio publication always equal an expensive, lavish book. These modern notions of literary folios are anachronistic, colored by the exhaustive attention scholars have paid to the first folios of Jonson and Shakespeare. When scholars use these folios as the standard by which other contemporary folios are measured, the results can be misleading.

The Folio Revisited

When it came to publishing literary work, English publishers reserved the folio format for the works of the most famous English authors, and even these were scarce in the sixteenth century. The works of Chaucer appeared in folio throughout the sixteenth and seventeenth centuries and were joined occasionally by writers such as John Gower.[42] Meanwhile, the great majority of English literary books appeared in quarto and octavo. It was not until the very end of the sixteenth century that stationers printed the literary works of contemporary English authors in folio. Two influential literary folios during this time were Sir Philip Sidney's *Arcadia* and Samuel Daniel's *Works*. Preceding Spenser's first folio by just a handful of years, these two books certainly influenced Lownes's publication of Spenser's works.

SIDNEY'S *ARCADIA*

William Ponsonby published the first folio edition of Sidney's *Arcadia* in 1593, three years after he had published the first edition in quarto.[43] The shift in format was accompanied by additions and revisions taken from the Old *Arcadia*, a new "To the Reader" penned by Hugh Sanford, and a decorative woodcut border commissioned specially for the folio's title page.[44] This border, described above, later appeared as the title page to Spenser's first folio and featured images corresponding to Sidney and his romance (fig. 2). Five years later, Ponsonby published a second folio edition of *Arcadia* to which he appended "Certaine Sonets Written by Sir Philip Sidney," *The Defence of Poesie*, *Astrophel and Stella*, and *The May Day Masque* (i.e., *The Lady of May*).[45] Although the title page does not identify the folio as a "works," the 1598 Sidney folio was the first collected literary works of a contemporary English author to appear in folio, in this case a little over a decade after Sidney's death. Considering how few English authors found their way into folio, this was a milestone in the English book trade.

Like Spenser's first folio, the 1598 Sidney folio works lacks the bibliographic features later found in the folios of Jonson and Shakespeare, which serve to monumentalize the author. There was no added preliminary material and no additional woodcuts beyond what had already appeared in the 1593 edition. The lack of new bibliographic features continued in 1605 when Matthew Lownes co-published the fourth edition of Sidney's *Arcadia* with Simon Waterson.[46] To this new edition, they added no new material, nor did they commission any new woodcuts. The folio simply constituted a "page for page" reprint of the 1598 edition.[47] Tellingly, even the title page border was an unrelated reuse. Replacing the border that had ornamented the 1593 and 1598 folios was an astrological-themed border featuring figures such as Ptolemy and Marinus, along with the person-ifications of Time, Geometry, and Arithmetic.[48]

The early print histories of Sidney's *Arcadia* and Spenser's *Faerie Queene* demonstrate that the two books tended to be associated with one another. Ponsonby published the first editions of both books in 1590 as a pair of quartos, which were linked typographically by roman type, an unusual choice for English literary works at the time.[49]

The 1596 *Faerie Queene*, however, did not immediately follow the example of *Arcadia* in undergoing a shift to folio. Nevertheless, the two texts continued to be linked. Just as one publisher, William Ponsonby, had held the rights to both texts in the 1590s, Matthew Lownes held the rights to both texts in collaboration with Simon Waterson in the early 1600s. Lownes co-published the fourth edition of *Arcadia* with Waterson only four years before he published the folio *Faerie Queene* in 1609. It is not surprising, therefore, that Lownes would follow the example of *Arcadia* and move *The Faerie Queene* from quarto to folio.

DANIEL'S *WORKS*

Three years after the publication of the folio edition of Sidney's works came another milestone in the English book trade: the first folio works of a living English literary author, namely *The Works of Samuel Daniel Newly Augmented*.[50] Daniel's *Works* consists of three sections: (1) title page, dedication to Elizabeth, and *The Civil Wars* books 1–6; (2) *Musophilus*, *A Letter from Octauia to Marcus Antonius*, *The Tragedie of Cleopatra*, and *The Complaint of Rosamond*; and (3) *To Delia*.[51] In addition to these three sections, some copies of the *Works* include Daniel's *A Panegyrike Congratulatorie*, which appeared two years later in the same format and with the same decorative title page border.[52]

In a manner not unlike Spenser's first folio, surviving copies of Daniel's folio *Works* exhibit a variation in contents from copy to copy, a bibliographical diversity which prompted an *STC* head note declaring: "Daniel's works are unusually awkward from a biblio-graphical point of view."[53] As John Pitcher observes:

> About eighty copies of the edition have survived, and from these we can make out a quite deliberate plan, on the part of the poet and his publisher, to cater for different readers. The

folio survives in two issues, with different dates on their title
pages (1601 and 1602); they were printed on two or three
distinct grades of paper; and they were presented and sold with
a variety of contents.[54]

An examination of four copies held at the Folger Shakespeare Library
and one copy held at the Library of Congress confirms the variety
of contents to which Pitcher refers.[55] Of the five copies, only two
contain all three sections of the *Works*. The Library of Congress's
copy lacks *To Delia*. One of the Folger copies contains only *The Civil
Wars*,[56] while another includes *A Panegyrike Congratulatorie*.[57]

Waterson must have been confident that a folio collection of Daniel's verse would sell. In an "Apology" written for the 1605 edition
of *The Tragedy of Philotas*, Daniel recalls "being called vpon by my
Printer for a new impression of my workes, with some additions to
the ciuill warres."[58] Subsequently, Waterson appears to have made a
significant investment in Daniel's *Works*.[59] An ornate title page border, complete with the Queen's royal arms, was commissioned specifically for the *Works*.[60] Even the layout of the book demanded
more of an investment. Although there was ample opportunity to set
Daniel's verse in double columns and subsequently save a great deal
of paper (as Lownes later did with Spenser's poetry), the whole of
the folio is set in the more ornate, but more paper-consuming, single
columns of great primer roman.

The physical appearance of Daniel's folio *Works* suggests that Daniel and Waterson intended to produce an elegant edition that was
suited for a distinguished audience and that would advance Daniel's
literary reputation. Surviving copies confirm that they produced copies for some of the most influential men and women in England. A
newly penned, verse dedication by Daniel to "Her Sacred Majesty"
heads the *Civil Wars*, supplanting the last edition's dedication to
Charles Blount, Lord Mountjoy. He also gave presentation copies to
important figures such as Sir Thomas Egerton and Sir Thomas Bodley.[61] In fact, Daniel's work "was one of the few volumes in English,
let alone English Verse, which Bodley allowed into his new library
in the University of Oxford."[62]

Spenser's first folio clearly falls more in the tradition of the earlier
folios of Sidney and Daniel than the later folios of Jonson and Shakespeare. Its print history is similar to that of Sidney's in that the major
work (i.e., *Arcadia* and *The Faerie Queene*) appeared first as a stand-
alone edition and was then followed by an edition that incorporated
the rest of the works. The print history of Spenser's first folio is also

similar to that of Daniel's *Works*. Like Waterson, Lownes produced a bibliographically flexible folio in sections, only he carried it further, reprinting the sections of Spenser's first folio over the course of a decade or more. Indeed, overall, Lownes went beyond his predecessors in taking measures to construct a flexible and economical folio. As we saw earlier, Lownes chose to save paper by printing in double columns of long primer roman type. Furthermore, unlike the publishers of the first folio edition of Sidney's *Arcadia* and Daniel's *Works*, he commissioned no new woodcuts or preliminary matter.

Lownes's choice to produce Spenser's first folio in a more flexible and economical fashion appears all the more pronounced when we compare his treatment of Spenser to his treatment of Michael Drayton in the publication of the first edition of *Poly-Olbion*.[63] Printed by Humphrey Lownes a year after the Spenser folio in 1611, this folio book begins with an elaborate frontispiece commissioned specifically for the book.[64]

This frontispiece is accompanied by a poem, "Vpon the Frontispiece" which explicates the illustration. Containing over a dozen maps, the book is heavily illustrated to the extent that the preliminaries even include an epistle "From the Author of the Illustrations." These woodcuts and preliminary materials drove up the cost of producing this book, creating a greater risk for Matthew Lownes. Why was he willing to take a financial risk with Drayton? There are at least two answers. The first is that the participation of co-publishers reduced Lownes's risks. The imprint reads: "Printed [by Humphrey Lownes] for M Lownes. I Browne. I Helme. I Busbie." The "for" designates the stationers who follow as co-publishers of the work, making Matthew Lownes one of four stationers investing in the folio. The second possible answer is that Drayton's career was still in full swing and his popularity demanded an elaborate publication.

The reluctance of Matthew Lownes, or any of the other men involved in the production of Spenser's first folio, to invest in Spenser to the extent that other publishers had invested in Sidney and Daniel, and would later invest in Drayton, Jonson, and Shakespeare, suggests that Spenser's reputation and popularity did not demand such investment. Demonstrating this point, folio editions of the works of each of the other authors would come out within the coming decades or much sooner.[65] The stationers who held the rights to Spenser's works could have followed suit, perhaps even producing a monumentalizing folio in the fashion of the Jonson and Shakespeare folios, but they chose not to. Instead, another half a century would pass before Spenser's collected works would again appear in a folio.

A Reluctance to Publish Spenser

Following the years of the production of Lownes's folios, Spenser's
works, for the most part, lay dormant. Prior to the publication of the
1679 folio edition of Spenser's *Works* by Jonathan Edwin, there were
only two Spenser publications: Sir James Ware's edition of *A View
of the Present State of Ireland* in 1633 and Theodore Bathurst's Latin
and English edition of *The Shepheardes Calender* in 1653. All the
while, the rights to Spenser's work continued to change hands.

In the years following Matthew Lownes's death in 1627, the *Stationers' Register* records a flurry of activity surrounding the rights to *The
Faerie Queene*. After Thomas Lownes inherited the rights from his
father in April of 1627, he assigned them to his uncle Humphrey
Lownes and Robert Young the following month.[66] This transaction
included a catalog of titles such as: Sidney's *Arcadia,* Drayton's *Poly-
Olbion*, and Ben Jonson's *Poetaster*. More than a year later, on Novem-
ber 6, 1628, Humphrey Lownes transferred his share of the rights
to his cousin George Latham and George Cole.[67] How these rights
transferred without the involvement of Robert Young is unknown.
Evidence does demonstrate that Young did assert his rights to these
titles and successfully arranged for their transfer back into his possession.[68] Though the 1630s, he published at least eight of the titles he
inherited from Lownes, yet he never exercised his prerogative to
publish *The Faerie Queene* or any of the other works of Spenser.[69]
When Robert Young died in 1643, his rights passed on to his son
James, who also never published any of Spenser's works.[70] After this,
no further record of *The Faerie Queene* appears in the *Stationers' Register*.

The Shepheardes Calender fared only slightly better; it was published
once before the folio of 1679. This was the aforementioned Bathurst
edition, published in 1653 by Mercy Meighen, Thomas Collins, and
Gabriell Bedell. No entry for this edition survives in the *Stationers'
Register*. The rights had transferred to John Harrison IV, who died
sometime around 1653.[71] Subsequently, his widow, Martha Harrison,
held the rights until April 28, 1660, when the *Stationers' Register*
records her transferring the rights to William Lee.[72] As in the case of
James Young, William Lee never published any of Spenser's work.

Ultimately, this ownership history demonstrates that stationers
who held the rights to Spenser's works in the middle of the seventeenth century were reluctant to publish them. As a result, *The Faerie
Queene* and the majority of Spenser's works remained out of print
or unsold on booksellers' shelves for decades.

"THE PRINCE OF POETS IN HIS OWN TYME": SPENSER IN THE SEVENTEENTH CENTURY

The publication history of Spenser's verse in the seventeenth century is quite telling, particularly when compared with that of the sixteenth century. From 1579 to 1597, there were fifteen printed editions of his work.[73] *The Shepheardes Calender* alone went through five editions before Spenser's death in 1599.[74] Conversely, in the time between the first folio of *The Faerie Queene* in 1609 and the end of the seventeenth century, there were only six new editions of Spenser's work.[75] If we were to gauge the popularity of Spenser's works by the number of editions printed, then the years from 1579 to 1597 eclipse the whole of the seventeenth century.

For seventeenth-century booksellers and book buyers, Spenser's works were no longer as popular as they had been while the poet was alive. Truth be told, the printing history suggests the seventeenth-century reading public lacked a driving interest in Spenser. This would explain why so many seventeenth-century stationers who held the rights to Spenser's works decided not to invest their money in new editions. It would also explain why, at the beginning of the century, Lownes did not see fit to invest a great deal of time and money in Spenser's first folio. It was not the right time. The right time would come in 1679 when Jonathan Edwin published *The Works of that Famous English Poet, Mr. Edmond Spenser. The Faery Queen, The Shepherds Calendar, The History of Ireland, &c. Whereunto is added, An Account of his Life; With other new Additions Never before in Print.*[76] As the title suggests, Edwin's folio edition was indeed a printed monument to Spenser. The book's engraved frontispiece is intriguing. It portrays the 1620 monument that had declared Spenser "the prince of poets in his tyme." With the publication of Edwin's 1679 folio, Spenser finally appears to have transcended beyond "his tyme."

The Ohio State University

NOTES

1. Quoted from Alexander C. Judson, *The Life of Edmund Spenser* [*Works of Edmund Spenser: A Variorum Edition, Vol. 8*] (Baltimore: John Hopkins University Press, 1945), 207.

2.   Fredson Bowers, *Bibliography and Textual Criticism* (Oxford: Clarendon Press, 1964), 76.

3.   Peter W. M. Blayney, *The First Folio of Shakespeare* (Washington, D.C.: Folger Library Publications, 1991), 1.

4.   Ben Jonson, *The Workes of Beniamin Ionson* (London: By Will Stansby, 1616). *STC* 14751.

5.   William Shakespeare, *Mr. VVilliam Shakespeares Comedies, Histories, & Tragedies Published According to the True Originall Copies* (London: Printed by Isaac Iaggard, and Ed. Blount [at the charges of W. Iaggard, Ed. Blount, I. Smithweeke, and W. Aspley], 1623). *STC* 22273.

6.   David Scott Kastan, *Shakespeare and the Book* (Cambridge: Cambridge University Press, 2001), 69.

7.   Edmund Spenser, *The Faerie Queene, Disposed into XII Bookes, Fashioning twelue Morall Vertues* (London: Printed by H.L. for Matthew Lownes, 1609). *STC* 23083.

8.   Edmund Spenser, *The Faerie Queen: The Shepheards Calendar: Together with the other Works of England's Arch-Poet, Edm. Spenser: Collected Into One Volume, And Carefully Corrected* (London: Printed by H.L. for Matthew Lownes, 1611). *STC* 23084–85. Even though Lownes published Spenser's folio works in parts over the course of nearly twenty years, I will refer to it as "Spenser's first folio" for purposes of convenience.

9.   The spelling of the title varies through the early editions. I will use the traditional uniform title of *The Shepheardes Calender* throughout this essay, except when quoting the titles of specific editions.

10.   Wayne Erickson, "William Ponsonby" in *The British Literary Book Trade, 1475–1700 (Dictionary of Literary Biography 170)* (Detroit: Gale Research, 1996), 212.

11.   I.e., Robert Greene's *Card of Fancy* or *Gwydonius*.

12.   Edward Arber, ed., *A Transcript of the Registers of the Company of Stationers of London, 1554–1640* (New York: P. Smith, 1950), III.269.

13.   Citing the absence of any dispute concerning Matthew Lownes's 1611 Spenser folio works, Francis R. Johnson speculates: "It is possible that there was a private understanding whereby the rights to the other poems were included" (*A Critical Bibliography of the Works of Edmund Spenser Printed before 1700*, [Baltimore: Johns Hopkins University Press, 1933], 44).

14.   Arber, *Transcript*, III.274.

15.   Ibid., III.274.

16.   Sir Philip Sidney, *The Countesse of Pembrokes Arcadia. Written by Sir Philip Sidney Knight. Now the fourth time published, with sundry nevv additions of the same author* (London: Imprinted [by George Eld and Humphrey Lownes] for Simon Waterson, 1605). *STC* 22543. This edition has two variant imprints. One reads "Imprinted for Simon Waterson," the other "Imprinted for Matthevv Lovvnes" (*STC* 22543, 22543a).

17.   Lownes appears to have merely substituted the title page of Ponsonby's remaining copies with one bearing his name. Fortunately for Lownes, there was nothing on the verso side. See note 37.

18.   Johnson, 23.

19.   The woodcut did not appear in any subsequent edition of *The Faerie Queene*.

20. A year or so later he also added *Prosopopoia or Mother Hubberds Tale*.

21. *The Shepheardes Calender* went through five editions from 1579 to 1597.

22. Johnson, 39.

23. Ibid., 39.

24. Although this imprint reads "Iohn Harrison the elder," it most certainly refers to John Harrison II. As Johnson notes, John Harrison the elder had died earlier that year, his will having been proved on February 11, 1617 (40).

25. Johnson dates the second printing of *Prosopopoia or Mother Hubberds Tale* after 1620, but no later than 1629, because the imprint names Humphrey Lownes (H.L.) and George Latham. Latham, who married Matthew Lownes's daughter, was freed from his apprenticeship in 1620. Humphrey Lownes died in 1630 (Johnson, 42).

26. As Johnson notes, "copies of the 1609 Folio of *The Faerie Queene*, when found separately, almost never contain it [i.e., the letter], and in most cases where it does appear it seems to have been inserted later" (38).

27. Johnson, 33–44. See note 25.

28. Ibid., 45–46.

29. Six if printed before the publication of *Prosopopoia* c.1612–13.

30. In his 1933 *Critical Bibliography of the Works of Edmund Spenser*, Johnson notes that individual sections of *The Shepheardes Calender* and of *Prosopopoia* often survive as freestanding editions (34). The Folger Library holds two single copies of the original 1609 *Faerie Queene* (Folger *STC* 23083 Copies 1 and 2), as well as two copies that contain only the 1617 editions of *The Shepheardes Calender*, the Letter to Ralegh and *Colin Clouts Come Home Again* and the minor poems (Folger *STC* 23094 Copies 1 and 2).

31. The question of binding arises when comparing the variant orders in which Spenser's first folio was bound. An examination of the bindings of the copies held at The Ohio State University is instructive. Three of the four copies are in their original, contemporary bindings (PR 2350 1611a, PR 2350 1611b, and PR 2350 1617). One of the three has been rebacked, but does not appear to have ever been disbound (PR 2350 1611a). Thus, the contents of all three folios remain as they were first bound near the time of publication. As Appendix 1 shows, none of the three copies are bound in the same order. This example, compounded by the sheer number of variant orders found throughout the samples from The Ohio State University and the Folger Shakespeare Library, precludes the notion that variant orders are the result of later rebinding. I would like to thank Harry Campbell for his aid in analyzing these bindings.

32. There is a list of contents on the verso to the title page for *Complaints Containing Sundry Small Poemes of the Worlds Vanitie*, a subsection of the *Colin Clouts* section.

33. For example, the signature collation of Ohio State's PR 2350 1611b group III copy breaks down as follows: (1) Title Page and Dedication, unsigned; (2) *Faerie Queen* parts one and two, A-2H6; (3) *Prosopopoia* A8; (4) *Shepheardes Calender*, A-E6, F4; (5) *Colin Clouts Come Home Again* and minor poems, A-L6, M2; letter to Ralegh, '8.

34. Not only do the imprints of each section of the folio identify Humphrey Lownes as their printer, the same ornamental woodcuts owned by Lownes repeat through each section. The only exception to this is the second printing of *The*

Shepheardes Calender, which, as its imprint tells us, was not printed by Humphrey Lownes, but by John Harrison II.

35.   Johnson first touched on this point, "separate sections could be assembled with the 1609 *Faerie Queene* and the new general title-page and issued as the collected works, or they could be sold separately to buyers who only wished to purchase certain individual works because they already had copies of the others" (Johnson, 47).

36.   The survival of *Prosopopoia or Mother Hubberds Tale* in single editions may also make sense if the authorities originally called in the first edition in 1591, as many scholars believe. Its publication in 1612 would have made this controversial text openly available for the first time.

37.   For a comparable example, see the publication history of Clement Edmondes, *Obseruations vpon Cæsars Comentaries* ([London]: printed for Math: Lownes, 1609). *STC* 7491. For earlier editions and states, see also *STC* 7488, 7490, 7490.3, and 7490.7. In this case, Matthew Lownes and the stationers who preceded him employed a similar strategy of producing a purposefully flexible, market-oriented folio edition. In fact, the headnote of the *STC* entry for Edmondes could very well describe Spenser's first folio: "While it is feasible to note a sequence in the printing of sections, it is impossible to say with certainty what combinations of them should be considered 'issues' or what one should expect to find with the purposefully ambiguous title-pages. Indeed, most copies as they survive today seem better to represent concatenations assembled by individual owners through the years" (Alfred W. Pollard and G. R. Redgrave, *A Short-title Catalogue of Books Printed in England, Scotland, & Ireland and of English books Printed Abroad, 1475–1640* [London: Bibliographical Society, 1976], Vol. 1, 338).

38.   See R. M. Cummings, *Spenser: The Critical Heritage* (New York: Barnes & Noble, 1971), 4–5; and Jewel Wurtsbaugh, *Two Centuries of Spenserian Scholarship (1609–1805)* (Baltimore: Johns Hopkins University Press, 1936), 6–8, 33.

39.   For a detailed discussion of the title page see Margery Corbett and Ronald Lightbown, *The Comely Frontispiece: The Emblematic Title-page in England, 1550–1660* (London: Routledge & Kegan Paul, 1979), 145–50.

40.   Ibid., 146.

41.   Interestingly enough, a Huntington Library copy of the folio provides an example in which a later owner of the book has affixed a Mezzotint portrait of Spenser to the flyleaf (Call #69580). This reader, no doubt influenced by later norms of folio production, found it necessary to correct Lownes's decision not to include a portrait of the author.

42.   For Chaucer folios, see: *STC* 5068–5076, 5076.3, 5077–5088, 5094, and 5096. For Gower, see: *STC* 12142–12144.

43.   Sir Philip Sidney, *The Countesse of Pembrokes Arcadia. Written by Sir Philip Sidney Knight. Now Since the First Edition Augmented and Ended* (London: Printed [by John Windet] for William Ponsonbie, 1593). *STC* 22540.

44.   See Bent Juel-Jensen, "Sir Philip Sidney, 1554–1586: A Check-List of Early Editions of His Works" in *Sir Philip Sidney: An Anthology of Modern Criticism*, ed. Dennis Kay (Oxford: Clarendon Press, 1987) 292–93; and Donald V. Stump, Jerome S. Dees, and C. Stuart Hunter, *Sir Philip Sidney: An Annotated Bibliography of Texts and Criticism (1554–1984)* (New York: G.K. Hall, 1994), 25.

45.   Sir Philip Sidney, *The Countesse of Pembrokes Arcadia. Written by Sir Philip Sidney Knight. Now the third time published, with sundry new additions of the same Author* (London: Imprinted [by R. Field] for William Ponsonbie, 1598). *STC* 22541.

46.   This does not include the controversial edition printed by Robert Waldegrave in 1599.

47.   Stump, 14.

48.   For the history of this woodcut, see Ronald Brunlees McKerrow and F. S. Ferguson, *Title-Page Borders used in England & Scotland 1485–1640* (London: Printed for the Bibliographical Society at the Oxford University Press, 1932) 93. The 1593 *Arcadia* border returned in the 1613 edition, also published by Lownes and Waterson.

49.   See Mark Bland, "The Appearance of the Text in Early Modern England," *TEXT* 11 (1998): 108–10.

50.   Samuel Daniel, *The vvorks of Samuel Daniel newly augmented* (London: Printed [by Valentine Simmes and W. White] for Simon Waterson, 1601). *STC* 6236–37. Although many scholars treat Jonson's 1616 folio as if it were the first collection of literary works in folio published by a living English author, Daniel's was the first. Daniel's collected works first came out in 1599 as a quarto under the title of *The Poeticall Essayes of Sam. Danyel* (*STC* 6261).

51.   The use of pagination and foliation in these sections reflects their independent signature runs. The *Civil Wars* section uses foliation; the section containing *Musophilus*, *A Letter from Octauia*, *The Tragedie of Cleopatra* and *The Complaint of Rosamond* uses neither foliation nor pagination; and the Delia section uses pagination.

52.   Samuel Daniel, *A Panegyrike Congratulatorie to the Kings Maiestie Also certaine epistles, by Samuel Daniel* (London: Printed by Valentine Simmes for Edward Blount, 1603). *STC* 6258. The design of *Panegyrike* appears "to complement (and be sold with) the *Works*," which explains why it can be found bound with the *Works* (John Pitcher, "Essays, Works and Small Poems: Divulging, Publishing and Augmenting the Elizabethan Poet, Samuel Daniel" in *The Renaissance Text: Theory, Editing, Textuality*, ed. Andrew Murphy [Manchester: Manchester University Press, 2000]), 14.

53.   Pollard and Redgrave, 1.281.

54.   Pitcher, *Essays*, 14.

55.   Forthcoming from the Clarendon Press, John Pitcher's critical edition of Daniel's work should provide the most detailed bibliographic analysis of Daniel's early editions.

56.   *STC* 6237 Copy 4

57.   *STC* 6237 Copy 2.

58.   See Samuel Daniel, *The Tragedy of Philotas*, ed. Laurence Michel (New Haven: Yale University Press, 1949), 156; and Pitcher, "Essays," 13. Although the "Apology" did not surface in print until the 1623 edition of the *Workes*, scholars have concluded "it *was* written in the fall of 1604 *for* publication with the '05 edition" (Daniel, *Tragedy*, 40, n. 7).

59.   As Pitcher observes "the cost of materials and labour to make this folio cannot have been a small thing for Waterson, and he would not have risked the investment unless he was anticipated enough demand for these expensive books of English poetry" (Pitcher, "Essays," 13).

60.   McKerrow and Ferguson record no earlier use of the compartments that comprise this title page border (180). Its only other reuse was in Daniel's *A Panegyrike Congratulatory* in 1603 (Pitcher, "Essays," 14; McKerrow and Ferguson, 180).

61. See Harry Sellers, "A Bibliography of the Works of Samuel Daniel 1585–1623," *Proceedings & Papers of the Oxford Bibliographical Society*, 2.1(1927): 35–36; and John Pitcher, "Samuel Daniel's Letter to Sir Thomas Egerton," *Huntington Library Quarterly* 47.1 (1984): 55–61.

62. Pitcher, "Essays," 13.

63. Michael Drayton, *Poly-Olbion* (London: Printed [by Humphrey Lownes] for M Lownes. I Browne. I Helme. I Busbie, 1612). *STC* 7266.

64. For an examination of the frontispiece, see Corbett and Lightbown (153–61) and Jean Brink, *Michael Drayton Revisited* (Boston: Twayne Publishers, 1990), 83–84.

65. The second Jonson folio was published in 1640, Shakespeare's in 1632. A folio edition of Drayton's poems was published in 1619, and a lavish edition of Daniel's *The Collection of the Historie of England* appeared in 1618. Editions of Sidney's *Arcadia* appeared in 1613, 1621, 1633, 1638, and beyond.

66. Arber, *Transcript*, IV.176, 180.

67. Ibid., IV.205.

68. Ibid., IV.245.

69. See *STC* 1383, 1633, 6562, 14472, 19985, 20641, 21654, and 22549.

70. H. R. Plomer, ed., *A Transcript of the Registers of the Worshipful Company of Stationers, from 1640–1708 A.D.* (London, Priv. print., 1913–14), I.122–26.

71. Johnson, 9.

72. Plomer, *Transcript*, II.261–62.

73. Not counting the Spenser-Harvey letters (1580), the editions are as follows: five editions of *The Shepheardes Calender* (1579, 1581, 1586, 1591, and 1597), two editions of *The Faerie Queene* (part 1 in 1590, parts 1 and 2 in 1596), *Complaints* (1591), two editions of *Daphnaïda*, (1591 and 1596 with *Fowre Hymns*), *Colin Clouts Come Home Againe* (1595), *Amoretti and Epithalamion* (1595), *Fowre Hymns* (1596), and *Prothalamion* (1596).

74. *STC* 23089, 23090, 23091, 23092, and 23093.

75. The 1609 edition of *The Faerie Queene*, the first and second editions of the folio works (1611–c.1625), *A View of the present State of Ireland* (1633), Bathurst's Latin and English edition of *The Shepheardes Calender* (1653), and the 1679 *Works*.

76. Edmund Spenser, *The Works of that Famous English Poet, Mr. Edmond Spenser. The Faery Queen, The Shepherds Calendar, The History of Ireland, &c. Whereunto is Added, An Account of His Life; With Other New Additions Never before in Print.* (London: Printed by Henry Hills for Jonathan Edwin, 1679). Wing S4965.

APPENDIX 1: COPIES OF SPENSER'S FIRST FOLIO
(1611–c.1625) AT THE RARE BOOKS AND MANUSCRIPTS
LIBRARY OF THE OHIO STATE UNIVERSITY:

PR 2350 1611:
1) General title page and dedication—First Printing (1611)
2) *The Faerie Queene* part 1–Second Printing (c.1613–17)
3) *The Faerie Queene* part 2–Second Printing (c.1612–13)
4) *The Shepheardes Calender*—First Printing (1611)
5) *Prosopopoia or Mother Hubberds Tale*—First Printing (c.1612–13)
6) *Colin Clouts Come Home Againe* and minor poems—First Printing (1611)
7) Letter to Ralegh, etc.—First Printing (c.1611)

PR 2350 1611a
1) General title page and dedication—First Printing (1611)
2) *The Faerie Queene* part 1–First Printing (1609)
3) *The Faerie Queene* part 2–First Printing (1609)
4) Letter to Ralegh, etc.—First Printing (c.1611)
5) *The Shepheardes Calender*—First Printing (1611)
6) *Colin Clouts Come Home Againe* and minor poems—First Printing (1611)

PR 2350 1611b
1) General title page and dedication—First Printing (1611)
2) *The Faerie Queene* part 1–Second Printing (c.1613–17)
3) *The Faerie Queene* part 2–Second Printing (c.1612–13)
4) *Prosopopoia or Mother Hubberds Tale*—First Printing (c.1612–13)
5) *The Shepheardes Calender*—First Printing (1611)
6) *Colin Clouts Come Home Againe* and minor poems—First Printing (1611)
7) Letter to Ralegh, etc.—First Printing (c.1611)

PR2350 1617:
1) General title page and dedication—Second Printing (1617)
2) *The Faerie Queene* part 1–Second Printing (c.1613–17)
3) *The Faerie Queene* part 2–Second Printing (c.1612–13)
4) *The Shepheardes Calender*—Second Printing (1617)
5) Letter to Ralegh, etc.—Second Printing (c.1617)
6) *Prosopopoia or Mother Hubberds Tale*—Second Printing (after 1620)
7) *Colin Clouts Come Home Againe* and minor poems—Second Printing (1617)

APPENDIX 2: COPIES OF SPENSER'S FIRST FOLIO
(1611–c.1625) AT THE FOLGER SHAKESPEARE LIBRARY:

STC 23083.8
1) *The Faerie Queene* part 1–First Printing (1609)
2) *The Faerie Queene* part 2–First Printing (1609)
3) *The Shepheardes Calender*—First Printing (1611)
4) *Colin Clouts Come Home Againe* and minor poems—First Printing (1611)
5) Letter to Ralegh, etc.—First Printing (c.1611)

STC 23083.9
1) General title page and dedication—First Printing (1611)
2) Letter to Ralegh, etc.—First Printing (c.1611)
3) *The Faerie Queene* part 1–First Printing (1609)
4) *The Faerie Queene* part 2–Second Printing (c.1612–13)
5) *The Shepheardes Calender*—First Printing (1611)
6) *Prosopopoia or Mother Hubberds Tale*—First Printing (c.1612–13)
7) *Colin Clouts Come Home Againe* and minor poems—First Printing (1611)

STC 23084 Copy 1
1) General title page and dedication—First Printing (1611)
2) *The Faerie Queene* part 1–Second Printing (c.1613–17)
3) *The Faerie Queene* part 2–Second Printing (c.1612–13)
4) *Letter to Ralegh, etc.—First Printing (c.1611)*
5) *The Shepheardes Calender*—First Printing (1611)
6) *Prosopopoia or Mother Hubberds Tale* — First Printing (c.1612–13)
7) *Colin Clouts Come Home Againe* and minor poems—First Printing (1611)

STC 23084 Copy 2
1) General title page and dedication—First Printing (1611)
2) *The Faerie Queene* part 1–Second Printing (c.1613–17)
3) *The Faerie Queene* part 2–Second Printing (c.1612–13)
4) *Letter to Ralegh, etc.—First Printing (c.1611)*
5) *Prosopopoia or Mother Hubberds Tale*—First Printing (c.1612–13)
6) *The Shepheardes Calender*—First Printing (1611)
7) *Colin Clouts Come Home Againe* and minor poems—First Printing (1611)

STC 23084 Copy 3

1) General title page and dedication—First Printing (1611)
2) *The Faerie Queene* part 1–Second Printing (c.1613–17)
3) *The Faerie Queene* part 2–Second Printing (c.1612–13)
4) Letter to Ralegh, etc.—First Printing (c.1611)
5) *The Shepheardes Calender*—First Printing (1611)
6) *Prosopopoia or Mother Hubberds Tale*—First Printing (c.1612–13)
7) *Colin Clouts Come Home Againe* and minor poems—First Printing (1611)

STC 23084 Copy 4

1) General title page and dedication—First Printing (1611)
2) *The Faerie Queene* part 1–Second Printing (c.1613–17)
3) *The Faerie Queene* part 2–Second Printing (c.1612–13)
4) *The Shepheardes Calender*—First Printing (1611)
5) *Prosopopoia or Mother Hubberds Tale*—First Printing (c.1612–13)
6) *Colin Clouts Come Home Againe* and minor poems—First Printing (1611)
7) Letter to Ralegh, etc.—First Printing (c.1611)

STC 23085 Copy 1

1) General title page and dedication—Second Printing (1617)
2) *The Faerie Queene* part 1–Second Printing (c.1613–17)
3) *The Faerie Queene* part 2–Second Printing (c.1612–13)
4) *The Shepheardes Calender*—Second Printing (1617)
5) *Prosopopoia or Mother Hubberds Tale*—First Printing (c.1612–13)
6) Letter to Ralegh, etc.—Second Printing (c.1617)
7) *Colin Clouts Come Home Againe* and minor poems—Second Printing (1617)

STC 23085 Copy 2

1) General title page and dedication—Second Printing (1617)
2) Letter to Ralegh, etc.—Second Printing (c.1617)
3) *The Faerie Queene* part 1–Second Printing (c.1613–17)
4) *The Faerie Queene* part 2–Second Printing (c.1612–13)
5) *The Shepheardes Calender*—Second Printing (1617)
6) *Prosopopoia or Mother Hubberds Tale*—First Printing (c.1612–13)
7) *Colin Clouts Come Home Againe* and minor poems—Second Printing (1617)

PATRICK PERKINS

Spenser's Dragon and the Law

This essay claims that the dragon curbing the liberty of the citizens of Eden in Book I of Spenser's *The Faerie Queene* is the last in a series of representations of the Law of God. Such a depiction of the Law, I argue, can be traced to Martin Luther's theology, and to his *Lectures on Galatians* in particular, where he claims that the Law is the principal weapon of "that 'great dragon, the ancient serpent, the devil, the deceiver of the whole world, who accuses our brethren day and night before God' (Rev. 12:9–10)."[1] Research for this essay was funded in part by the 2003 NEH Summer Seminar on Literature of the English Reformation at Ohio State University.

*L*AW IS EMERGING, IN THE LIGHT of recent interpretations, as a central theme of Book I," Carol V. Kaske observes as she concludes her careful study of the Red Cross knight's struggle with the dragon in Edmund Spenser's *The Faerie Queene*.[2] A number of readers have indeed called attention to Spenser's treatment of the Christian's relationship to the Law of God in this initial legend of the poem, both before and after Kaske's article, and while discussing various episodes from it. Maurice Evans, like A. C. Hamilton, reads Arthur's rescue of Red Cross from the dungeon of the Papal giant, Orgoglio, as an allegory "of the Gospel redeeming man from the prison of Law."[3] James Nohrnberg notes that Despaire well nigh damns Red Cross simply by insisting on the primacy of the Law.[4] Scholars also see allegories that serve to distinguish between Law and grace active elsewhere in Book I. Abessa, Kathryn Walls argues, is reminiscent of Hagar, and represents *Synagoga*, a Roman Catholic "reversion to the legalism and ceremonial of Judaism."[5] Ake Bergvall, advancing the

---

Spenser Studies: A Renaissance Poetry Annual, Volume XXI, Copyright © 2006 by AMS Press, Inc. All rights reserved.

arguments of both Kaske and Walls, claims that Spenser follows Augustine in dividing human history into four periods made distinct by specific relationships to the Law. The satyrs who rescue Una in Canto vi, says Bergvall, represent "pagans living according to natural religion," or before the advent of divine law as received by Moses, while Una's imprisoned parents, like Abessa, figure those living *sub lege* or "under the law."[6]

How can we account for this seeming repetition in Spenser's allegory? First of all, we need not see repetition, whether generated by the author or the single-minded interpreter, as a shortcoming. In an inventive reading of Psalm 23 translated into English by Myles Coverdale in 1523, Martin Luther contends that "the prophet giveth the word of God divers names," that he "calleth it goodly pleasant grass, fresh water, the right way, a staff, a sheep hook, a table, balm, or pleasant oil, and a cup that is always full."[7] All of the figures in the psalm, says Luther, figures which he identifies as allegories, serve solely to amplify or expound one idea: the saving power of God's Word. Second, we might remind ourselves that allegory was a controversial topic for Reformation theology. Protestants certainly did write allegories, but they also accused Catholics of spinning diabolical ones.[8] "Our miserable captivity and persecution under Antichrist the Pope," writes William Tyndale in the penultimate section of *The Obedience of a Christian Man*, is traceable to a single device. This "captivity and the decay of faith and this blindness wherein we now are," says Tyndale, "sprang first of allegories." Though he opposes the reading practices of "Origen and those of his time," who supposed that "scripture served but to feign allegories upon," who "with an antetheme of half an inch" were able to "draw a thread of nine days long,"[9] Tyndale wholeheartedly approves of allegories that distinguish between the Law and the gospel. Noting that abusive allegorists defend their practice by pointing to 2 Corinthians 3:6—"the letter killeth but the spirit giveth life"—Tyndale argues that "letter" does not refer to the literal sense, and neither does "spirit" refer to the allegorical sense. "Paul," writes Tyndale,

> by the letter meaneth Moses' law. Which the process of the text following declareth more bright than the sun. . . . Paul maketh a comparison between the law and the gospel and calleth the law the letter, because it was but letters graven in two tables of cold stone. For the law doth but kill and damn consciences, as long as there is no lust in the heart to do that which the law commandeth. Contrarywise he calleth the gospel the administration of

the spirit and of righteousness or justifying. For when Christ is preached and the promises which God hath made in Christ are believed, the spirit entereth the heart and looseth the heart and giveth lust to do the law and maketh the law a lively thing in the heart.[10]

What Tyndale develops, and he follows Luther's *Lectures on Galatians* (hereafter *Galatians*) when he does this, is not an attack on allegory as a literary device or as an interpretive practice, but rather a distinction between good and bad allegory. Good or sound theological allegory, Pauline allegory, say Luther and Tyndale, restricts itself to illustrating the difference between grace (or what Luther and Tyndale often call "promises")[11] and the Law, to depicting the triumph of faith over legalism and moralism, thereby propagating the gospel; bad allegory, developed by Antichrist to keep man enslaved, obscures this difference.[12]

St. Paul's Epistle to the Galatians 3:19–31 was a touchstone for Protestant discussion of allegory, for here Paul supports his position on the Law by employing an allegory. Luther concedes that "allegories do not provide solid proofs in theology" (*LW* 26: 435) and warns us to be careful when handling them, yet he has high praise for Paul's claim that Hagar represents the earthly Jerusalem in bondage to the Law and Sarah the heavenly Jerusalem free from the Law. "Sarah, or Jerusalem, our free mother," writes Luther,

is the church, the bride of Christ who gives birth to all. She goes on giving birth to children without interruption until the end of the world, as long as she exercises the ministry of the Word, that is, as long as she preaches and propagates the Gospel; for this is what it means for her to give birth. . . . Therefore this allegory teaches in a beautiful way that the church should not do anything but preach the Gospel correctly and purely and thus give birth to children. In this way we are all fathers and children to one another, for we are born of one another. I was born of others through the Gospel, and now I am a father to still others, who will be fathers to still others; and so this giving birth will endure until the end of the world.

(*LW* 26: 441)

This allegory appears to be echoing through Spenser's House of Holiness, as the three sisters in I.x. of *The Faerie Queene* are party to the knight's being reborn and finally getting a glimpse of the New Hierusalem. The ultra-prolific Charissa recalls Sarah, who, says Luther, like the church,

> teaches, cherishes, and carries us in her womb, her bosom, and her arms; she shapes and perfects us to the form of Christ, until we grow into perfect manhood (Eph. 4:13). . . . It is the duty of a free woman to go on giving birth to children endlessly, that is, to sons who know that they are justified by faith, not by the Law.
>
> (*LW* 26: 441–42)

If, in fact, Spenser has modeled Charissa on Sarah as figured in Galatians, this says much about Spenser's position on the relationship between charity and faith: charity, properly understood, would be another version or an embodiment of faith, and its essential purpose would be to propagate that faith. Spenser himself, one would assume, is likewise engaged in such work, as are St. Paul and Luther. St. Paul prefaces his allegory by identifying himself as one ready to bear children.[13] What Paul immediately brings forth is an allegory that distinguishes between faith and the Law, such allegory being an effective way to give spiritual birth to new believers.

Luther's *Galatians* (first translated into English in 1575 and reprinted in 1577, 1580, and 1588) is itself an extended analogy, one where Luther figures himself as a second Paul admonishing "sectarians" and "fanatics" who have lost sight of the doctrine of justification and are preaching the Law in lieu of the promises of God. Like the Papists, says Luther, the "sectarians" preach

> that Moses is Christ and Christ is Moses. This is their main proposition. Then they ridicule us for inculcating and emphasizing faith with such diligence. . . . So they have become nothing but legalists and Mosaists, defecting from Christ to Moses and calling the people back from Baptism, faith, and the promises of Christ to the Law and works, changing grace into the Law and the Law into grace.
>
> (*LW* 26: 143)

Influenced by St. Paul, Luther argues that the works required by the

Law are beyond the capabilities of fallen man, and that man can be saved solely through faith and grace. The self-righteous who believe they do the works of the Law on their own, those who do not recognize the primacy of faith, are, says Luther, doomed to both failure and damnation. "[I]t is abundantly clear," writes Luther in *Galatians*,

> what harm is caused by a righteousness that comes from the Law or is one's own, namely, that those who put their trust in it immediately lose inestimable possessions. . . . [S]omeone could write an encomium of the righteousness that comes from the Law or from oneself and develop it at great length by dwelling on each item individually.
>
> (*LW* 26: 218)

One must concede from the start that Spenser's allegorical practice, which generates a myriad of meanings, differs from that promoted by Tyndale and Luther. His entire poem is not, after all, solely a theological treatise. Yet in "The Legend of Holiness" Spenser takes up Luther's suggestion and provides a rigorous delineation of Christian righteousness and its essentially adversarial relationship with the Law. Spenser's knight struggles against enemies who are, at bottom, avatars of the Law, of conscience, of a natural, reasonable, unholy self-righteousness. Whether battling pride, the papacy, personal despair, or the devil, Red Cross is always battling with the Law and with a particularly deadly attitude toward the Law: that it can be kept.

Scholars investigating the theological positions reflected in Spenser's poetry have generated an array of opinions. Early in the twentieth century Frederick Morgan Padelford sought to establish Spenser as a Calvinist poet with Puritan tendencies.[14] Virgil A. Whitaker later countered that Spenser's work indicates he favors a theology influenced more by Luther than John Calvin, one that anticipates conservative Anglicanism. Among many of Whitaker's strong points is his observation that Una, Red Cross, and Arthur do not have any desire to raze Orgoglio's castle or altar after the giant has been overthrown. In fact, says Spenser, they "Did in that castle afterwards abide,/To rest them selues, and weary powres repaire,/Where store they fownd of al, that dainty was and rare" (I.viii.50).[15] Kaske, who, like Whitaker, claims "Spenser's treatments of images and of the monastic life . . . are so favorable that they cannot be reconciled with the Calvinist hegemony," sees Spenser as a "positive adiaphorist," or as one advocating for freedom or liberty regarding "practices neither commanded nor forbidden in Scripture."[16] More recently, some of Spenser's attentive readers have discovered Catholic elements or moments in Spenser's poem, in spite of the presence of Orgoglio and Duessa. Harold Weatherby, for example, argues that Spenser's treatments of images and the sacraments are more Catholic than Calvinist, and that his House of Holiness resembles a Catholic monastery.[17]

The theology that the scholars (excluding Padelford) have uncovered in Spenser's poetry is, paradoxically, one that insists upon drawing a sharp distinction between Law and gospel and that identifies Papal Rome with Antichrist, yet one that is adamantly indifferent to many traditional Roman Catholic rites and practices. In this, Spenser's theology resembles that of Luther, whose understanding of the Lord's Supper was much closer to that of the Catholics than to that of Huldrych Zwingli, and who shared little of the iconoclasm of Zwingli or Calvin.[18] And though Luther breaks his monastic vows and holds that others should do so as well, arguing that monasticism is a form of self-righteousness,[19] he does not condemn fasting and other methods of restraining the flesh absolutely.[20] For Luther, the model Christian is Bernard, "a man so pious, holy, and chaste," writes Luther,

> that I think he deserves to be put ahead of all other monks. Once, when he was gravely ill and despaired of his life, he did not place his trust in the celibacy that he had observed so chastely, or in the good works and acts of piety that he had performed in such quantity; but he put all these far from sight and took hold of the blessing of Christ by faith. . . . He did not set his monkery or his angelic life against the wrath and judgment of God but took hold of the one thing that is needful and thus was saved. I believe that Jerome, Gregory, and many other fathers and hermits were saved the same way.
>
> (*LW* 26: 460)

These holy fathers were saved, Luther allows, not by their pious works or their impressive attempts to adhere to the Law, but because they were able to put this form of righteousness behind them and adopt another. Their "angelic" works themselves are fine and good, provided that they are weighed correctly and are not understood as being spiritually meritorious.

Section one of this essay, which first contrasts the teachings of Luther and Calvin regarding Christian righteousness and its relationship to the Law and then discusses select moments in Red Cross's career, argues that the theology informing Book I of Spenser's poem is more Lutheran than Calvinist. Section two explores Luther's novel understanding of the conscience and claims that the dragon troubling the citizens of Eden be read as yet another figure for the Law and its spiritual effects.

I

There are two primary strains in sixteenth-century Protestantism, strains pulling in opposite directions. The fideists attempt to break free from what they see as a self-righteous, works-driven legalism, while the moralists, emphasizing the depravity of the Catholic hierarchy, seek to purify the Church. Alister E. McGrath reminds us that, though Luther's break with the Catholic Church was propelled exclusively by soteriological matters, such was not the case with other sixteenth-century reformers such as Ulrich Zwingli, Martin Bucer and John Calvin, who were strongly influenced by Erasmian humanism. Luther's insistence that passive or alien righteousness (sometimes called "imputed righteousness"), as opposed to active righteousness, is *the* Christian righteousness, though of considerable theological significance, had, according to McGrath, "relatively little, if anything, to do with the origins of the Reformation." "The Reformed wing of the Reformation," says McGrath, "was not initially concerned with the general question of man's justification."[21] Calvin, while he follows Luther in distinguishing between the civil and spiritual functions of the Law—the former restrains the wicked, and the latter reveals and multiplies our sins and drives us toward reliance on grace—also develops a positive third use of the law, one he calls the "principal" and "proper purpose of the law."[22] E. David Willis claims that

the use of the law as a guide for believers, is, according to Calvin, its principal one. . . . Where Luther would say Christ is no new Moses and mean that Christ does not leave the law in full force, Calvin means that Christ does not undo the law and substitute his new law for it. He does not set aside the old law at all, but rather is its faithful expounder; it never ceases to

have a salutary role in aiding the Christian to live freely in
obedience to God.[23]

Merwyn S. Johnson holds that Calvin's third use of the Law undermines Luther's teaching that sinners are justified solely through faith.
"If justification comes by the gospel or faith-union with the righteousness of Jesus Christ, *apart from* the works of the law (Romans
3:23)," writes Johnson, "then the possibility of a further use of the
law for those who are justified threatens the whole dialectic of law
and gospel and the efficacy of justification as well."[24]

When commenting on Galatians 3:19, "Wherefore then serveth
the law? It was added because of transgressions," Calvin claims that
"The law has manifold uses," and that Paul does not bring them up
here simply because they are not his topic. "It is necessary to put
readers on their guard on this point," Calvin warns,

> for very many, I find, have fallen into the mistake of acknowl-
> edging no other advantage belonging to the law, but what is
> expressed in this passage. Paul himself elsewhere speaks of the
> precepts of the law as profitable for doctrine and exhortations.
> (2 Tim. 3:16) The definition here given of the use of the law
> is not complete, and those who refuse to make any other ac-
> knowledgment in favor of the law do wrong.[25]

Calvin's principal target here may be antinomianism, but he simultaneously distances himself from those who, like Luther, recognize no
positive spiritual role for the Law in their theology. Luther, it is
true, does recognize that the Law has a civil purpose, namely, to
restrain the wicked. His primary concern, however, is to insist upon
the deadly spiritual side effects of seeking righteousness through the
Law. Whereas Calvin takes pains to rescue and preserve the Law,
Luther wishes to reveal the limits of its spiritual efficacy. In his
Galatians Luther addresses the Galatian-like sectarians, who, misled
by false teachers, have lost sight of the doctrine of justification and
are busy reviving the Law.[26] He is less interested, finally, in addressing
the corruption of the Catholic Church than in exposing the false
doctrine being preached both by Rome and by "fanatics" within
the Reform movement.[27] When he does attack Rome, he carefully
distinguishes between doctrinal error, which matters (and which cannot be redressed through force), and immoral behavior, which, he

argues, is beside the point theologically. "We should," writes Luther, "pay attention not so much to the sinful lives of the papists as to their wicked doctrine and their hypocrisy, and this is what we chiefly attack" (*LW* 26: 459).[28]

Luther recognizes two uses of the Law, one civil, the other spiritual—two uses, he argues, which must not be confused. The civil Law places a necessary "restraint upon those who are unspiritual and uncivilized" (*LW* 26: 314), says Luther, and though it is instituted by God and is beneficial, it has nothing to do with salvation. It is the domain of princes, executioners, and other ministers of state.[29] What Luther has to say about obedience to the Law parallels what Contemplation says about service in Gloriana's army: it is good to do, one should do it, but nevertheless, spiritually it remains a deadly sin.[30] The spiritual and primary purpose of the Law, according to Luther, which is wholly negative, is the exclusive concern of theologians and Christians. The spiritual Law reveals our "sin, blindness, misery, wickedness, ignorance, hate and contempt of God, death, hell, judgment and the well-deserved wrath of God" (*LW* 26: 309). The Law is necessary for salvation, for it humbles man, robs him of his monstrous self-righteousness, and prepares him for grace. And that is all the Law should do. There is a point, says Luther, after it has performed the Herculean task of humbling and destroying man's wicked righteousness and preparing the way for God's righteousness, when the Law must be absolutely abandoned, forgotten, and Moses regarded "as an excommunicated and condemned heretic, worse than the pope and the devil" (*LW* 26: 365). Worse than the devil! For Luther, the Law becomes more than diabolical when "it ascend[s] into the conscience and exert[s] its rule there" (*LW* 26: 11).

Central to Luther's theology is the doctrine of alien or passive righteousness, a "righteousness hidden in a mystery," says Luther, "which the world does not understand." "Human reason," Luther explains, "cannot refrain from looking at active righteousness, that is, its own righteousness" (*LW* 26: 5). It is human nature to desire to redress one's sins by repenting and vowing to behave more virtuously in the future. But since the Law can do nothing but terrify one's conscience and drive one to despair, the "afflicted conscience has no remedy . . . except to take hold of the promise of grace offered in Christ, that is, this righteousness of faith, this passive or Christian righteousness" (*LW* 26: 5–6). "Then do we do nothing and work nothing in order to obtain this righteousness?" asks Luther; he answers: "Nothing at all. For this righteousness means to do nothing, to hear nothing, and to know nothing about the Law or about works" (*LW* 26: 8).

Luther insists that justification is solely a theological or divine matter, and that therefore it has nothing to do with ethics or morality, the domain of the philosopher. Aware that there are many passages in Scripture that talk about "working" and "doing," Luther, in an extended commentary on Galatians 3:10,[31] claims that there are three kinds of "doing": natural, moral, and spiritual. Natural doing, says Luther, is a matter of performing a deed, while moral doing requires performing the deed with a good heart or pure intention; spiritual doing, however, requires faith. And as in the case of a moral deed, where the intention is the essence or form of the deed, and the deed itself but an instance or accident of the intention, so with the faithful deed it is faith itself that informs the deed. Whenever a Christian comes across the words "doing" and "working" in Scripture, says Luther, he should read them spiritually or theologically, as opposed to morally or philosophically, and understand that the words refer to *faithful* doing or working (*LW* 26: 248–68).

This is something that Red Cross appears unaware of prior to visiting the House of Holiness in Canto x; as a number of readers have noted, in his first adventure the knight relies on his force in lieu of his faith. "Add faith vnto your force, and be not faint," Una advises Red Cross, who, "in great perplexitie"—both because he is entangled in Errour and because he does not see the relevance of her suggestion—responds by summoning "all his force" (I.i.19). Thomas A. Dughi, commenting on the fact that Redcrosse's chokehold induces Errour to spew her "floud of poyson horrible and blacke" (I.i.20), claims that this initial battle with Errour "dramatizes the doctrine of justification by faith alone," for though the knight's use of force "initially *seems* to help him in his struggle, it quickly proves to have been worse than useless."[32]

The knight's "failure" here is no local one, but the first in a series of acts that privilege works and moral behavior over faith. Red Cross, I argue, is a Galatian, and his conscience is repeatedly troubled while he pursues an active righteousness. Luther claims that Paul puns on the word "Galatians" in 1:6 when he writes "I am astonished that so quickly you are removed from Him who called you in the grace of Christ to a different gospel." St. Jerome, Luther notes, tells us that the word "Galatian" means "removed" or "fallen or carried away" (*LW* 26: 47). Red Cross behaves like a Galatian as he abandons the Truth, or Una, only to be bewitched by the seemingly attractive and virtuous "Lady Law,"[33] Duessa, who describes herself as a work-righteous creature. Red Cross falls for Duessa not only because of her outward appearance, but also because she claims to be a spotless dame on an endless quest to retrieve the "blessed body" of her "dearest Lord" (I.ii.24, 23), whose death she understands as a defeat instead of the final triumph that fulfills or satisfies the Law. Spenser warns his readers in Canto iv not to imitate the behavior of Red Cross:

> Young knight, what euer that dost armes professe,
> And through long labours huntest after fame,
> Beware of fraud, beware of ficklenesse,
> In choice, and chaunge of thy deare loued Dame,
> Least thou of her belieue too lightly blame,
> And rash misweening doe thy hart *remoue*.
>
> (I.iv.1, italics mine)

Paul's Galatians, says Luther, "when they had been led astray by the false apostles and were forsaking the truth completely, . . . were so bewitched by these false arguments that they believed their whole life was moving along and running very successfully" (27: 33). We might remind ourselves that chapter 3 of Paul's Galatians begins "O foolish Galatians, who has bewitched you so that you do not obey the truth?" The self-righteous, Luther explains later in his commentary, are all bewitched. "Just as witches cast spells upon cattle and people," writes Luther,

> so idolaters, that is, all self-righteous men, would like to cast a spell upon God, to make Him the way they imagine Him in their ideas; that is, they do not want Him to justify us by mere grace and faith in Christ but to regard their acts of worship and self-chosen works and to grant them righteousness and eternal life on account of these. But they are actually casting a spell upon themselves rather than upon God; for if they persist in this wicked notion of theirs about God, they will die in their idolatry and will be damned.
>
> (*LW* 27: 90)

Red Cross, like his spiritual brother Fradubio, fails to distinguish properly between the promise of salvation through faith alone and the Law. Active righteousness, warns Luther, will always appear more attractive and holy than passive righteousness, for reason tells us that we must do something to merit salvation and thereby casts a pall over passive righteousness or true faith, making it seem sinful. Luther admits that he has "had considerable experience of this." "I know how often," writes Luther, sounding much like Fradubio, "I suddenly lose sight of the rays of the Gospel and of grace, which have been obscured for me by thick, dark clouds" (*LW* 26: 63–64).[34]

It is the Red Cross Knight's mission to rescue Una's parents, and with every adventure he pursues, with every victory he earns, he goes further astray. And he is never more lost than when he feels good about his accomplishments. Red Cross's weakness is clearly evident as he wrestles with Despaire, and his experience in Orgoglio's dungeon all but undoes him, but he is furthest from grace (and most distant from Una) at the start of Canto vi as he congratulates himself on escaping from the House of Pride.[35] "Yet sad he was," says Spenser,

> that his too hastie speed
> The fayre *Duess'* had forst him leaue behind;
> And yet more sad, that *Vna* his deare dreed
> Her truth had staynd with treason so vnkind;
> Yet cryme in her could neuer creature find,
> But for his loue, and for her own selfe sake,
> She wandred had from one to other *Ynd*,
> Him for to seeke, ne euer would forsake.
>
> (I.vi.2)

Spenser's narrative presents us with a self-righteous adventurer fleeing simultaneously from sin and from grace; fleeing from sin necessarily involves Red Cross in a flight from grace. In fact, it seems that every time Red Cross behaves virtuously (in the traditional sense of the word), he ends up in big trouble. (The one *Sans* brother who never manages to touch Red Cross is *Sans Loy*; occasionally Red Cross demonstrates a lack of faith, and he often seems less than joyful, but he remains quite attentive to the Law.) His moral indignation, which arises as he responds first to the advances and then to the escapades of Archimago's sprightly Una, only drives him into the arms of Fidessa/Duessa. The seemingly righteous decision to flee the House of Pride and reject the worldly power that leads to the grave soon lands the knight in Orgoglio's dungeon, a spiritual wasteland; Red Cross simply replaces one dunghill with another. Undoubtedly Red Cross is right to leave the House of Pride, but this, it appears, is but a "moral doing," and as it is done without faith, it is deadly, as is everything Red Cross does outside the presence of Una.[36] "From the darkness and night of their hypocrisy," writes Luther—in a sentence that could effectively gloss the fallen knight, Orgoglio, and the false Duessa—"we must drag them [the self-righteous] into the light, in order that the doctrine of justification, like the sun, may reveal their infamy and shame" (*LW* 26: 136). In Spenser's poem, the chivalric do-gooder must be tracked down and rescued by the damsel preaching grace[37] and by the knight with the enchanted shield figuring the doctrine of justification, or, as M. Pauline Parker describes it, true "humility" (89–90),[38] which finally reduces Red Cross's pride to nought.

The oft-cited lines with which Spenser opens Canto x, lines that clearly distinguish between earthly and spiritual battles, explicitly attribute man's spiritual welfare to grace alone. "What man is he, that boasts of fleshly might," writes Spenser, "And vaine assuraunce of mortality,"

> Which all so soone, as it doth come to fight,
> Against spirituall foes, yields by and by,
> Or from the fielde most cowardly doth fly?
> Ne let the man ascribe it to his skill,
> That thorough grace hath gained victory.
> If any strength we haue, it is to ill,
> But all the good is Gods, both power and eke will.
>
> (I.x.1)

In addition to anticipating Red Cross's final battle with the dragon, the lines point back to the knight's failure in the Cave of Despaire, where his spiritual foe, an advocate of the Law, makes a "secrete breach" in the knight's "conscience" (I.ix.48). Despaire convinces Red Cross that, given his sinful behavior, he is certainly damned. "Is not he iust, that all this doth behold," says Despaire. "Shall he thy sins vp in his knowledge fold,/And guilty be of thine impietie?" (I.ix.47). The "correct" answer to these rhetorical questions is "Yes,"[39] but as Despaire's framing of the questions indicates, such an answer is irrational. Red Cross is saved only when Una insists upon prioritizing the promise of grace.

> In heauenly mercies hast thou not a part?
> Why shouldst thou then despeire, that chosen art?
> Where iustice growes, there grows eke greter grace,
> The which doth quench the brond of hellish smart,
> And that accurst hand-writing doth deface.
> Arise, Sir knight arise, and leaue this cursed place.
>
> (I.ix.53)

Red Cross is no match for Despaire; given the fact that he enters the
cave demanding "iustice," he is doomed to lose this argument from
the start. The scene illustrates that justice, at least on the spiritual
level, is the last thing one needs. "Grace and peace," writes Luther,

—these two words embrace the whole of Christianity. Grace
forgives sin, and peace stills the conscience. The two devils who
plague us are sin and conscience, the power of the Law and the
sting of sin (1 Cor. 15:56). But Christ has conquered these two
monsters and trodden them underfoot, both in this age and in
the age to come. The world does not know this; therefore it
cannot teach anything sure about how to overcome sin, conscience, and death. Only Christians have this kind of teaching
and are equipped and armed with it, so that they can overcome
sin, despair, and eternal death. It is a teaching that is given only
by God; it does not proceed from free will, nor was it invented
by human reason or wisdom.

(*LW* 26: 26)

Though Red Cross fights but a single foe in Canto xi and not two
devils, the ideas expressed here by Luther frame my understanding
of Red Cross's project. At bottom, both Red Cross and those imprisoned in Eden are beset by "the power of the Law" (which both
reveals our sin and makes it abound)[40] and the exacerbating effect
that it has on the conscience. If, in fact, the final battle with the
dragon is yet another struggle with the Law, this would suggest that
Spenser understands the Law, and not immorality, nor the Papal
Antichrist, to be mankind's central foe. Such a portrayal of the power
of the Law would indicate that Spenser is closer to Luther than Calvin
when treating this central tenet of Reformation theology.

II

There is widespread critical agreement that Book I of *The Faerie
Queene* directly alludes to and is influenced by the Revelation of St.
John. Josephine Waters Bennett, noting that Book I of Spenser's
poem is indebted "both structurally and allegorically" to Revelation,
claims that "the Protestant interpretation of the Revelation should
be our guide in the study of the primary meaning" of the poem.[41]

John Erskine Hankins, following Bennett, marks additional parallels between Spenser's poem and Protestant treatments of Revelation.[42] Bennett and Hankins are most persuasive when tracing Canto viii of Book I of *The Faerie Queene* to Revelation 12–17; however, they both encounter difficulties when they come to Canto xi. Bennett says that a more immediate source for this dragon fight might be the St. George legend, and Hankins suggests that this last dragon should be traced to Daniel 7 and Job 41 instead of Revelation.[43] Neither Bennett nor Hankins can comment effectively on the state of Una's parents, whose imprisonment, after all, is the immediate cause of the adventure. Hankins offers that Una's parents "represent Adam, Eve, and the patriarchs . . . delivered by Christ from hell and the jaws of death," but soon acknowledges that the tower in which they take refuge cannot be a figure for hell, for they enter it to escape the dragon rather than to serve him. Hankins concludes suggesting that "the tower represents the Limbo of the Fathers, in which the souls of the patriarchs were preserved until Christ's earthly incarnation."[44] Yet there is an awkwardness to claiming that Red Cross has been chosen by Una to rescue the Church Fathers from Limbo, for Una's parents appear to dwell on earth.

Two scholars who negotiate the allegory in Canto xi more convincingly are Carol Kaske and Ake Bergvall, both of whom filter their readings of Book I through St. Paul's Galatians and Luther's theology. Kaske says that "the brazen tower" in which Una's parents have taken refuge, which serves "as both a defense and a prison, both keeping out and keeping in," is a "portrayal of Mosaic law in Gal. 3.23 and its commentators." "Before faith came," writes St. Paul, "we were confined under the Law, kept under restraint until faith should be revealed." Luther's commentary on this verse, Kaske writes, "emphasizes the negative aspect of law," asserting that though the law does help to maintain order in the secular realm, it "is also a spiritual prison, and a very hell."[45] This tower, if we follow Kaske, is another form of Orgoglio's dungeon, or even Fradubio's tree.[46]

Bergvall, who, as mentioned previously, argues that Spenser's poem follows Augustine and Luther's close associate Philipp Melanchthon in dividing human history into four periods,[47] likewise glosses the "mighty brasen wall" in which Una's parents have been "fast embard" for "fowr years" (I.vii.44) with Galatians 3:23. Bergvall also notes that as Una and Red Cross approach Eden they are spied by "The watchman wayting tydings glad to heare" (I.xi.3); this verse, claims Bergvall, alludes to Isaiah 52:7–8, a passage often read by reformers as prophesying both the Messiah's arrival and the transition to the third period of history, where humanity is no longer under the Law but under grace.[48] Una and her knight arrive with the intent of delivering the glad tidings that will "ease" her city of its "misery," (I.xi.3), and "With that," writes Spenser, "they heard a roaring hideous sound,"

> That all the ayre with terror filled wide,
> And seemd vneath to shake the stedfast ground.
> Eftsoones that dreadful Dragon they espyde,
> Where stretcht he lay vpon the sunny side,
> Of a great hill, himselfe like a great hill.
> But all so soone, as he from far descryde
> Those glistring armes, that heuen with light did fill,
> He rousd himselfe full blyth, and hastned them vntill.
>
> > (I.xi.4)

Spenser's phrase "with that" suggests a causal relationship between the appearance of the gospel and the awakening of the dragon. It is Luther's contention that nothing so enrages the devil as the gospel; when the gospel arrives, says Luther, the devil begins to shake us with the Law. "Let us remember this well in our personal temptations," writes Luther,

> when the devil accuses and terrifies our conscience to bring it to the point of despair. He is the father of lies (John 8:44) and the enemy of Christian freedom. At every moment, therefore, he troubles us with false terrors, so that when this freedom has been lost, the conscience is in continual fear and feels guilt and anxiety. *When that "great dragon, the ancient serpent, the devil, the deceiver of the whole world, who accuses our brethren day and night before God" (Rev. 12:9–10)*—when, I say, he comes to you and accuses you not only of failing to do anything good but of transgressing against the Law of God, then you must say: "You are troubling me with the memory of my past sins; in addition, you are telling me that I have not done anything good. This does not concern me. For if I either trusted in my performance of good works or lost my trust because I failed to perform them, in either case Christ would be of no avail to me. Therefore whether you base your objections to me on my sins or on my good works, I do not care; for I put them out of sight and depend only on the freedom for which Christ has set me free."[49]
>
> > (*LW* 27: 11, italics mine)

Luther's use of this verse from Revelation is of importance, and not only because it is the verse to which Spenser alludes in his epigram to Canto xi.[50] The Christian's ultimate nemesis, Luther argues, is not the Pope, and much less is it immoral behavior; rather, it is his easily bedeviled conscience. Heiko A. Oberman reminds us that for Luther "the conscience . . . is the natural kingdom of the Devil." Luther's devil, says Oberman,

> attacks us ceaselessly, not only from without, through fanatics and party spirit, but also from within—via the conscience. We find not a trace in Luther of what is both a medieval and a secularized modern understanding of the conscience: that there is a spot in the human soul that remains untouched by sin, that is always directed toward God, just as a compass points north, immovable and infallible, the voice of God inside us. For Luther, the conscience is so clearly the Devil's prize that the Devil appears, boring into us and gnawing us when we go to bed at night and look back on the day's events. He cites the Ten Commandments, as he knows the Bible well, in order to condemn us and claim us as his own.[51]

In his *Galatians* Luther figures the Law in three distinct ways: (1) as a divine spectacle designed to terrify and destroy monstrous self-righteousness and drive man toward grace,[52] (2) as a temporary prison where man is restrained and humbled until grace has come, or as a grammar school presided over by a fifteenth-century schoolmaster not afraid to use his whip,[53] and (3) as a great dragon that continuously accuses us of sin and thereby keeps us imprisoned and in despair. The first two of these are, according to Luther, proper manifestations of the Law, provided that they remain temporary states or preliminary stages; they last, Luther explains, only "Till the Offspring should come to whom the promise had been made" (Galatians 3:19), until the moment Christ began to preach on earth and until the individual believer, fully convinced of his or her sinfulness, begins "to blanch and to despair" (*LW* 26: 317). The third guise of the Law, however, which appears relentlessly permanent, is a satanic abuse of the Law, and a sign of an afflicted conscience that has yet to let go of its own righteousness. This abuse of the Law can be understood in two ways: as the devil perverting the Law by overextending its purpose, and as the Law itself overstaying its welcome and metamorphosing into something demonic, the devil being close kin to that part of ourselves that refuses to accept that we are wholly without merit, or our all but insurmountable self-righteousness. Luther's dragon is that which "prowls around and seeks to devour us (1 Peter 5:8)" by obscuring "the pure doctrine of faith" (*LW* 26: 3).[54]

The prison of the Law, Luther argues, ought to be temporary; it should last only until one has been broken and faith has arrived. After the Law has completely destroyed our belief that we can do better, that we can behave righteously, we are open to grace. Once grace has come, Luther argues, we must not turn back to the Law, for to do so is to turn our back on grace and thereby re-imprison ourselves. When the Law attempts to do more than its office, it becomes a dragon that keeps us imprisoned in despair. If we did not still cling to our belief in our own self-righteousness, however, this dragon could not trouble us; the presence of the dragon indicates that self-righteousness has not been completely overthrown, that it has grudgingly settled down in the prison of the Law. This dragon is, in part if not in whole, a projection of a tortured conscience that tenaciously refuses to let go of its belief in its own righteousness. The more we insist on our own righteousness, Luther holds, the bigger and noisier the dragon grows. Luther describes his own battles with a guilty conscience in *Galatians*, saying:

> Outwardly I was not like other men: extortioners, unjust, adulterers (Luke 18:11). I observed chastity, poverty, and obedience. In addition, I was free of the cares of this present life and was devoted only to fasting, vigils, prayers, reading Mass, and things like that. Nevertheless, under the cover of this sanctity and confidence I was nursing incessant mistrust, doubt, fear, hatred, and blasphemy against God. This righteousness of mine was nothing but a cesspool and the delightful kingdom of the devil. For Satan loves such saints and treats as his own beloved those who destroy their own bodies and souls, and who deprive themselves of all the blessings of the gifts of God. Even as they do this, however, malice, blindness, contempt for God, ignorance of the Gospel, profanation of the Sacraments, blasphemy and abuse of Christ, and the neglect of all the blessings of God hold full sway in them. In short, such saints are the slaves of Satan.
>
> (*LW* 26: 70)

Luther's understanding of the behavior of the afflicted conscience anticipates Sigmund Freud's discussion of unconscious guilt. Luther's dragon is much like Freud's "harsh taskmaster," the superego or ego ideal, which makes impossible moral demands, and which, because of its privileged relationship with the Id, knows full well that we begrudge them.[55] Freud claims that the "severity of the superego does not—or does not so much—represent the severity which one has experienced from it, . . . or which one attributes to it; it represents rather one's own aggressiveness towards it."[56] This hidden animosity towards the superego, which serves but to strengthen the superego, is, says Freud, only intensified by instinctual renunciations.[57]

Early in her analysis of Red Cross's struggle with the dragon, Kaske notes that Spenser employs a pun that can also be found in Luther's *Galatians.* "Although the Galatians had been illumined, were believers, and had received the Holy Spirit through the preaching of faith," writes Luther,

> there still remained in them this shred of their old vice, this tinder [*fomes*] that so easily caught the flame of false teaching. Therefore let no one be so confident of himself as to suppose that when he has received grace, he is completely cleansed of his old vices. Many things are indeed cleansed, especially the head of the serpent—that is, unbelief and ignorance of God are cut off and crushed (Gen. 3:15)—but the scaly body and the remnants of sin still remain in us.
>
> (*LW* 26: 189)

Kaske claims that Spenser, too, is punning on the Latin word *fomes* (which, in addition to "tinder," also stands for man's natural corruption or concupiscence) in I.xi.26, when the dragon sends forth a spark and Red Cross's beard becomes enflamed. "Spenser's curious detail of the beard in which the spark catches," claims Kaske, " . . . dramatizes tinder, the literal meaning of Latin *fomes*."[58] Kaske then proceeds to read the knight's three-day battle with the dragon as an allegory tracing the stages of the sin of concupiscence. If, however, Spenser is indeed thinking of Luther's passage above, or of Luther's theology in general, Red Cross's Galatian-like sin would be less indicative of a natural concupiscence than of a natural inclination to pursue an active righteousness, that is, a "false teaching," and to eschew the doctrine of justification. "If works are sought after as a means to righteousness, are burdened with this perverse leviathan, and are done under the false impression that through them one is justified," writes Luther,

they are made necessary and freedom and faith are destroyed;
and this addition to them makes them no longer good but
truly damnable works. . . . This leviathan, or perverse notion
concerning works, is unconquerable where sincere faith is
wanting. Those work-saints cannot get rid of it unless faith, its
destroyer, comes and rules in their hearts. Nature of itself cannot
drive it out or even recognize it, but rather regards it as a mark
of the most holy will. If the influence of custom is added and
confirms this perverseness of nature, as wicked teachers have
caused it to do, it becomes an incurable evil and leads astray
and destroys countless men beyond all hope of restoration.[59]

Spenser's dragon, like Luther's "perverse leviathan" or self-righteousness, can not be defeated actively. Red Cross can only defeat the
Law by dying to it,[60] as he does two times over; his final victory over
the dragon is directly attributable to his being defeated on each of
the first two days. There is but one thing that "knocks out the teeth
of the Law, blunts its sting and all its weapons, and utterly disables
it" (*LW* 26: 161), says Luther while commenting on Galatians 2:19
(For I through the Law died to the Law, that I might live in God).
One must become dead to the law by admitting one's guilt and
clinging exclusively to faith and grace.

John N. King notes that Red Cross's triumph over the dragon in
Canto xi little resembles the common graphic portrayal of the knight
charging the beast and "driving the spear through its neck." Spenser's
account of the battle, King says, alludes instead to Revelation
19:11–15, where one called "Faithful and true" arrives with a sword
issuing from his mouth.[61] This sword, King says, oft interpreted as a
figure for the Word of God, coincides with the sword which Una
has presented to Red Cross: the sword from Ephesians 7:17, which
Paul calls the Word of God. King's point here is that "Redcrosse's
role in the dragon combat is no more than instrumental," that it is
not the knight but the "blade personifying the power of the Word
that slays the beast." Though he may have passed through the House
of Holiness, the Christian knight, as King argues, is still incapable of
performing spiritual works, for they are "wholly a gift of divine
grace" (199).[62]

Red Cross's victory over the dragon illustrates Luther's concept of
alien or passive righteousness. "This righteousness," Luther explains
in a passage that could gloss I.xi.29–36, where the knight demonstrates a new vigor after having been bathed in "*The well of life*"

(I.xi.29), "is given to men in baptism and whenever they are truly repentant. Therefore a man can with confidence boast in Christ and say: 'Mine are Christ's living, doing, and speaking, his suffering and dying, mine as much as if I had lived, done, spoken, suffered, and died as he did.' "[63] Red Cross becomes a figure for Christ, replaying Christ's victory over sin and death, through imputed righteousness. Despite the apocalyptic tone of the canto, though, Red Cross's local victory over his dragon remains partial or incomplete. The citizens of Eden are not absolutely foolish to fear that there remains "some lingring life within" the dragon's "hollow brest," or that their children may yet be scratched by his "talants" (I.xii.10–11). Even after the Law has been disabled, Luther argues, it "remains a Law for the wicked and unbelieving" and "also for us who are weak, to the extent that we do not believe. Here it still has its sharpness and its teeth" (*LW* 26: 161–62). "Christ daily drives out the old Adam more and more," writes Luther, "in accordance with the extent to which faith and knowledge of Christ grow. For alien righteousness is not instilled all at once, but it begins, makes progress, and is finally perfected at the end through death."[64]

Spenser's dragon, "horrible and stearne" (I.i.3), the "cruell cursed enemy" of the citizens of Eden, has "long opprest" them "with tort" (I.xii.4), and "spoild" and "wasted" their land. "Themselues, for feare into his iawes to fall," writes Spenser,

> He forst to castle strong to take their flight,
> Where fast embard in mighty brasen wall,
> He has them now fowr years besiegd to make them thrall.
>
> Full many knights aduenturous and stout
> Haue enterprizd that Monster to subdew;
> From euery coast that heauen walks about,
> Haue thither come the noble Martial crew,
> That famous harde atchieuements still pursew,
> Yet neuer any could that girlond win,
> But all still shronke, and still he greater grew:
> All they for want of faith, or guilt of sin,
> The piteous pray of his fiers cruelty haue bin.

(I.vii.44–45)

Una's parents and all the citizens of Eden have retreated into a castle that has become a prison, and there they remain, not because there is a dearth of brave, heroic knights—in fact, there appears to be an abundance of them, the remains of which Red Cross will spot between the dragon's teeth—but because the knights who challenged this dragon were either guilty of sin or lacked the necessary faith. The fact that Red Cross has proven himself to be a sinner does not seem to have disqualified him as a combatant, though, so either "guilt of sin" is less significant than "want of faith" (that is, his faith covers his guilt with an imputed righteousness), or the phrases "want of faith" and "guilt of sin" are synonymous (a lack of faith makes one feel guilty or sinful, "guilt" here referring to a psychological state rather than to culpability). It is this lack of faith or shrinking, this guilty feeling resulting from reliance on self-righteousness, that feeds the dragon.

All the remarkable weapons of Spenser's fire-breathing dragon—tail, claws, teeth, his terror-breeding roar[65]—are, to borrow from Luther's "Exposition upon the 23rd Psalm," allegories for the deadly aspects of the Law. The dominant *b* rhyme in stanzas 12 and 41 of Canto xi, which echoes "laws," suggests this on the purely acoustic level.[66] The dragon, whom we are told is "himselfe like a great hill" (I.xi.4), and who sends "smoothering smoke and sulphure seare / Out of his stinking gorge" in order to engender and heighten "cold congealed feare" (I.xi.13), seems designed to recall Mt. Sinai as described in Exodus 19–20.[67] Spenser tells us that when the dragon would take to the air, "The clowdes before him fledd for terror great, / And all the heuens stood still amazed with his threat" (I.xi.10). Kaske suggests that the dragon's sting alludes to I Corinthians 15:55–56—"The sting of death is sinne, and the strength of sinne is the Lawe"—and notes that Augustine, following Romans 7.8, argues, "concupiscence is aggravated by the law" (614). We might further gloss the dragon's "two stings" with Luther's allusion to I Corinthians 15:56 cited above: "The two devils who plague us are sin and conscience, the power of the Law and the sting of sin" (*LW* 26: 26).

The knight's real spiritual advances, both during the dragon fight and elsewhere in the poem, are marked not by his own diligence or willpower, but rather by his being reluctantly dragged forward or unwillingly knocked backward into unanticipated grace. When Arthur rescues Red Cross from Orgoglio's dungeon, the imprisoned knight calls out for death; as Red Cross prepares to comply with Despaire's behest, Una must forcefully disarm him and remind him of his purpose. Hamilton glosses Red Cross's fortunate fall beneath the Tree of Life in I.xi.45 by noting "now the Knight co-operates with saving grace,"[68] but he then adds that the knight's "backsliding" marks the extent of his cooperation. This is a special partnership, for the knight participates against his will. His cooperation consists of nothing more than a failure to retain his balance. Moreover, as he is unaware that grace awaits him beneath the tree, he wholeheartedly struggles to avoid encountering it; he falls "with dread of shame sore terrifide" (I.xi.45), in spite of his previous experience at the end of the first day's battle.

At the close of the second day, the knight lies beneath the Tree of Life "as in a dreame of deepe delight,/Besmeard with pretious Balme, whose vertuous might/Did heale his woundes, and scorching heat alay" (I.xi.50). The lines recall and reverse Red Cross's previous misadventure with Duessa, where he drinks from the cursed fountain and finds himself "Pourd out in loosnesse on the grassy grownd" (I.vii.7), and perhaps his initial dreams of Una in Canto i as well. His "dreame of deepe delight" also echoes Arthur's account of his being visited by the Faerie Queene, a visitation which likewise occurs against the dreamer's will. Arthur reveals that as he had been instructed to "subdew" the "creeping flames" of love with "reason" (I.ix.9), he long resisted it, regarding "loue, and louers life,/As losse of time, and vertues enimy" (I.ix.10). But, as he is fond of noting:

> Nothing is sure, that growes on earthly grownd:
> And who most trustes in arme of fleshly might,
> And boasts, in beauties chaine not to be bouwnd,
> Doth soonest fall in disauentrous fight,
> And yeeldes his caytiue neck to victours most despight.[69]
>
> (I.ix.11)

As Arthur dreams, he receives an unexpected promise from Gloriana that he has been chosen by her, and his "hart" is quickly "rauisht with delight" (I.ix.14). Arthur awakens with a new purpose and resolve, as does Red Cross after receiving the sacramental grace at the close of days one and two.[70] The "dreame of deepe delight," the poem insists, is where the real "action" rests, for it is there that the promise quickens the spirit and silences the Law.

Nicholls State University

NOTES

1. *Lectures on Galatians, 1535, Luther's Works* (*LW*), vols. 26 and 27, eds. Jaroslav Pelikan and Walter A Hansen, trans. Jaroslav Pelikan (St. Louis: Concordia Publishing House, 1963, 1964), 27: 11.

2. "The Dragon's Spark and Sting and the Structure of Red Cross's Dragonfight: *The Faerie Queene*, I.xi–xii," *Studies in Philology* 66 (1969): 636.

3. *Spenser's Anatomy of Heroism* (Cambridge: Cambridge University Press, 1970), 105. A. C. Hamilton claims that "the rending of the veil of Arthur's shield marks the violent irruption of divine grace into the natural world through which man may be freed from the bondage of the Law to live under the covenant of Mercy." *The Structure of Allegory in "The Faerie Queene"* (Oxford: Clarendon Press, 1961), 78. See also S. K. Heninger, Jr., "The Orgoglio Episode in *The Faerie Queene*," *ELH* 26 (1959): 171–87.

4. Nohrnberg views Despaire as "an interpreter of the Law," who "contemplates . . . the old covenant to the exclusion of the new one." *The Analogy of "The Faerie Queene"* (Princeton: Princeton University Press, 1976), 152. See also Daryll Gless, *Interpretation and Theology in Spenser* (Cambridge: Cambridge University Press, 1994), 143–45. Nohrnberg and Gless also associate Ignaro, the keeper of the keys to Orgoglio's dungeon, with the Law. See *Analogy*, 152 and *Interpretation*, 139. Susan Snyder argues that Despaire is a distinctly Lutheran figure for the Law. See "The Left Hand of God: Despair in Medieval and Renaissance Tradition," *Studies in the Renaissance* 12 (1965): 18–59. Vern Torczon holds that Orgoglio represents the sin of "presumption," or "over-reliance on one's own abilities" (126), the flip side of the sin of despair, or the belief that one's sin's are so great that they cannot be forgiven. See "Spenser's Orgoglio and Despaire," *Texas Studies in Literature and Language* 3 (1961): 123–28.

5. "Abessa and the Lion: *The Faerie Queene*, I.3.1–12," *Spenser Studies* 5 (1984): 10.

6. *Augustinian Perspectives in the Renaissance* (Uppsala: Studia Anglistica Upsaliensia, 2001), 205, 202. Kaske says that Spenser follows Luther's *Lectures on Galatians* by figuring the Law as a prison. See "Dragon's Spark and Sting," 632. Richard Douglas Jordan offers an alternate reading of the satyrs, claiming that "Una's sojourn among the satyrs is meant to be read as an account of Truth among the Jews in Old Testament times" (124). "Una Among the Satyrs: *The Faerie Queene*, 1.6," *Modern Language Quarterly* 38 (1977): 123–31.

7. "Exposition upon the 23rd Psalm," trans. Myles Coverdale, *Remains of Myles Coverdale*, ed. George Pearson (Cambridge: Cambridge University Press, 1846), 282.

8. John N. King says that "it is erroneous to presume that 'Protestant suspicion' of allegory makes this mode 'a peculiar form' for Spenser to use as a 'self-consciously Reformed poet.' His contemporaries and the English Protestant authors of the preceding generation found ample precedent in the writings of William Tyndale for their use of allegorical fiction as a pleasing vehicle for conveying religious and moral truth." *Spenser's Poetry and the Reformation Tradition* (Princeton: Princeton University Press, 1990), 76–77.

9. *The Obedience of a Christian Man*, ed. David Daniell (New York: Penguin, 2000), 160.

10. *Obedience*, 160–61.

11. Luther distinguishes between promises and the Law throughout his commentary on Galatians; the distinction receives particular attention as Luther treats Galatians 3:8–10, where Paul identifies Abraham as being a man of faith. See *LW* 26: 241–55. For an account of how Luther's theology is shaped by his "discovery" of such promises in the Hebrew Bible, see James Samuel Preus, *From Shadow to Promise:*

Old Testament Interpretation from Augustine to Young Luther (Cambridge: Harvard University Press, 1969).

12.   For more on the allegorical practices developed in response to 2 Corinthians 3:6 see H. R. MacCallum, "Milton and the Figurative Interpretation of the Bible," *University of Toronto Quarterly* 31 (1962): 397–415.

13.   See Galatians 4:19, "My little children, with whom I am again in travail until Christ be formed in you!"

14.   See "Spenser and the Theology of Calvin," *Modern Philology* 12 (1914): 1–18, "Spenser and the Spirit of Puritanism," *Modern Philology* 14 (1916): 31–44, and "The Spiritual Allegory of *The Faerie Queene*, Book One," *Journal of English and Germanic Philology* 22 (1923): 1–17.

15.   *The Religious Basis of Spenser's Thought* (Stanford: Stanford University Press, 1950), 27. All passages quoted from *The Faerie Queene* come from *Spenser: The Faerie Queene*, ed. A. C. Hamilton, 2nd ed. (New York: Longman, 2001). See also John N. King, "Was Spenser a Puritan?" *Spenser Studies* 6 (1985): 1–31. King identifies Spenser as a "progressive Protestant" less interested in "Puritan issues involving ecclesiastical polity and discipline, clerical vestments, the use of candles, kneeling during communion, and the playing of music during services" than in "broad Reformation problems of faith, spiritual regeneration, and salvation" (3).

16.   "The Audiences of *The Faerie Queene*: Iconoclasm and Related Issues in Books I, V, and VI," *Literature & History* 3 (1994): 16, 25.

17.   "Holy Things," *English Literary Renaissance* 29 (1999): 422–42. Anne Lake Prescott likewise says that "Spenser seems strangely friendly toward some Catholic practices and texts" (10). See "Complicating the Allegory: Spenser and Religion in Recent Scholarship," *Renaissance and Reformation / Renaissance et Reforme* 25 (2001): 9–23.

18.   Regarding Luther's insistence on the real physical presence of Christ in the Lord's Supper, and his heated disagreement with his fellow reformers on this matter, see *The Sacrament of the Body and Blood of Christ—Against the Fanatics*, *LW*, vol. 36, ed. Abdel Ross Wentz, trans. A. T. W. Steinhauser and revised by Frederick C. Ahrens and Abdel Ross Wentz (Philadelphia: Fortress Press, 1959), 329–61 and *Confession Concerning Christ's Supper* and *That These Words of Christ, "This Is My Body," etc., Still Stand Firm Against the Fanatics*, *LW*, vol. 37, ed. and trans. Robert H. Fischer (Philadelphia: Muhlenberg Press, 1961), 3–150 and 151–372. For a discussion of the difference between Luther and Calvin regarding the danger of images see Margaret Aston's *England's Iconoclasts*, vol. 1 (Oxford: Clarendon Press, 1980), 391–92. "Would to God," says Luther "that I could persuade the rich and the mighty that they would permit the whole Bible to be painted on houses, on the inside and outside, so that all can see it. That would be a Christian work." See *Against the Heavenly Prophets in the Matter of Images and Sacraments*, *LW*, vol. 40, ed. and trans. Conrad Bergendoff (Philadelphia: Muhlenberg Press, 1958), 99.

19.   "[W]hoever seeks righteousness apart from faith in Christ," Luther writes, "—whether it be through works or satisfactions or afflictions or the Law of God—is nullifying the grace of God and despising the death of Christ, even though he may speak otherwise with his mouth" (*LW* 26: 185).

20.   "[W]e . . . do not reject fasting," says Luther, "and other pious practices as something damnable, but we do teach that by these practices we do not obtain the forgiveness of sins" (*LW* 26: 84).

21. *Iusticia Dei: A History of the Doctrine of Justification*, vol. 2 (Cambridge: Cambridge University Press, 1986), 8. See also McGrath's "Humanist Elements in the Early Reformed Doctrine of Justification," *Archiv fur Reformatiosgeschichte* 73 (1982): 5–19. Karl Barth writes that "one thing at least is certain—that if the theology of Calvin has a center at all, it does not lie in the doctrine of justification." See *Church Dogmatics*, vol. 4, trans. Rev. G. W. Bromiley (Edinburgh: T. & T. Clark, 1956), 525. William J. Bouwsma argues that Calvin, while following Augustine in teaching that man is absolutely dependent on God's grace for salvation, was also influenced by a Stoic strain in Renaissance humanism that held reason to be a "legitimate source of religious insight" (20). Calvin's doctrine of Election, Bouwsma claims, is rooted in Stoic thought. "One of the marks of the Stoic humanist," says Bouwsma, "was his constant, rather nervous concern to differentiate himself from the vulgar crowd and to reassure himself, somewhat in the manner at times of the Protestant elect, of his spiritual superiority" (32). See "The Two Faces of Humanism," *Itinerarium Italicum: The Profile of the Italian Renaissance in the Mirror of its European Transformations*, eds. Heiko A. Oberman and Thomas A. Brady, Jr. (Leiden: E. J. Brill, 1975), 3–60.

22. *Institutes of the Christian Religion*, vol. 2, ed. John T. McNeil, trans. Ford Lewis Battles (Philadelphia: Westminster Press, 1960), 2.7.12.

23. *Calvin's Catholic Christology: The Function of the So-Called Extra Calvinisticum in Calvin's Theology* (Leiden: E. J. Brill, 1966), 140. See also Ernst Troeltsch's *The Social Teaching of the Christian Churches*, trans. Olive Wyon (New York: Harper Torchbooks, 1960), where Troeltsch claims that "in Lutheranism the moral law of Scripture was regarded as having been instituted solely in order to produce conviction of sin," whereas in Calvinism "the Law was regarded as a positive Christian moral law, as the standard of personal and congregational discipline" (594).

24. "Calvin's Handling of the Third Use of the Law and Its Problems," *Calviniana: Ideas and Influence of John Calvin*, ed. Robert V. Schnucker (Kirksville: Sixteenth Century Studies, 1988), 33. Edward A. Dowey likewise recognizes that Luther and Calvin have a fundamental disagreement over the nature and purpose of the Law. "Luther's apprehension of the law as a curse and a killer, from Scripture in correlation with his own experience as a monk and a priest," writes Dowey, "made it forever impossible for him to consider a third, positive 'use' for the law. . . . It is precisely here that the great debate with Calvin and Calvinism begins. For all the agreement on various designations for law in these two theologies, and even that it is the law that curses and kills, there is a very different fundamental apprehension of the law in Calvin." See "Law in Luther and Calvin," *Theology Today* 41 (1984): 151. I. John Hesselink claims that "Calvin recognizes fully the negative function of the law" and that he holds this negative function to be "a proper function of the law *in so far as* the ministry of Moses is opposed to the ministry of Christ and the gospel." Calvin, however, adds Hesselink, does not hold this to be "the complete picture," for "only an aspect or part of the law is dealt with when the law is so portrayed." See *Calvin's Concept of the Law* (Allison Park: Pickwick Publications, 1992), 193. Heiko A. Oberman also sees Luther as standing apart from other Reformation theologians (whom he claims are all Erasmian) who seek a moral reformation. The moralists "won out," says Oberman, "and pulled a gray veil over all of Europe—a veil that spread from

Switzerland and France to the Netherlands, England and finally to the United States." *The Reformation: Roots and Ramifications*, trans. Andrew Colin Gow (Grand Rapids: William B. Eerdmans, 1994), 73.

25.   *Calvin's Commentaries*, vol. 21, ed. and trans. Rev. William Pringle (Grand Rapids: Baker Book House, 1984), 99–100.

26.   Luther first makes this claim in the "Argument" that prefaces his commentary (see *LW* 26: 9), and he repeats it throughout *Galatians*.

27.   Luther sometimes singles out the Anabaptists, sometimes the Zwinglians; his enemy, finally, is anyone who does not accept the doctrine of justification and his teachings on the purpose of the Law.

28.   See also *LW* 26: 221–25, where Luther suggests that Christians say to the Pope: "I am willing to kiss your feet, pope, and to acknowledge you as the supreme pontiff, if you adore my Christ and grant that we have the forgiveness of sins and eternal life through His death and resurrection and not through the observance of your traditions. If you yield here, I shall not take away your crown and power. But if you do not, I shall constantly cry out that you are the Antichrist." "The sectarians," writes Luther, who are not focused exclusively on doctrinal error, "do not do this; they only try to take away the crown and power of the pope by external force. Therefore their effort is useless" (224–25).

29.   See Luther's *Temporal Authority: To What Extent It Should Be Obeyed* in *Martin Luther's Basic Theological Writings*, ed. Timothy F. Lull (Minneapolis: Fortress Press, 1989), 655–703.

30.   See Bergvall, *Augustinian Perspectives*, 196.

31.   "For all who rely on works of the Law are under a curse. For it is written: Cursed be everyone who does not abide by all things written in the book of the Law, and do them."

32.   "Redcrosse's Springing Well of Faith," *Studies in English Literature, 1500–1900* 37 (1997): 26. See also Gless, *Interpretation*, 65–66, King, *Spenser's Poetry*, 187, 197, and Richard Mallette, *Spenser and the Discourses of Reformation England* (Lincoln: University of Nebraska Press, 1997), 25.

33.   Luther uses the term "Lady Law" disparagingly when distinguishing between "the promise" (the free gift of grace), and the Law. See *LW* 26: 302.

34.   See *The Faerie Queene*, I.ii.34–43.

35.   Maurice Evans notes that though Red Cross "has the sense to escape from the Palace of Pride, it is through the merely prudential advice of the dwarf who reminds him of the lessons of history, not through any principle of ultimate truth derived from his understanding." See *Spenser's Anatomy*, 99.

36.   The third thesis in Luther's "Heidelberg Disputation" claims that "Although the works of man always seem attractive and good, they are nevertheless likely to be mortal sins." "Human works appear attractive outwardly," Luther elaborates, "but within they are filthy." See *Martin Luther's Basic Theological Writings*, 30, 34. See also Gless's *Interpretation*, where he argues that Red Cross's disdain for Lucifera's court "includes a moralistic element which some theological perspectives would judge to be culpable" (92). Gless also suggests that Red Cross's "aloofness" upon arrival at Lucifera's court "springs from injured vanity" (93).

37.   Though Una may be said to stand for other things (such as truth, the true church, and Elizabeth), she also is repeatedly associated with faith, grace, and the

gospel. See 1.1.19, 1.8.1, 1.9.53, and1.11.3. C. S. Lewis notes that "throughout the book Una encourages, even rescues" Redcrosse, "and at one point she is associated very closely with divine grace." See *Spenser's Images of Life*, ed. Alastair Fowler (Cambridge: Cambridge University Press, 1967), 111.

38. Arthur's "shield is the immediate symbol of humility in action," writes Parker, "that dreadful shield which he so seldom unveils deliberately; it is the shield of humility because it shows things as they are." *The Allegory of "The Faerie Queene"* (Oxford: Clarendon Press, 1960), 90.

39. See Nohrnberg, Analogy, 152.

40. See Romans 5:20.

41. *The Evolution of "The Faerie Queene,"* (Chicago: University of Chicago Press, 1942; reprint, New York: B. Franklin, 1960), 109, 119.

42. *Source and Meaning in Spenser's Allegory: A Study of "The Faerie Queene,"* (Oxford: Clarendon Press, 1971).

43. Bennett, *Evolution of "The Faerie Queene,"* 117 and Hankins, *Source and Meaning*, 110.

44. Hankins, *Source and Meaning*, 112.

45. Kaske, "Dragon's Spark and Sting," 632. "The Law," writes Luther, "is our tormentor and our prison. . . . Therefore, anyone who says that he loves the Law is lying and does not know what he is saying. A thief or a robber who loved his prison and his shackles would be insane and out of his mind. But since . . . the Law confines us, it is certain that we are its bitterest enemies. In other words, we love the Law and its righteousness just as much as a murderer loves prison" (*LW* 26: 340).

46. William Nelson suggests that the condition of Fradubio and Fraelissa recalls that of Adam and Eve immediately after their act of disobedience. "According to the Vulgate," writes Nelson, "when the disobedient pair heard the voice of God in the Garden they hid themselves 'in medio ligni paradisi.' The singular *ligni* is usually translated 'of the trees' or 'of the forest' but the interpretation which made Adam and Eve hide inside a *tree* or within the shade of it is a persistent one." See *The Poetry of Edmund Spenser: A Study* (New York: Columbia University Press, 1963), 163.

47. The four stages or periods that Augustine recognizes, says Bergvall, are before the law, under the law, under grace, and in peace, the first three of which are each to last two thousand years. Bergvall notes that the "Elizabethan reader had easy access to this progression even without going back to Augustine. It had become common property long before the sixteenth century, and the reformers adopted it for their own ends" (201). See also Kaske, "Dragon's Spark and Sting," 632–33.

48. Bergvall, *Augustinian Perspectives*, 202 and Kaske, "Dragon's Spark and Sting," 632. Anne Lake Prescott reminds me that the verse may also allude to illustrations in the Sarum Missal depicting St. George slaying the dragon as the King and Queen watch from behind the castle walls. See "Una's lamb Fig 1" in *The Spenser Encyclopedia*, ed. A. C. Hamilton (Toronto: University of Toronto Press, 1990; reprint 1997).

49. Luther figures the Law as a dragon in his *Commentary on Psalm 110* as well. Here he argues that "the devil and his scales" seek to suppress "the Word of the Gospel" and replace it with the terrors of the Law (*LW* 13: 280). Luther's gloss of Revelation 12: 9–10 as a figure for the Law rather than a figure for the Roman

Catholic church is noteworthy, for it indicates he sees self-righteousness as the greatest enemy of the Christian, the papacy being but an instance or manifestation of this sin.

50. "The knight with that old Dragon fights/two days incessantly." See Hamilton's note, 137.

51. *The Reformation: Roots and Ramifications*, 65–66. See also George W. Forell, "Luther and Conscience," *The Lutheran Theological Seminary at Gettysburg Bulletin* 55 (1994): 3–11. Forell says that Luther breaks with traditional Christian teaching and develops a novel understanding of the conscience, one that holds that the faculty is a tool of the devil. Only when the conscience is completely free of the Law can it become something other than the devil's plaything. We might note as well that the seventeenth-century allegorist John Bunyan witnesses to the great comfort he found in Luther's argument in *Galatians*. Luther, Bunyan reports, "in that book debate[s] of the rise of these temptations, namely, Blasphemy, Desperation, and the like, shewing that the law of *Moses*, as well as the Devil, Death, and Hell, hath a very great hand therein; the which at first was very strange to me, but considering and watching, I found it so indeed. . . . [T]his methinks I must let fall before all men, I do prefer this book of Mr. *Luther* upon the *Galathians*, (excepting the Holy Bible) before all the books that ever I have seen, as most fit for a wounded Conscience" (43). *Grace Abounding to the Chief of Sinners*, ed. Roger Sharrock (London: Oxford University Press, 1966).

52. Luther cites God's revelation of the Law on Mt. Sinai as an instance of this function of the Law. "To curb and crush this monster and raging beast," writes Luther, "that is, the presumption of religion, God is obliged, on Mt. Sinai, to give a new Law with such pomp and with such an awesome spectacle that the entire people is crushed with fear. For since the reason becomes haughty with this human presumption of righteousness and imagines that on account of this it is pleasing to God, therefore God has to send some Hercules, namely, the Law, to attack, subdue, and destroy this monster with full force" (*LW* 26: 309–10).

53. See *LW* 26: 336–37, 345–49.

54. "The law, truly understood," says Willliam Tyndale while translating Luther's commentary on Matthew 5–7, "is those fiery serpents that stung the children of Israel with present death." The reference is to Numbers 21:6, where God punishes the Israelites for demonstrating a lack of faith as Moses leads them through the desert. Tyndale and Luther use the verse to distinguish between Moses' law, which condemns, and Christ's grace, which saves. See "An Exposition upon the V. VI. VII. Chapters of Mathew," *Expositions and Notes on Sundry Portions of Holy Scriptures*, vol. 43, ed. Rev. Henry Walter (Cambridge: Cambridge University Press, 1849), 4.

55. See *The Ego and The Id* in *The Standard Edition of the Complete Psychological Works of Sigmund Freud*, vol. 21, ed. and trans. James Strachey (London: Hogarth Press, 1961; reprint 1968), 52–53. In chapter 5 of *The Ego and the Id*, Freud distinguishes between two illnesses in which the patient's sense of guilt is particularly pronounced: obsessional neurosis and melancholia. "In certain forms of obsessional neurosis," writes Freud, "the sense of guilt is over-noisy but cannot justify itself to the ego. Consequently the patient's ego rebels against the imputation of guilt and seeks the physician's support in repudiating it." Freud notes that "it would be folly

to acquiesce in this, for to do so would have no effect. Analysis eventually shows that the super-ego is being influenced by processes that have remained unknown to the ego. It is possible to discover the repressed impulses which are really at the bottom of the sense of guilt." The ego of the melancholic, however, Freud claims, "ventures no objection" when charged by the super-ego. [I]t admits its guilt," says Freud, "and submits to punishment" (52). Perhaps we might draw a rough analogy between these two maladies and specific religious doctrines and practices; obsessional neurosis is to Catholicism (or any belief system that emphasizes ceremonies and works) as melancholia is to Lutheranism (or any faith-based creed). Freud explores the relationship between obsessional neurosis and religious ceremonies, compulsions, and prohibitions at length in his essay "Obsessive Actions and Religious Practices," *The Standard Edition of the Complete Psychological Works of Sigmund Freud*, vol. 9, ed. and trans. James Strachey (London: Hogarth Press, 1959; reprint 1968), 115–39.

56.   *Civilization and Its Discontents*, *The Standard Edition of the Complete Psychological Works of Sigmund Freud*, ed. and trans. James Strachey (London: Hogarth Press, 1961; reprint 1968), 92.

57.   Freud explains that "when saints call themselves sinners, they are not so wrong, considering the temptations to instinctual satisfaction to which they are exposed in a specially high degree—since, as is well known, temptations are merely increased by constant frustration, whereas an occasional satisfaction of them causes them to diminish, at least for the time being" (*Civilization*, 87). For further discussion of the ways Luther's thought prefigures Freud's see Erik H. Erikson, *Young Man Luther: A Study in Psychoanalysis and History* (New York: W.W. Norton, 1962) and Norman O. Brown, *Life against Death: The Psychoanalytical Meaning of History* (Middletown, Conn.: Wesleyan University Press, 1985), 202–304.

58.   Kaske "Dragon's Spark and Sting," 611.

59.   Luther, "The Freedom of a Christian," *Basic Theological Writings*, 615.

60.   See Galatians 2:19. "For I through the Law died to the Law, that I might live to God." Luther insists that "human reason and wisdom do not understand this doctrine. Therefore they always teach the opposite . . . . This is a principle and maxim of all theologians: 'He who lives according to the Law lives to God,' " Luther complains. But Paul, Luther tells us, "says the exact opposite, namely, that we cannot live to God unless we have died to the Law" (*LW* 26: 156).

61.   This passage, as King points out, is portrayed in the penultimate woodcut of Jan van der Noot's *A Theatre for Worldlings*. See King, *Spenser's Poetry*, 200 and *A Theatre for Worldlings* in Edmund Spenser, *The Yale Edition of the Shorter Poems of Edmund Spenser*, eds. William A. Oram, Einar Bjorvand, Ronald Bond, Thomas H. Cain, Alexander Dunlop, and Richard Schell (New Haven: Yale University Press, 1989), 483.

62.   King calls attention to the syntax of 1.11.53 of *The Faerie Queene*, where Spenser's lines "The weapon bright/Taking aduantage of his open jaw,/Ran through his mouth" indicate that the dragon is felled by the weapon rather than the knight wielding it. *Spenser's Poetry*, 199. See also A. C. Hamilton's note on I.xi.42 in his 1977 edition of *The Faerie Queene*, where he argues that once Red Cross's native strength is exhausted, he turns to his "trustie sword," or the Word of God. See Kaske, "Dragon's Spark and Sting," 616 as well.

63. "Two Kinds of Righteousness," *Basic Theological Writings*, 155.

64. *Ibid.*, 157.

65. In a gloss on Galatians 2, Tyndale writes: "Deeds of the law justify not: but faith justifieth. The law uttereth my sin and damnation, and maketh me flee to Christ for mercy and life. As the law roared unto me that I was damned for my sins: so faith certifieth me that I am forgiven and shall live through Christ." See *Tyndale's New Testament*, ed. David Daniell (New Haven: Yale University Press, 1989).

66. See also the *a* rhyme of I.xi.13.

67. The dragon is associated with a mountain again in I.xi.8 and 44. In *Galatians* Luther repeatedly emphasizes the terror surrounding the dispensation of the Law to Moses. "The terrors" that the Law "arouses in the conscience," writes Luther, "are no smaller than was the tremendous and horrible spectacle on Mt. Sinai" (*LW* 26: 64). See also *LW* 26: 309–311, 321.

68. *The Faerie Queene*, 145.

69. See also *The Faerie Queene*, I.vii.44.

70. For discussions of the sacramental nature of "the well of life" and "the tree of life" see James Schiavoni, "Predestination and Free Will: The Crux of Canto Ten," *Spenser Studies* 10 (1989): 175–95 and John N. Wall, Jr., *Transformations of the Word: Spenser, Herbert, Vaughan* (Athens: University of Georgia Press, 1988). Schiavoni and Wall both claim that Spenser's treatment of the sacraments is not wholly Calvinist. Schiavoni notes that "since Red Cross is unconscious when he receives the balm, he cannot be receiving the sacrament through the conscious faith which Calvinists believed necessary to make the sacrament beneficial" (190). Wall argues that Spenser's emphasis on the bestowal of grace through the sacraments is foreign to "the Calvinist traditions" where "an emphasis on divine omnipotence" resulted in "a vestigial role for the Sacraments in parish life" (125). For the relationship between I.xi.50, I.i.47, and I.ix.14, see Hamilton's note, *The Faerie Queene*, 146.

KIRSTEN TRANTER

"The sea it selfe doest thou not plainely see?": Reading *The Faerie Queene*, Book V

Book V of *The Faerie Queene* represents contemporary events and aspects of Elizabethan policy in mostly unmistakable form. However, as Spenser moves the matter of his allegory closer to such recognizable historical referents, his insistence on the instability of reference intensifies. In Canto ii, Artegall's encounter with the Mighty Gyant introduces uncertainty around the interpretation of "plaine" appearance and the status of figurative language as a representational device. Malfont, the tortured poet of Canto ix, is read as a model of how irony and ambiguity may be mobilized as a defense against potentially disastrous misreading. The question of how to read Malfont shows how *The Faerie Queene's* typical recommendation of skeptical reading is reshaped in Book V in response to the political pressures of history.

BOOK V, THE LEGEND OF JUSTICE, has been of critical interest mainly for its unusual status in *The Faerie Queene* as an allegory that bears close, sustained correspondence to contemporary events and controversial aspects of Elizabethan policy. The judgment of Duessa in Canto ix seems to represent the trial and execution of Mary, Queen of Scots in a transparent way; Artegall himself at times appears to stand for Elizabeth's notoriously ruthless Irish deputy, Lord Grey de Wilton. However, as Spenser moves the matter of his allegory closer to recognizable historical referents in this book, his insistence on the

Spenser Studies: A Renaissance Poetry Annual, Volume XXI, Copyright © 2006 by AMS Press, Inc. All rights reserved.

instability of reference intensifies. Like the Gyant's vision of the sea
cited in my title, the historical allegory of Book V presents itself as
"plaine" to see. Yet the Gyant's perspective is presented as danger-
ously wrong in Artegall's forceful rejection of his "plaine" analogies.
Spenser's interrogation of the nature of "plaine" appearance and analogical signification in this scene raises significant questions for the
interpretation of Book V, with its apparently self-evident correspondence between history and poetry.

In the book where Spenser's allegory appears most determinate,
the task of reading the relation between history and figure, sign and
signified, becomes increasingly complicated. Book V returns repeatedly to concerns with the conditions—and limits—of correct interpretation, and how we are to understand, read or judge what appears
to be "plaine" in the text and in the world that it mirrors. In Book
V Spenser's emphasis on the instability of language seems strongly
motivated by his fears about the political consequences of misinterpretation. He does not want to meet the terrible fate of Malfont, the
court poet who has his tongue nailed to a post as punishment for
angering the queen. As a result, in Book V Spenser questions the
kind of "plaine" correspondence he seems also to recommend, and
mobilizes irony and ambiguity as a defense against potentially disastrous misreading. While this book is in some ways a didactic demon-
stration of the "plaine" relationship between Faeryland and the
contemporary world, it also contains it own warnings against a reading that would judge too quickly whatever is "plainely to be red"
(V.ix.26).[1]

The bluntness of Book V's historical allegory has led readers to
associate it with a sense of closure and determinate meaning on the
level of narrative and poetic signification in contrast to the rest of
The Faerie Queene.[2] Although interest in Book V has been revived
recently by new ways of thinking about the politics of Spenser's
work, it is still somehow hard to approach the complexity of the
poetry, as the close correspondence between allegory and history
seems to crowd out the rich, dazzling layers of imaginative possibility
that characterize the poetry of other books.[3] Book V can seem disap-
pointingly reductive: whatever Britomart meant before, when she
meets Radigund in Book V she is simply translated to Elizabeth in
the minds of many readers. She "falls into history," as Lauren Silberman puts it, and never escapes back into poetry.[4]

It is by now commonplace to acknowledge that the allegory of
The Faerie Queene leads readers to question first impressions, as things
are consistently proved to be other than what they seem. Discouraged
from trusting their initial interpretations, Spenser's readers assume a

form of skeptical reading, an interpretive position that actively questions the relationship between sign and signified in the allegorical
figure.[5] The process of active engagement with the production of
meaning that is produced by this strategy is often regarded as part of
the redemptive aspect of Spenser's allegory. By being encouraged to
choose among several possible meanings (and choose again, and revise
those choices), the reader ideally reflects on the process of making
meaning in a way that is intended to produce eventually enlightened
understanding, according to Maureen Quilligan's influential account.
Book I provides the best example of the way the text produces a
valued "self-consciousness" on the part of readers, who are forced to
revise their own readings in a "process of retroactive qualification."[6]
There is a sense underlying these accounts, however, that the poem
will eventually offer a reading that can be qualified enough to be
trusted. The poem may encourage readers to suspend or defer judgment, but not indefinitely.

Spenser's strategy takes an important turn in Book V as the recommendation of skeptical reading which has been a defining feature of
the poem's figurative strategy is transformed under the pressure of
the historical and political issues at stake: while the earlier books may
demonstrate Spenser's faith in the possibility of "right" reading, the
intensified level of irony and insistence on irresolvable ambiguity in
Book V undermine this possibility. Quilligan notes the shift that takes
place between the first and last books of the poem, "as if Spenser
had lost faith in language itself to reveal the truth" by Book VI.[7]
Such disillusionment with the revelatory powers of language can be
found earlier, in Book V.

1. How to See the Sea

The encounter between Artegall, the Knight of Justice, and the Gyant
in Canto ii provides a key example of the problems of judgment
and interpretation, reading and representation that arise repeatedly
throughout Book V. Riding along the cliffs that border the sea, Artegall notices a crowd of people gathered around a Gyant armed with
a pair of scales who is holding forth about the unjust state of the
world and his plans to fix it. The Gyant suggests that the world is
out of balance, which he proposes to remedy by restoring all things
to their original state of equality. This plan takes on an apocalyptic
cast as the Gyant threatens to level mountains, redistribute wealth

and property, and destroy all distinction including that between the separate elements of earth, air, fire, and water. Artegall argues with the Gyant's arrogant assumption of such authority, invoking scripture at every line. In a torturous series of experiments Artegall demonstrates that the Gyant is incapable of using his scales to achieve true judgment due to the faulty bases of the comparisons that underlie his analysis. When the Gyant is not convinced by Artegall's arguments and demonstrations, Talus intervenes and throws the Gyant over the cliff to his death in the sea below, then chases away his crowd of followers.

As this brief sketch shows, the episode with the Gyant presents itself as an important lesson in distinguishing proper and improper forms of judgment. Spenser here provides Artegall with a chance to demonstrate the correct use of the set of balances, the icon of his patron Astrea, Goddess of Justice, that has been falsely appropriated by the popular Gyant. However, it becomes difficult to distinguish between proper and improper forms of interpretation and judgment in this episode, even after Artegall's bluster of biblical citations against the Gyant and his clumsy experiments with the Gyant's pair of scales. This scene is a key text for Judith H. Anderson's study of Renaissance perceptions of the relationship between words and what they represent. As she observes, Artegall's argument with the Gyant condenses the "signs of strain in this book between metaphorical and material dimensions of meaning . . . concept and history . . . words and things."[8] The encounter with the Gyant turns out to be an argument over how to read or "see" what appears to be "plaine," with a special focus on the proper basis of comparison between related terms.

Spenser clearly presents the Gyant as wrong-headed, "admired much of fooles, women, and boys," (V.ii.30) and as a threat that needs to be removed. The Gyant's doctrine of social equality stands in direct opposition to the divinely-ordered hierarchy that Artegall invokes against him. However, in one of the most problematic (and remarked-upon) aspects of this episode, the Gyant also appears to echo figures of authority we recognize in the text, both Artegall and the poet-narrator himself.[9] This makes it all the more difficult to discern exactly what point is being made through the dismissal and destruction of the Gyant and his followers. The Gyant appears as something of a grotesque parody of Artegall, with his passionate desire to right all the wrongs in the world, armed with a balance, the iconic instrument of judgment. The Gyant's forms of expression also closely recall those of the poet in the Proem to Book V in some significant ways, particularly in his use of extended analogies to describe the disordered state of the universe.

The Proem opens Book V with a series of pessimistic statements about the state of the contemporary world. The poet describes a pervasive sense of decay and disorder in the universe, generated by his comparison of an "image of the antique world" in its original state with the "state of present time":

> Such oddes I finde twixt those, and these which are,
> As that, through long continuance of his course,
> Me seemes the world is runne quite out of square,
> From the first point of his appointed sourse,
> And being once amisse growes daily wourse and wourse.
>
> (V.Proem.1)

The poet's observations have much in common with the Gyant's view of things, especially his sense that things in the world have visibly fallen away from their original state of order and perfection. "Thou foolish Elfe," the Gyant says to Artegall, "Seest not, how badly all things present bee, / And each estate quite out of order goth?" (V.ii.37).

At the heart of Artegall's argument with the Gyant is a debate over the nature of seeing and interpretation, a question of how to read or "see" what "plaine appeares" to the eye. Both the poet-narrator and the Gyant come to their conclusions about the disordered state of the world through a signifying system of resemblance that works through analogy, indicated by visible marks of correspondence.[10] For the poet, the disjointed state of the world is mirrored, through analogy, in the place of the constellations, widening the sphere of disorder to a cosmic level:

> . . . all things else in time are chaunged quight.
> Ne wonder; for the heauens reuolution
> Is wandred farre from where it first was pight,
> And so doe make contrarie constitution,
> Of all this lower world, toward his dissolution
>
> (V.Proem.4)

The poet's "Ne wonder; for . . . and so" establishes a relationship of obvious correspondence between these two things, the constellations and the state of the world. Most importantly, this is an analogy, and a sign, that can be clearly seen and interpreted. The poet argues that the constellations have "wandered much" from their original placement in space: "that plaine appeares" to anyone who looks

(V.Proem.5). The analogy of the stars to the state of the world "plaine appeares" as much as the stars themselves.

The Gyant also finds disorder inscribed "plaine" on the world. For him as well as the poet, to see is to read and understand a system of significant analogies that are clearly apparent, and that point to cosmic disorder. The Gyant finds that all the elements have assumed "vnequall" status with each other, and this state of disorder is reflected, through visible analogy, in the inequality that dominates all the world, from topical features of the landscape to social relations of power and wealth:

> For why, he sayd they all vnequall were,
> And had encroached upon each others share
> Like as the sea (which plaine he shewed there)
> Had worn the earth, so did the fire the aire,
> So all the rest did others parts empaire.
> And so were realmes and nations run awry.
>
> (V.ii.32)

"Like as . . . so did . . . So all . . . And so": like the poet's "Ne wonder, for," the Gyant's assertion of similitude leads automatically to a world of correspondences that show the consequences of likeness.

As this stanza shows, the sea provides the Gyant's favorite example of the self-evident disorder and analogy for which he argues. The actions of this element more than any other are plainly apparent to his eyes, in the waves that wash away and erode the land and thus produce an unequal relationship between the elements: "Like as the sea (which plaine he shewed there)." In this line we hear two homophones or puns that relate elements of the landscape ("sea" and "plain" as nouns) to visual appearance ("see" as verb and "plain" as adjective). These two terms are juxtaposed again several stanzas later, in another of the Gyant's desperate appeals to Artegall to perceive the signs of self-evident disorder in the universe: "The sea it selfe doest thou not plainely see / Encroch vppon the land there under thee [?]" (V.ii.37). A. C. Hamilton suggests that the Gyant's "atrocious pun determines his punishment," as he is thrown into the sea to drown.[11] The Giant's punishment is somewhat related to this pun, but he is not punished for its lack of aptness. In fact, this pun seems highly apt. The double sense of "see" and "sea" may alert us to the reason for this element's favored status in the Gyant's range of examples. With its phonic homology to "see," the "sea" contains within itself a word for the mark of the visible that is the guarantee of analogy and "plaine" signification.

While both the poet of the Proem to Book V and the Gyant understand the world according to a vision of divinely ordered correspondence and analogy, Artegall challenges this vision in a way that questions the basis of such structures of comparison. Artegall's rebuke to the Gyant takes the form of an attack on both his system of visible analogy and his way of reading it. The sea does not simply take away from the land, Artegall suggests, but redistributes matter elsewhere, maintaining some kind of natural equilibrium in an action that is not immediately perceptible:

> Of things unseene how canst thou deeme aright . . .
> Sith thou misdeem'st so much of things in sight?
> What though the sea with waues continuall
> Doe eate the earth, it is no more at all:
> Ne is the earth the lesse, or loseth ought,
> For whatsoever from one place doth fall,
> Is with the tide vnto an other brought:
> For there is nothing lost, that may be found, if sought.
>
> (V.ii.39)

Artegall draws a distinction here between material "things in sight" and more abstract "things unseene," and suggests that the Gyant is incompetent in judging either. In fact, the Gyant's inability to judge the material, visible world ("things in sight") precludes him from metaphysical judgment. Artegall's following actions attempt to conceive the difference between the abstract and the material and how they might be compared, signified, and thereby judged.

Artegall embarks on a series of experiments to convince the Gyant of his error in comparing things that do not bear proper comparison, in what becomes a lesson in how to construct proper analogies. The two try to weigh right and wrong, true and false, but the scales fail to achieve balance. The problem seems to lie both in the Gyant's attempt to subject non-material things to the judgment of material weight, and in his attempt to compare or balance opposing elements. At stanza 47 Artegall concludes that the scales are in fact useless: they are simply a figure which "doe nought but right or wrong betoken" (V.ii.47).[12] He thus rejects the figure of the scales in favor of the actual judging mind: "[I]n the mind the doome of right must bee" (V.ii.47).

The confusion in this passage over the status of the scales as literal or metaphorical suggests a significant breakdown in the allegory, a culmination of the tension between material and abstract categories in the episode.[13] Artegall argues that issues of justice are weighed "in the mind," but if the scales are a functional sign of the mental process of judgment, then they should be able to perform within the allegorical frame. What do the scales represent, if not the weighing of issues "in the mind"? Artegall's rejection of the figure of the scales suggests the failure of allegory itself as a vehicle for establishing and communicating the truth. Figurative language, including allegory, depends on balancing a relationship of similitude and difference between separate elements: thus, the scales are conventionally able to signify mental judgment. Artegall's insistence on the "the mind" as the only proper place of judgment disturbs this process of figuration. By his reasoning all figurative language might be cast, as the Gyant's finally is, as catachresis or improper association.

The problematic status of words in this system of comparison and evaluation points to a deep concern with verbal interpretation and judgment, and one that is not fully resolved in the experiments that follow. When the Gyant first tries to measure right and wrong, true and false, these terms take the form of "words" that the scales are unable to accommodate. The Gyant throws the words into his balance, where they refuse to be weighed: "But straight the winged words out of his ballaunce flew" (V.ii.44). This angers the Gyant, and he blames the failure on the fact that the words are "light" (V.ii.45). He then tries to weigh the same concepts without the form of words: this time, he simply places "the true" and "the false" into the balance. How this new version of true and false differs from the version of them as "words" is not explained, but we must assume that they are somehow distinct. A further twist appears when Artegall explains that the "eare" must judge words like "the mind" must judge right and wrong: "And so likewise of words, the which be spoken, / The eare must be the ballance, to decree, / And iudge, whether with truth or falsehood they agree" (V.ii.47). After rejecting the figure of the scales, Artegall turns to the ear as synecdoche for the mind, and then turns back to the metaphor of the scales. This new "ballance" will presumably measure words more effectively than the Gyant's, but how is unclear

The Gyant's framework for understanding the world and its signs is undermined and forcefully rejected, but the poem does not offer a clear recommendation for an alternative model of reading, judgment, and interpretation. Artegall's use of the scales to achieve proper judgment proves even more confusing than his previous arguments against the Gyant. He is finally able to achieve results by weighing things according to a different rule: a rule of resemblance, rather than difference. Rather than weighing right against wrong, Artegall recommends that the Gyant should "put two wrongs together to be tride; / Or else two falses, each of equall share; / And then together doe them both compare" (V.ii.48). In this way Artegall constructs his own system of comparison that also relies on a signature or "visible mark" to signify its meaning. This visible sign is the mark of its authenticity: in a phrase that strongly echoes the Proem, we find that when Artegall's "two wrongs . . . or two falses" are placed in the scales, "then *plaine it did appeare,* / Whether of them the greater were attone. / But right sate in the middest of the beame alone" (V.ii.48, my emphasis). The Gyant is not satisfied with this result, we are told, because "it was not the right, which he did seeke" and he does not want to contemplate the "meane" between the "extremes" to which he is dedicated (V.ii.49).

This scene can be interpreted as Artegall's enunciation of a theory of distributive justice that follows Aristotle's *Nichomachean Ethics* 5.3,[14] but it remains an obscure series of arguments, "enmeshed in ironic or otherwise disturbing nuances."[15] The Gyant's concrete instances of disorder in the world, examples of material inequality and the political abuse of power, are replaced by a highly abstract, non-material order of right and wrong which seems difficult to apply. By the time Artegall has finished his torturous series of experiments we are quite willing to be skeptical of whatever "plaine appeares" from his example. The Gyant's initial experiments, where "truth" and "right" can be both words and not words, undermine Artegall's insistence on the very unity of truth—"truth is one, and right is ever one" (V.ii.48). It has become clear or "plaine" to "see" at least, that words are hard to weigh, their relationship to what they represent is unstable, and they can be manipulated. The appearances of things, and apparent relationships of correspondence between things, are also not as stable as they seem. The adequacy of figuration itself is questioned by Artegall's initial dismissal of the scales as only useful to "betoken" right and wrong.

2. EFFACING ECONOMICS

At the heart of the confusion over judgment and interpretation in this episode is a struggle over forms of comparison and the proper basis of correspondence between things. The text appears to ask what kind of things can properly be compared with others, and interrogates the basis of likeness and resemblance that underlie the poem's own processes of signification. Both the poet of the Proem and the Gyant understand the world through a system of correspondences that visibly displays the disordered state of the world. The rejection of the

Gyant's analogical world view encourages a revision of the claims of the Proem and to some extent undermines the authority of the poet's voice, since their perspectives seem so closely aligned. Yet where the poet sees a state of moral decay, the Gyant's concerns are primarily political and economic. The unequal state of the elements, whereby one encroaches on another producing a state of inequality, corresponds to a social order of inequality. The Gyant sees a clear need to remedy this situation in order to produce equality between persons in the here and now: "Were it not good that wrong were then surceast,/And from the most, that some were given to the least?" (V.ii.37). The Gyant suggests a program of political change, a radical redistribution of property, power, and wealth that will find its correspondence in the leveling of every hill and valley and the erasure of distinction between the elements.

The Gyant's political message has been persuasively connected to discourses of popular radical politics in England and Europe. Frederick Padelford's influential work relates the Gyant to the subversive, communitarian Anabaptist sect, who were persecuted in England,[16] while Stephen Greenblatt draws parallels with the Peasant Wars in Germany in 1525 and related aspects of "radical protest in the early modern period."[17] The Gyant's arguments revolve around the role of the distribution of land in the unequal state of the world he describes, echoing the arguments against land enclosure that were the basis of many revolts in England. The Gyant expresses political ideas about the distribution of wealth, power, and property that were circulating in various forms, especially through radical religious sects in the late sixteenth century. In England in the late 1580s and early 1590s, food shortages and economic hardship produced a rise in popular discontent both in the countryside and the city that could have provided a specific context for concern about rebellion.[18]

Spenser presents the Gyant as a parody of rebellious politics that is discredited by the structures of comparison that underlie his reasoning. Greenblatt observes that the Gyant's ideas are not too far away from the poet's own as they are expressed in the Proem—close enough, as he suggests, to require some forceful distancing from the radical ideas of the Gyant through the establishment of a "firm boundary between acceptable and subversive versions of the same perceptions."[19] In Greenblatt's view, this boundary is finally drawn in the construction of a poetic project that separates rhetoric from its real-world counterpart of actual, physical force. Yet the Gyant's politics appear to be already undermined from within, presented as a wrong-headed version of a theory that locates the causes of oppression in the distribution of goods and property in the material world.

Fundamentally, the Gyant's mistakes are mistakes in reading, judgment, and interpretation; he is wrong because his faulty comparisons lead to the wrong conclusions.

The Gyant is very close to sounding like a contemporary peasant rebel in his suggestion of an intimate relation between the distribution of land and corresponding unequal social relations. However, his expression of this correspondence presents some strange problems. In the Gyant's rhetorical constructions the land reflects the social relations that it grounds, but does not explain them. The problem with the distribution of land, for the Gyant, is not that some is enclosed and some common, for example, or even that some have more than others; rather, he complains that there are differences that mirror divides in social status, so that some areas of land are higher than others. He aligns "These mountains hie," and "[t]hese towering rocks, which reach unto the skie" with the "Tyrants that make men subject to their law" (V.ii.38). In this catalogue of evils the high mountains and "lowly plaine" are neatly analogous to great divides in social status.

For all his concern about the shape and meaning of the land, the Gyant does not complain about the actual things men do with it that produce the inequalities he wants to correct. The image of the sea encroaching on the land, eating away at what belongs to that other element, is suggestive of a greedy landlord, enclosing and appropriating land that was once common to all, but the Gyant does not make this comparison explicit. In the Gyant's view, people are high and low *like* mountains and valleys are, a reasoning that takes its cue from the "Like *x*, so *y*" formula introduced most strongly in the Proem's similitudes. The Gyant desires to take from those that have most, and give to those that have least (V.ii.37); "*Therefore* I will throw down these mountains hie, / and make them level with the lowly plaine. . . . And all the wealth of rich men to the poore will draw" (V.ii.38, my emphasis).

Why does the Gyant want to level the actual mountains, an action that will be analogous to his goal of social leveling, but will bear no material relationship to it? By his reasoning, by which things reflect each other and figural similitude has cosmic consequences, his program of social equality will logically involve leveling the mountains which reflect oppressive distinction in the social world. Like the German peasant rebels and English enclosure rioters, the Gyant sees a relationship between land and social relations; yet in the Gyant's view differences in social status are not caused by a material base, the distribution of land, but are instead shadowed by topical features of the landscape. The Gyant's analogical formula reduces the causal relation between the institution of property and the social order perceived by contemporary rebels to a logic of visible analogy that evacuates economics. The material base of social inequality is displaced onto the image of the sea wearing away the beach, while social inequality itself is allegorized, not analyzed, in the images of high mountains and low plains. The redistribution of land that would serve the Gyant's overtly stated political purpose is not the leveling of mountains but the reversal of enclosures, the undoing of feudal relations, and finally the abolition of the institution of private property (all radical demands voiced by popular rebellions in England and Europe). To put it another way, the image that would make a more materialist analogue to his arguments about economic oppression is not the sea wearing away the beach but the common field transformed by a fence into enclosed property; the squatter's fen drained for a private pasture; the longstanding forest felled for landlord's timber. "Like as . . . so did . . . So all . . . And so."

Indeed, contemporary accounts of one significant sixteenth-century English rebellion instigated by discontent over enclosures provide a counterpoint to these images. Alexander Neville's account of Kett's Rebellion of 1549 was published in Latin in 1575 as *De furoribus Norfolciensum Ketto duce* and translated into English in 1615.[20] Neville includes a speech in the voice of one of the rebel instigators that calls for the destruction of hedges and the eradication of ditches (the two main methods of enclosure): "We see that now it is come to extremitie, we will also prove extremity, rend down hedges, fill up ditches, make way for every man into the common pasture: Finally, lay all even with the ground, which they no less wickedly, then cruelly and covetously have inclosed."[21] This passage suggests a complex constellation of allusions: on the one hand, the Norfolk rebels' plan to "lay all even with the ground" is a translation and appropriation of biblical apocalyptic language in its echo of Luke 3.5: "Everie valley shalbe filled, and everie mountaine, and hil shalbe broght lowe." Neville is an opponent of their beliefs, so we should treat his representation of their language carefully. From his perspective, their translation of biblical language could seem, like the Gyant's, wicked and presumptuous. Nevertheless, it seems that the biblical apocalyptic language of "leveling" had been translated into material, political statement and event by sixteenth-century rebels in their accommodation of hill to hedge, valley to ditch, in the context of private versus common land. Rather than tearing down hedges and filling up ditches, actions which have the material effect of restoring common property, the Gyant wants to "throw downe these mountaines hie, /

And make them level with the lowly plaine" (V.ii.38). He returns
to the biblical terms and takes them literally rather than performing
the political interpretation of the rebels.[22] The Gyant's beliefs are
only "materialist" in the sense that they demand change in the realm
of the present material world, despite his echo of materialist popular politics

Artegall easily points out the absurdities in the Gyant's construct,
as the Gyant's apocalyptic plan of leveling the mountains with the
plaine is simply one of a string of monumental reforms that includes
redistribution of wealth and power. Dismantling one of these elements of reform effects them all, strung together as they are in a chain
of similitude that gives them all the meaning they have. Thus, Artegall
says, "The hils doe not the lowly dales disdaine; / The dales do not
the lofty hills enuy" (V.ii.41). Artegall is right to suggest that no
problems would be solved by the leveling of mountains and valleys;
the human, social symptoms of disdain and envy would not be affected by the Gyant's proposed landscaping actions. The Gyant's view
of correspondence between the material and political worlds is faulty,
and yet Artegall presents no convincing alternative model of interpretation or judgment.

3. RETURNING TO THE PLAIN

We have at least learnt through our encounter with the Gyant that
there is nothing "plaine" about the way we might "see" the "sea." In
fact, the status of "plaine" appearance has itself become questionable
through its association with the Gyant's derogated, analogical episteme. The sea is not a space of transparent signification as the Gyant
wishes it to be, but a far more complicated zone of meaning, "the
chaotic element" as Angus Fletcher describes it.[23] The pun in the
sound of the word seems now like a trick. Not what he thinks he
sees at all, the meaning of the sea escapes the Gyant's attempts to
make it "plaine." His final drowning in it enacts a horrible kind of
poetic justice.[24]

The problems of interpretation and appearance registered by the
"sea"-which-is-not-"plaine" are familiar to readers of *The Faerie
Queene*, and relate to the poem's typical recommendation of skeptical
reading. To the extent that anything "plaine appeares" at any time
in *The Faerie Queene*, its meaning must be questioned. Red Cross
Knight's early encounter with the monster of Error in Book I establishes the potential dangers of faith in "plaine" sight: when he enters

Error's cave, we are told that "he saw the ugly monster plaine" (1.1.14) even though she has deliberately shrouded herself in the cave's darkness "where plaine none might see her, nor she see any plaine" (1.1.16). Red Cross happily thinks he has vanquished Error at the end of this scene, only to find that he is still capable of erring over and over again. We can only think that he was mistaken when he thought "he saw the ugly monster plaine"; rather, it seems that he did not really perceive her or the truth of the situation at all. Whatever appears in "plaine" sight is potentially misleading. Allegory itself can be understood as a mode that is established against "plaine" speech, through its etymology, as described by Fletcher, from "*allos + agoruein (other + speak openly, speak in the assembly or market). Agoruein* connotes public, open, declarative speech. This sense is inverted by the prefix *allos.*"[25]

"Plaine," like the term "sea" or "see" that it is paired with, also registers a pun on space or location and an aspect of interpretation. In considering Spenser's interest in the term "plaine" in Book V, we should not overlook a pun on the "plaine" that provides the favored landscape surface of Spenser's poem. It offers the proper place of opening into the time and space of allegorical narrative, as indicated by its place in the first line of Book I, "A Gentle Knight was pricking on the plaine." The "plaine" of Faeryland provides a clear space of open signification upon which the encounter of meaning in allegory can take place. By Book V, however, the plaine itself has become invested with meaning. It does not simply provide a blank surface, analogous to a blank page, upon which significant features present themselves (woods, caves, a fountain, a bower) and through which narrative and allegory may move forward. Instead, the landscape itself is identified with particular, actual places as a result of the move to historical specificity in Book V. This move is most visible in the use of names which are close to their "real" referents: Belge is unmistakably Belgium; Irena is clearly read as Ireland—or, at least, some aspect of that place. The plaine's status as a symbolic surface means that it begins to lose its affinity with the "material" of allegory as Gordon Teskey describes it, "that which gives meaning a place to occur while remaining heterogeneous to it."[26] The plaine of Book V is not heterogeneous to allegorical meaning; rather, the topical specificity of the plaine is integral to the meaning of what takes place on its ground.

The first stanzas of Canto XII that set the scene for Artegall's climactic encounter with Grantorto emphasize the plaine's quality of openness: "That night Sir Artegall did cause his tent / There to be pitched on the open plaine" (V.xii.10); then, Irena waits, "Like as a tender Rose in open plaine" (V.xii.13). The open quality of the "plaine" is foregrounded, ironically, as its range of signification closes down, moving away from its status as blank matter and closer to the status of what is signified by matter. The land—the plaine—upon which Artegall's encounter with Grantorto takes place is itself full of meaning as the material land of Ireland, suppressed in the allegorical figure of Irena. Grantorto's execution takes place once Artegall sees his body flat against the background of this "plaine": "when he saw prostrated on the plaine, / He lightly reft his head, to ease him of his paine" (V.xii.23). Grantorto's body and his affective state have become pressed into proximity with the plaine: his "paine," a rhyming word, is only one letter away from the "plaine" his body is "prostrated" upon. The immediate proximity of the plain to the allegorical figures it supports demonstrates its figurative closeness to them. The plain has become folded into the allegory.

Towards the end of Book I a confusion emerges between the two zones, "plaine" and "sea," that in the Gyant's imagination encroach upon each other but that should be rightfully separate. The first appearance of the word "plaine" in Canto xii engages two meanings of the word: "when as nigh vnto the shore they drew, / That foot of man might sound the bottom plaine, / *Talus* into the sea did forth issew" (V.xii.5). The adverbial sense of the word is present here (i.e., "plainly" or "clearly sound the bottom") but it may also operate as a noun, suggesting the idea of the actual bottom of the sea (so that "bottom" is an adjective modifying the noun "plaine"), drawing on the definition of "plain" as any level surface.[27] The poem usually refers to the plain as ground in distinction to the sea, but the idea of an underwater "plaine" paradoxically links the land with the sea that should be its border and its other. Canto xi also suggests a figural meeting of land and sea in the "green" that provides the setting for the fight with the Souldan, representing England's naval battle with the Spanish Armada. The material "plaine" is not only folded into allegory, but folded into the "sea," "the chaotic element," suggesting a fundamental problem of distinction in language situated allegorically where the sea meets and is confused with the "plaine."[28] The status of these two terms as ironic puns mirrors this problem of distinction: one cannot clearly "see" the "sea"; the "plaine" itself is not "plaine."[29]

Spenser's complication of the "plaine" occurs where allegory meets history in the most violent way so far encountered in the poem. The folding of Grantorto into the plain that is plainly the ground of Ireland suggests the proximity of Spenser's allegory to the contemporary world of historical compromise that it mirrors. Jacqueline T.

Miller describes this sense of proximity and "congruence" that increasingly characterizes Spenser's sense of the relation of his Faeryland
to the actual world and "disturbing reality": "The poet does not
see conflict between Faeryland and actuality," she writes, "he sees
congruence; he does not so much acknowledge that 'real life' contra-
dicts his art as that it defines and structures it."[30] Yet even as Book
V suggests "congruence" with history, it also questions the exact
nature of such correspondence. The relationship between the allegorical structures of the poem and what they represent is both plain
and problematic.

4. How to Read ''Malfont''

Spenser's complication of the meaning of the "plaine" is an extension
of his meditation, in Book V, of what "plaine" might mean, and
what it might mean for something to "plaine appeare." This concern
relates to worries about the reception of his own text. *A Letter of the
Authors* prefaced to the 1590 edition of the *Faerie Queene* gives a
strong indication of Spenser's anxieties about the way the poem may
be misinterpreted.[31] This document, addressed to Sir Walter Ralegh,
functions as an introduction to how the poem should be read, with
a defense of the choice of allegory as a device and an explanatory
description of some of the narrative action. The problem of misinterpretation is a priority from the outset. Spenser opens the *Letter*
"knowing how doubtfully all Allegories may be construed" and it is
immediately clear that "doubt" here indicates not only a response to
the possible obscurity of the poem's "darke conceit" but a more
hostile interpretive approach.[32] The *Letter* offers not only an aid towards right reading and an explication of the poet's "general intention and meaning" but also an attempt to defend against misreading,
a device "for auoiding of gealous opinions and misconstructions."[33]
Spenser addresses Ralegh, a reader imagined as being sympathetic,
but also has in mind a sphere of less generous potential readers.

Hostile misinterpretation is memorably embodied in the figures
of Envy and Detraction and their companion the Blatant Beast in
the last canto of Book V. The description of Detraction's special aim
recalls the language of the *Letter* in telling ways: "to misconstrue of
a man's intent" (V.xii.34). The target of Envy and Detraction here
is not the poet himself but Artegall, who here appears to represent
the historical person of Lord Grey, Elizabeth's deputy in Ireland.

Their graphic abuse of Artegall stands for the criticism leveled at Grey back in England for his violent policies, particularly the notorious massacre he ordered at Smerwick. While the historical allegory of Book V invites these apparently simple correspondences (Artegall = Grey), the poem has also called that kind of reading into question. The poem's recommendation of skeptical reading appears in the context of Book V to be a defense against a certain kind of reception. Better, perhaps, to read "doubtfully" than "to misconstrue."

Spenser's anxieties about the reception of his own work are most graphically dramatized in the figure of the poet Malfont, who has been cruelly punished for insulting the queen. As Artegall and Talus pass through the castle towards Mercilla's chamber of judgment, they see:

> Some one, whose tongue was for his trespasse vyle
> Nayld to a post, adjudged so by law:
> For that therewith he falsely did reuyle,
> And foule blaspheme that *Queene* for forged guyle,
> Both with bold speaches, which he blazed had,
> And with lewd poems, which he did compyle;
> For the bold title of a Poet bad
> He on himselfe had ta'en, and rayling rymes had sprad.
>
> (V.ix.25)

Malfont's place in the castle implies his prior position as a court poet. His role is now simply that of a didactic, living *exemplum*, condemned to display the punishment he received for circulating slanderous texts against the queen. The mutilated tongue offers a version of actual punishments handed out to authors of seditious or libelous literature such as John Stubbes, who underwent the mutilation of organs of communication such as ears and hands and the public display of their suffering bodies. It also suggests the image of a verse libel or other notice pinned to a public wall or post, as verse libels often were.[35] In this sense, Malfont has been turned into a text that describes the consequence of his original poems and "speaches."

Malfont presents a nightmarish image of a poet punished for his verses, a vision of the worst possible consequences of the kind of misreading Spenser dreaded. As Andrew Hadfield observes, Malfont is a type of poet like Spenser, "grimly prophetic of a never-realized but possible history."[36] Artegall encounters Malfont immediately prior to one of the more controversial episodes in the book: several stanzas on, Mercilla oversees the trial and execution of Duessa, commonly identified as Mary, Queen of Scots. Canto ix was understood

by at least one reader as the same kind of "bold" poetry that earned
Malfont his "bad" name: Mary's son, James VI of Scotland (later
James I of England) took offense at what he understood to be a
representation of his mother and appealed to Elizabeth for Spenser
to be punished.[37] This episode seems to signify Spenser's fear that
the good may well be read as bad, and that the poet's own words
may be misconstrued with disastrous consequences. The lines above
suggest that Malfont has taken "the bold title of a Poet bad" upon
himself, but it is not exactly clear how he might have done so. It is
also far from obvious, as A. Leigh Deneef points out, who has judged
Bonfont. He has been judged "by law" and so presumably by Mercilla, but the nature of this judgment suggests that it could just have
easily been made by the figures of Envy and Detraction who appear
later in Book V.[38]

The following stanza that describes the movement from Bonfont
to Malfont is further steeped in ambiguity:

> Thus there he stood, whylest high ouer his head,
> There written was the purport of his sin,
> In cyphers strange, that few could rightly read,
> BON FONT: but *bon* that once had written bin,
> Was raced out, and *Mal* was now put in.
> So now *Malfont* was plainely to be red,
> Eyther for th'euill, which he did therein,
> Or that he likened was to a welhed
> Of euill words, and wicked sclaunders by him shed.
>
> (V.ix.26)

The agent of these inscriptions is absent, adding to the sense of mystery around the poet's judgments. The presence of the original name
seems essential to understanding the meaning of the bad poet's new
status, but "BON FONT" is the name that is hardest to decipher.
The poet's "good" name is written "in cyphers strange" (although,
ironically, set in capitals, the clearest of letters) and legible only by a
"few." Although we are told that "*Malfont* was plainely to be red,"
this name itself incorporates at least two possible descriptions: "Eyther
for th'euill, which he did therein, / Or that he likened was to a
welhed / Of euill words." The poet can no longer speak to explain
himself: the nail through the tongue ensures this. The organ of speech
has been immobilized, leaving the hands free—oddly, in a way, since
those writing hands would have been responsible for the "lewd
poems" and "rayling rymes" he is punished for. The writing that
explains his condition to the reader is far from clear, even when we
are told it might be "plainely . . . red."

Malfont's punishment has also been read as an example of the total imposition of the monarch's power and the total submission of the subject poet. However, the ambiguous terms in which his punishment is presented trouble this equation. For Jonathan Goldberg, Malfont stands as evidence of the effective imposition of the monarch's version of the truth in place of any other, an example of the "obliterative justice" enacted in Book V "which leaves nothing but the truth—their truth—behind."[39] Book V does favor a justice of obliteration: Talus is mostly employed to destroy and erase evidence of bad things such as the castle of Lady Munera. However, Bonfont's original name is not obliterated, and the continued visibility of the name "Bonfont" unsettles any idea of the new name as a total replacement of the old.[40] Malfont stands as an example of the enactment of the monarch's power, but the presence of his original name could indicate a failure of the monarch's "justice" to obliterate it rather than a complete erasure and replacement.

It is possible to read the continued presence of Bonfont's original name as necessary evidence of the monarch's power to replace and reinscribe. Without the somewhat obscure presence of the old name, Artegall would not know that any such renaming had taken place, although this narrative could surely have been supplied in other ways. The presence of the old name is somehow necessary to the narrative that makes him an instructive example: we must know that he was once good in order to appreciate the treasonable nature of his turn towards the bad. "The purport of his sin," as Spenser describes it, requires an evident move from the good to the bad, from "Bon" to "Mal." But why exactly is this narrative of renaming and reinscription necessary? Malfont could conceivably have been presented simply as a bad poet. Instead, he is represented as a poet who has forfeited the good name he once owned. His status as "good" poet who turns critical of the queen emphasizes the parallel with Spenser and his poem of carefully qualified praise and counsel verging on criticism. The fact that "few could rightly read" the good in Bonfont's name suggests that a positive interpretation is least likely: he is read as "good" only by a "few." This leaves open the distinctly disturbing possibility that the good poet has been misread.

Allegory's potential for ambiguity leaves it especially open to misinterpretation, which Spenser evidently feared. In his discussion of Spenser's *Letter*, Kenneth Gross argues that allegory's "hiddenness of meaning . . . is the very thing that leaves it open to the threat of violation by willfull or slanderous misinterpreters"; in this context, "mere semantic uncertainty becomes something potentially more

dangerous."[41] However, "semantic uncertainty" can also be mar-
shaled in the poet's defense, here through the trope of irony implicit
in the assertion that Malfont is "plainely to be read." The reader of
Book V is rightly suspicious of anything that appears to be "plaine,"
a term that has come to be invested with skeptical uncertainty. This
is not only an acknowledgment of the inherent ambiguity of language
as a referential system, but a recommendation of the suspension of
interpretive judgment in the context of controversial representations
of history: a political choice. Richard McCabe asks, in the context
of Spenser's veiled criticism of Elizabeth, "Is it possible that Bonfont
and Malfont are one and the same person seen from different political
perspectives?"[42] Possibly, yes; the passage asks the reader at least to
hold the two names as potentially valid in his or her mind. What
might it mean to join, however provisionally, with those "few" who
"could rightly read" the poet's good name? Definite judgment is
here symbolized by the nail through the tongue of the silenced poet:
a picture of Spenser's possible fate if he were to be read in such a way.

5. READING BOOK V

After the wandering, fragmented narrative of Book IV and, to a lesser
extent, Book III, Book V provides something of a sense of a return
to a more linear narrative. We have one obvious (male) hero, Artegall, with a fairly clear mission. It soon begins to seem, however, that
this return to linearity has a price. Artegall's way is cleared for him
by the "iron man" Talus, who slaughters all who stand in the path
of Artegall's progress. Any sense of fragmentation that affected the
narrative of earlier books has been displaced onto the crowds of
"rabble" that populate Book V. The ruthless dismemberment, massacre, and threshing into tiny pieces of their bodies enables Artegall,
and the narrative of the book, to move on their relentless way. This
sense of a clear, uninterrupted line also characterizes the direction of
allegorical signification in Book V, which directs us straight to mostly
unmistakable historical referents. Deneef suggests that "the poet no
longer trusts the reader to make the historical connection—as he
does, say, with Timias and Belphoebe—but makes the necessity of
connection a condition of the narrative itself."[43] In a sense, we cannot
help but see Mary, Queen of Scots in the figure of Duessa in Book
V, and Artegall as Lord Grey in Ireland, at times. But this most
transparent incident, Duessa's trial, is immediately prefaced by the

figure of Bonfont, and preceded by several episodes including the encounter with the popular Gyant that demonstrate the problems that might attend our understanding of what we first see, what "plaine appeares" and what might be "plainely red."

Book V suggests that what seems "plaine" is never so, and leaves the possibility of irony always present. The very ground under our feet—"the land there under thee," the allegorical "plaine"—might always shift its meaning beneath us, becoming more like the chaotic sea than solid ground. Duessa resembles Mary, but the poem has asked us to question the meaning of resemblance. Radigund, the Amazon Queen who represents a misogynistic vision of uncontrolled female power, is also like Mary, while Britomart, who vanquishes her, is typically taken to be one of Elizabeth's "shadows" in another allegory of Mary's defeat. But Radigund is more like Elizabeth than this account of the episode suggests: as Hadfield has observed, Radigund dies childless and unmarried, while Britomart—although she is a virgin warrior for now—has marriage and descendants firmly fixed in her future, like Mary.[44] The neat chiasmus of Radigund-Mary/ Britomart-Elizabeth is not so very stable. The way one is judged to be like the other could make all the difference, between Spenser retaining his good name or being given a bad one. But the poet's bad name is also something he apparently, boldly, takes on himself

Where to, from the unsettled landscape of Book V? It ends with Artegall's attack by Envy and Detraction, but Artegall continues on his way "and seem'd of them to take no keepe" (V.xii.42). His refusal to acknowledge them is no protection, though; he is bitten by Envy's snake, which leaves its own physical sign. In an image that recalls Malfont's sentence, we are told that "long the marke was to be read" (V.xii.39). Artegall continues his journey to "Faery Court," and it is to the virtue of "Courtesie" that Spenser turns in Book VI. The Proem of the new book comes as something of a shock to the reader traumatized by the harrowing violence of V. The poet's description of his "weary steps" along the "waies" of Faeryland is continuous with Artegall's steadfast movement long his "course," but these "waies" of Book VI are a drastic revision of the bloodied landscape of V: now, they are "delightfull . . . sprinckled with such sweet variety, / Of all that pleasant is to eare or eye" (VI.Proem.1). He contemplates the flower of "comely courtesie," which grows in the "sacred noursery of vertue," planted with "heavenly seeds" (VI. Proem.3–4). These positive images of gardening and growth seem like an attempt to revise the gruesome aspect of V, but how effective are they when the "plaine" of the final canto of V is fresh in the reader's mind, itself a monstrous planter's field of death? There the "battred" corpses of the Irish "lay scattred over all the land, / As thicke as doth the seed after the sower's hand" (V.xii.7). Book VI starts, in a sense, on ground poisoned not only by the venom of Envy and Detraction but also contaminated with actual blood that cannot be effectively erased.

Rutgers University

NOTES

1.   All quotations from Edmund Spenser, *The Faerie Queene,* refer to the edition edited by A. C. Hamilton (London: Longman, 1977).

2.   Post-structuralist readings of Spenser have emphasized elements of inconclusiveness and open signification in the text, but the historical allegory of Book V can challenge the idea of a text generated by instability. For Jonathan Goldberg, Book V is the authoritarian opposite of the productively unstable text. Narrative fragmentation is banished along with poetry itself as the text is "limited semantically, straitened so that it speaks only the language of power." *Endlesse Work: Spenser and the Structures of Discourse* (Baltimore: Johns Hopkins University Press, 1981), 168.

3.   Lauren Silberman's recent work acknowledges the need to focus on the "poetic complications in the way Spenser represents sixteenth-century history in Book V," and performs a subtle reading of the politics of the Radigund episode, but she nonetheless finds that the historical allegory of the book closes down imaginative possibilities. "*The Faerie Queene,* Book V, and the Politics of the Text," *Spenser Studies* XIX (2004): 1–16 (16). Anne Lake Prescott's reading of the Burbon episode makes a strong case for the complex relation between history, politics, and allegory in Book V: "Foreign Policy in Fairyland: Henri IV and Spenser's Burbon," *Spenser Studies* XIV (2000): 189–214.

4.   Silberman, "*The Faerie Queene,* Book V," 7.

5.   David Norbrook summarizes the reader's predicament in this way: "Spenser problematises the act of reading, discouraging his audience from taking the interpretations they are offered immediately on trust. It is the idolatrous magicians Archimago and Acrasia who encourage readers to take sign for reality, representation for thing represented." *Poetry and Politics in the English Renaissance* (London: Routledge, 1984), 111.

6.   Maureen Quilligan, *The Language of Allegory: Defining the Genre* (Ithaca: Cornell University Press, 1979), 229, 235.

7.   Quilligan, *The Language of Allegory,* 51.

8.   Judith Anderson, *Words That Matter: Linguistic Perception in Renaissance English* (Stanford: Stanford University Press, 1996), 167.

9.   See especially Stephen Greenblatt, "Murdering Peasants: Status, Genre, and the Representation of Rebellion," *Representing the English Renaissance,* ed. Stephen

Greenblatt (Berkeley: University of California Press, 1988), 1–29 (20–21), and Annabel Patterson, "The Egalitarian Giant: Representations of Justice in History/Literature," *Journal of British Studies* 31 (1992): 97–132 (113).

10.   This way of understanding the world fits closely with the sixteenth-century "episteme" of resemblance described by Michel Foucault in *The Order of Things: An Archaelogy of the Human Sciences* (New York: Random, 1994): "It was resemblance that organized the play of symbols, made possible knowledge of things visible and invisible, and controlled the art of representing them" (17). Resemblance could be recognized by visible "signatures": "these buried similitudes must be indicated on the surface of things; there must be visible marks for the invisible analogies" (26). While the Proem and the Gyant conform to Foucault's model, the outcome of Artegall's challenge to the Gyant suggests a far more skeptical attitude to the idea of cosmic correspondence and the congruence between words and the things they represent than Foucault describes.

11.   Hamilton, *The Faerie Queene,* note to V.ii.37.4.

12.   Anderson discusses the ambivalence of the word "betoken," which means chiefly that the scales "prove nothing" but also suggests that they might indicate the truth (*Words*, 182).

13.   Annabel Patterson describes the effect as a "blurring of registers" as Artegall forces the Gyant to "weigh abstractions . . . in his materialist scale." Patterson, "The Egalitarian Giant," 113.

14.   Edmund Spenser, *Works: a Variorum Edition*, ed. E. A. Greenlaw et al., 10 vols. (Baltimore: Johns Hopkins University Press, 1932–49), 5:175.

15.   Anderson, *Words,* 167.

16.   Frederick Morgan Padelford, "Spenser's Arraignment of the Anabaptists," *Journal of English and Germanic Philology* XII (1913): 434–48. The Anabaptists rejected infant baptism and the concept of a state church, favoring instead "voluntary congregations"; they held egalitarian beliefs and some denied the right to private property, according to Christopher Hill in *The World Turned Upside Down: Radical Ideas During the English Revolution* (London: Penguin, 1972), 26.

17.   M. Pauline Parker also notes references to the German peasant revolt in *The Allegory of The Faerie Queene* (Oxford: Clarendon, 1960), 210, note 1.

18.   See Penry Williams, *The Tudor Regime* (Oxford: Clarendon, 1979), 328–29, and John Guy, *Tudor England* (Oxford: Oxford University Press, 1988), 405.

19.   Greenblatt, "Murdering Peasants," 21.

20.   Alexander Neville, *De furoribus Norfolciensium Ketto duce* (London, 1575); *Norfolkes furies, or a view of Ketts campe*, trans. Richard Woods (London, 1615).

21.   Neville, *Norfolkes furies*, sig. B3.

22.   Biblical citation is primarily reserved for Artegall, who makes himself the voice of scriptural authority with a long collection of biblical paraphrases in his refutation of the Gyant. Spenser makes little or no use of the many biblical texts that could support the Gyant's views on social equality, only those that make him a presumptuous, apocalyptic agent.

23.   Angus Fletcher, *The Prophetic Moment: An Essay on Spenser* (Chicago: University of Chicago Press, 1971), 246.

24.   The sea reappears in the guise of Fortuna in Canto iv in the story of the two brothers whose disagreement is adjudicated by Artegall. The sea has worn away one

brother's patch of land and deposited it upon the others, making one poor and the other rich. As a result, the poor brother has lost his fiancée to the richer brother. In a further twist, the chest containing the fiancée's dowry, lost in the process of shipping, has been deposited by the sea on the beach belonging to the poorer brother. Artegall rules "That what the sea vnto you sent, your own should deeme" (V.iv.17). On one level, this story proves one of Artegall's arguments against the Gyant, namely his suggestion in Canto 39 that whatever the sea takes from one place it puts back in another, being more of a force of redistribution than of encroaching gain or loss. The sea in this story has produced a kind of equilibrium, but only after it has engendered a situation of discord and division between brothers.

25.   Angus Fletcher, *Allegory: The Theory of a Symbolic Mode* (Ithaca: Cornell University Press, 1964), 2, note 1.

26.   Gordon Teskey, "Allegory, Materialism, Violence," *The Production of English Renaissance Culture*, eds. David Lee Miller, Sharon O'Dair, and Harold Weber (Ithaca: Cornell University Press, 1994) 293–318, 303.

27.   *Oxford English Dictionary*, s.v. "plain," n1, def. 4.c "A level (horizontal) area." The *OED* provides no examples of the word being used to describe the bottom of the sea.

28.   In Spenser's time the word "plaine" was used not only to describe flat land, but also the flat surface of the sea (*Oxford English Dictionary*, s.v. "plain," n1, def. 1c). However, Spenser avoids this usage in Book V, which is remarkable in the context of his interest in the term "plaine" and its relationship to the sea.

29.   Andrew Hadfield discusses different puns in Spenser's poetry in his work on the significance of the words "salvage" and "sacred" and their relationship to Ireland in "The 'Sacred Hunger of Ambitious Minds': Spenser's Savage Religion," *Religion, Literature and Politics in Post-Reformation England, 1540–1688*, eds. Donna B. Hamilton and Richard Strier (Cambridge: Cambridge University Press, 1996), 27–45. The instability that surrounds these puns indicates the powerfully destabilizing impact of Spenser's attempts to control the contradictions inherent in his position on Ireland ("Savage Religion," 30–33). I have tried to show that the problems that attend the representation of history extend beyond Ireland, even though it is one of the key referents.

30.   Jacqueline T. Miller, *Poetic License: Authority and Authorship in Medieval and Renaissance Contexts* (New York: Oxford University Press, 1986), 99, 100, 101.

31.   Spenser, *A Letter of the Authors* in Hamilton, 737–38.

32.   Spenser, *Letter*, 737.

33.   Spenser, *Letter,* 737.

34.   Recent critical interest in the importance of Ireland in Spenser's life and work has drawn attention to the representation of Ireland and Grey in Book V (see Hadfield, *Edmund Spenser's Irish Experience: Wilde Fruit and Salvage Soil* [Oxford: Clarendon, 1997] and "Savage Religion"). Spenser believed that Grey's conduct in Ireland was justified and should not have been censured as it was by Elizabeth.

35.   See Alastair Bellany, " 'Railing Rhymes and Vaunting Verse': Libellous Politics in Early Stuart England, 1603–1628," *Culture and Politics in Early Stuart England*, eds. Kevin Sharpe and Peter Lake (Stanford: Stanford University Press, 1993), 285–310, 291.

36.   Hadfield, *Irish Experience*, 165.

37.   Hadfield, *Irish Experience,* 165. Jonathan Goldberg also discusses James's reaction to this representation of Mary, and Elizabeth's decision not to enforce the type of punishment he called for, in "The Poet's Authority: Spenser, Jonson, and James VI and I." *Genre* 15.2–3 (1982): 81–99, 81–83.

38.   A. Leigh Deneef, *Spenser and the Motives of Metaphor* (Durham: Duke University Press, 1982), 132.

39.   Goldberg, "Poet's Authority," 87.

40.   Elizabeth Bieman (*Plato Baptized: Towards the Interpretation of Spenser's Mimetic Fictions* [Toronto: University of Toronto Press, 1988]), 182–85, Theresa Krier (*Gazing on Secret Sights: Spenser, Classical Imitation, and the Decorums of Vision* [Ithaca: Cornell University Press, 1990]), 214, and Mihiko Suzuki (*Metamorphoses of Helen: Authority, Difference and the Epic* [Ithaca: Cornell University Press, 1989]), 193–94, all observe the inscrutability of this episode and the difficulties of interpretation it presents. Bieman and Suzuki also argue that the presence of the original name unsettles its replacement with the new.

41.   Kenneth Gross, *Spenserian Poetics: Idolatry, Iconoclasm, and Magic* (Ithaca: Cornell University Press, 1986), 16.

42.   Richard McCabe, *The Pillars of Eternity: Time and Providence in The Faerie Queene.* (Blackrock: Irish Academic Press, 1989), 78.

43.   DeNeef, *Motives,* 131.

44.   Hadfield, "Duessa's Trial and Elizabeth's Error: Judging Elizabeth in Spenser's *Faerie Queene*," *The Myth of Elizabeth*, eds. Susan Doran and Thomas S. Freeman (Houndmills: Palgrave Macmillan, 2003), 56–76, 62. Suzuki also argues that Radigund and Britomart are not strictly distinct, and finds similarities between Radigund and Elizabeth, particularly in the representations of Elizabeth as Amazon warrior that circulated after the defeat of the Spanish Armada (*Metamorphoses of Helen,* 177–82).

A. E. B. COLDIRON

The Widow's Mite and the Value of Praise: Commendatory Verses and an Unrecorded Marginal Poem in LSU's Copy of *The Faerie Qveene* 1590

This essay introduces a previously unstudied commendatory poem inscribed in a first edition copy of *The Faerie Qveene* (London: Ponsonby, 1590). Bound with a copy of 1596, this volume also contains corrections in the same hand that exceed those of the errata slip. Although the available evidence is not sufficient to establish the poem's authorship, the poem is inscribed in the middle of an important epideictic literary context, the Commendatory Verses and Dedicatory Sonnets. While adopting some conventions of Renaissance praise poetry—allusiveness, *aemulatio*, treatment of the poet's Muse and chosen genres—it ignores others. The margin poem, as script poems often do, challenges the literary conventions and values of the printed poems, inviting reconsideration of its commendatory context. This poem takes its cue from the mercantile implications of the final Commendatory Verse, Ignoto's skeptical "To looke vpon a worke of rare deuise" (CV 7). By means of the familiar parable of the widow's mite, the handwritten poem inverts Ignoto's trade-based poetic economy and recalibrates the literary worth of the Commendatory Verses.

*W*HAT IS A POEM WORTH, and what is poetic praise of it worth? These questions are central to the Commendatory Verses and Dedicatory Sonnets added to *The Faerie Queene*, and they seem to have inspired a manuscript poem written in the margins of one copy of the edition of 1590 (fig. 1). This essay introduces the manuscript

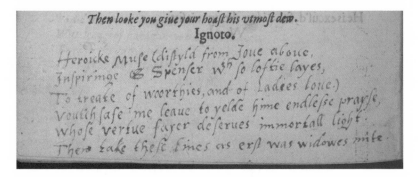

Fig. 1. Courtesy of Elaine Smyth, Curator of Special Collections, Hill Memorial Library, Louisiana State University.

poem and investigates its answers to these questions of poetic value, answers that differ clearly from those given by the printed poems among which it is inscribed. In addition, the essay discusses the evidentiary problems in, and the interpretive implications of, trying to establish the poem's authorship.

This unidentified, unstudied commentary sixain is written in what looks like a late-sixteenth- or early-seventeenth-century italic hand, in a first edition *Faerie Queene* (London: Ponsonby, 1590/1596), now held in Special Collections of Louisiana State University.[1] Although current evidence about the poem is insufficient to establish its author or date, the poem is inscribed at the center of an important epideictic circle composed of Spenser's readers, friends, commenders, and patrons. The poem is written between the Commendatory Verses (by Ralegh, Harvey, "Ignoto," and others) and the Dedicatory Sonnets, Spenser's seventeen poems to important Elizabethans (see fig. 2). In allusively and imitatively praising Spenser and *The Faerie Queene,* the margin poem, like much of the commendatory and dedicatory material surrounding it, participates in the conventions of Renaissance praise poetry. But the margin poem also challenges the printed praises. It ignores Elizabeth, for instance, and presents a recalcitrant Muse. The margin poem, furthermore, extends the mercantile implications of the final poem in the printed group, "Ignoto"'s commendation, "To looke upon a worke of rare devise." The central image of the handwritten poem, the widow's mite, inverts the system of literary valuation that guides the printed poems surrounding it.

I begin with a transcription of the margin poem and a reading of its widow's-mite topos:

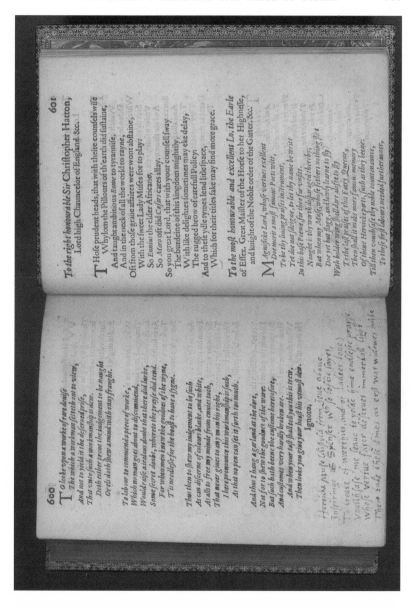

Fig. 2. Courtesy of Elaine Smyth, Curator of Special Collections, Hill Memorial Library, Louisiana State University.

Heroicke Muse (distyld from Ioue aboue,
Inspiringe ★Spenser wth so loftie layes,
To treate of woorthies, and of Ladies loue.)
Voutchsafe me leaue to yelde him endlesse prayse,
Whose vertue fayer deserues immortal light.
Then take these lines as erst was widowes mite.
(★ = capital S, crossed out)

The writer first appeals to Spenser's Muse, asking permission to praise
him endlessly. An epic or heroic commendation should follow, filling
many margins. But in the pointed silence after line 5, the Muse
apparently says "no" to this writer. Line 6 follows with a fallback
position: no epic? Then take these lines of praise, as once was taken
a widow's mite. What the poem actually says about Spenser is, as in
most of the printed Commendatory Verses, conventional enough on
its surface. We have here an epic Muse (unusual because "distyld"
—no Muse of Fire, but a condensed, liquid Muse); a poet inspired
with "loftie layes," to "treate of woorthies, and of Ladies Loue"; a
poet whose vertue fayer deserues immortall light"; and a commender
who wishes to "yelde hime endlesse prayse." The lines praise *The
Faerie Queene* as a high narrative poem with both romance and epic
elements, and Spenser as infinitely worthy. Less typical of Renaissance praise poetry, however, are the poem's self-justifications: first,
the Muse's implicit denial of permission for the deserved endless
praise, and second, the use of the widow's mite image.

   Here, the widow's mite parable (Mark 12:41–44; Luke 21:1–4) is
compressed to an image that achieves an unusual recalibration of
poetic scale and literary value. In the New Testament parable, a poor
widow puts her mite, her tiny coins, into the Lord's treasury along-
side the richer gifts of rich givers. They scorn her, but Jesus says,
"Truly I say to you, this poor widow has put in more than all those
who are contributing to the treasury; For they all contributed out of
their abundance, but she out of her poverty has put in everything
she had" (Mark 12:43–44). This image had a wide currency in the
Renaissance, as we will see later in the essay; it describes the elevation
of a lowly gift. A typical Christian paradox in its inversion of the
world's hierarchy of value—the last shall be first; the meek shall
inherit the earth—it also suggests what would later be identified as
a Marxist system of valuation and circulation ("from each according
to his abilities, to each according to his needs."[2] The widow's tiny
coin seems a small offering compared to others' gifts, but in terms of
the giver's limited abilities, it is significant, more meaningful than

the larger gifts of the wealthier givers. The re-evaluation of this gift, in other words, occurs not in terms of absolute value, and not relative to the recipient, but relative to the giver's own store; applied to poetry, this recalibration disrupts normal epideictic hierarchies (epic a higher form than pastoral or georgic, and "great" poets not generally those with a small oeuvre). Presenting him- or herself as a poor widow, whose pentameter sixain looks relatively worthless in context (humbly written in as it is after the richer commendatory poems printed in the volume), the writer uses the parable to effect a reappraisal of the poem as a small token that is nevertheless a significant literary offering. Thus the poem explains its own existence: the writer sets out to praise Spenser endlessly, but, Muse-denied, can only manage this token two-cents' worth. The poem also manages to justify its small scale and make itself valuable, even in such a rich literary context as the Commendatory Verses to *The Faerie Queene*. The competitive drives and anxiety of influence that haunt poetic commendation-writers: banished with one image.

ULTIMUS INTER PARES? THE POEM IN THE CONTEXT OF THE COMMENDATORY VERSES

This bold recalibration of literary value is inscribed right in the middle of *The Faerie Queene*'s "virtual" literary community, as figure 2 shows, between critical praises and the patronage critical to *TFQ*'s success.[3] The widow's mite figure is a perfect choice for a writer on the margins of such an impressive epideictic gathering. The writer enters the company of commendatory contributors like Walter Ralegh and Gabriel Harvey, and of dedicatees like the countess of Pembroke and Lord Burghley, and, over them all, the looming shade of Philip Sidney. With the widow's mite image, the poet reimagines this commendatory context as a "treasury" of opinion into which a modest praise-poem can be cast. Like the other printed poems here, this poem foregrounds the question of poetic value and reputation. Unlike all but one of the printed commendations, this poem focuses not just on Spenser and *The Faerie Queene,* but on the value of praise—rather, on the revaluing of praise. This small, anonymous, possibly female-authored poem thereby improves its position in this impressive literary context.

Surprisingly little has been written about one side of this literary context, the Commendatory Verses. Wayne Erickson's article on them is the most recent and effective treatment I have found.[4] Some research on them has been biographical and textual, focused on identifying the authors and placing them in what Erickson calls "one of the signal publishing events of English literary history" (13), focused on how to read and praise Spenser and his epic. The inscribed poem, which we might call a post-publishing event, raises instead the question of how to read the readers reading Spenser. Erickson notes the "ironic play . . . at work in the 1590 *Faerie Queene's* ancillary texts" (16) and further points out that "part of Spenser's rhetorical strategy in the [Dedicatory] Sonnets—to deprecate his poem while asserting its value to those willing to sanction . . . it—participates in conventional poetic false modesty" (14). This margin-writer's unconventional strategy is rather the elevation of modesty. As margin marks often do, this poem challenges the printed poems, inviting us to reconsider the Commendatory Verses' conventionally epideictic forms and themes.

Formally, the Commendatory Verses work on a plan of balanced variety. Two sonnets, a six-sixain poem, two ten-line epigrams, and two four-stanza poems, appear as a parade of (mostly) pairs inviting comparison. First come Ralegh's two poems, showing two kinds of fourteen-line sonnet, both in form[5] and theme: a poem on literary laureation and reputation, "Methought I saw the grave where Laura lay," is followed by the native, natural imagery of "The praise of meaner wits this worke like profit brings." Erickson reads this pair as a deliberate and meaningful juxtaposition of kinds of praise: praise from Elizabeth and from "meaner wits" (17–19). Next is Gabriel Harvey's poem in six sixains, "To The Learned Shepheard."[6] Addressed to "Collyn" and signed "Hobbynoll," Harvey's poem treats a recurring theme of the commendatory verses, Spenser's move from pastoral to epic poetry. Then come two ten-line epigrams, one by R. S. ("Fayre Thamis streame, that from Ludds stately towne"), and one by H. B. ("Graue Muses march in triumph and with prayses"). This pair, one a river-poem and one a Muse-procession, presents two aspects of an idea of motion or passage; the natural and topographical imagery of the river poem is paired with classical allusions and puns.[7] "Faire Thamis' Streme" is to be silent while the English Orpheus (Spenser) plays; in the next poem, the "Grave Muses" may land for a laureation ceremony before the great patroness Elizabeth, compared to Augustus. Erickson reads the pair as "two views of the problem of the queen, a subject notably absent from the final two poems" (20). Those final two poems, each in four *ababcc* sixains, also make a formal pair ("When stout Achilles heard of Helen's rape," by W. L., and "To looke upon a worke of rare devise," by "Ignoto"). This final pair seems somewhat like Ralegh's opening pair, in that one poem with classical emphasis is followed by another formally linked to it that is more nativist or "Deep English" in character, featuring proverbial and commonsensical arguments. The Homeric and the homely poem each look to the poetic art or craft (respectively): the former presents an elaborate analogy of how Spenser moved from pastoral to epic mode, and the latter, to be discussed further below, more directly treats how the crafted work is to be bought and valued.[8] Overall, then, the formal arrangement of the Commendatory Verses is not perfectly architectural or numerological, but uses patterns of formal likeness and difference to invite comparisons among the kinds of praise in these poems. The laureate and more folkloric sonnets contrast with one another; the natural river-images and the Muse-triumphs show variety; the epic intertexts of "When stout Achilles" stand in modal contrast to the georgic-mode shopkeeper's garlands and customer-readers of Ignoto's poem.

Thematically, too, these poems answer and extend one another in several specific ways, and their content aligns well with general conventions of praise poetry. Some Commendatory Verses treat the Muses, and some more conventionally than others.[9] Most poems here treat Elizabeth as chief reader and interpreter, source of inspiration (in one case, as source of the Muses), and patron.[10] Most allude to Spenser or imitate his style, as is conventional in Renaissance praise-poetry.[11] Several of the Commendatory Verses allude to or treat Spenser's genres and in particular his progression from pastoral to epic. For instance, CV6 is built on an analogy to the story of Achilles. Just as Ulysses helps Achilles out of feminine disguise into warlike heroism, Sidney helps Spenser move from sweet pastoral to heroic epic. Spenser's shedding of pastoral drag, or rather, his coming-out as an epic poet, is a frequent theme in other commendations, as well, though it is most memorably expressed in CV6.[12]

Our margin-poet responds to the formal and thematic patterning of the collection by adopting its dominant epigrammatic mode and its predominant form (the pentameter sixain), and by using allusive and imitative style, syntax, and diction.[13] But the poem largely ig-nores the main themes and content of the Commendatory Verses. The handwritten poem notably does not mention Elizabeth. Spens-er's Muse only appears in the opening invocation, and there, self-referentially, invoked for leave to praise Spenser endlessly. The poem does point lightly to Spenser's multiple modes within the *Faerie Queene*: epic ("Heroicke Muse"), romance ("ladies loue"), exem-plary historiography ("woorthies"); "loftie layes" may glance at all three. But there is no reference here to a main theme of the printed

Commendatory Verses, Spenser's literary progress through the *rota virgiliana,* and no notice that the pastoral *Calender* gave way to the epic *Faerie Queene.* The margin writer's concern with literary valuation renders the poem more direct, occasion-conscious, and self-conscious than the printed poems. This poem's central work is to reimagine and revise the action and value of poetic commendation into which it inscribes itself.

POETRY AS COMMERCE: THE VALUE OF PRAISE

In reimagining the action and value of poetic commendation, the margin poem may take its cue from the last printed commendatory poem, CV7, "To looke upon a worke of rare devise" by "Ignoto." This final commendatory poem is the immediate provoking context for the handwritten poem,[14] and it too revises commendatory conventions. While Commendatory Verses 1 through 6 allow for contrasting forms and kinds of praise, for the mixed genres of Spenser's oeuvre, for varying conceptions of the Muse and for the varying roles of Elizabeth, Ignoto's CV7 figures poetry strictly as a commercial enterprise. CV7 addresses the readers and their judgment, and its conceit is that poetry is a workers' product, a piece of craft implicitly to be sold and bought. It is a homely and practical poem, commonsensical in comparison with the preceding six commendatory poems:

> To looke upon a worke of rare deuise
> The which a workman setteth out to view
> And not to yield it the deserued prise
> That vnto such a workmanship is dew,
> Doth either proue the judgement to be naught
> Or els doth show a mind with enuy fraught.

> To labour to commend a peece of worke,
> Whiche no man goes about to discommend,
> Would raise a iealous doubt that there did lurke,
> Some secret doubt wherto the prayse did tend.
> 　　For when men know the goodnes of the wyne,
> 　　T'is needlesse for the hoast to haue a sygne.

> Thus then to shew my judgement to be such
> As can discerne of colours blacke, and white,

As alls to free my minde from enuies tuch,
That neuer giues to any man his right,
　　I here pronounce this workmanship is such,
　　As that no pen can set it forth too much.
And thus I hang a garland at the dore,
Not for to shew the goodnes of the ware:
But such hath beene the custome heretofore,
And customes very hardly broken are.
　　And when your tast shall tell you this is trew,
　　Then looke you giue your hoast his vtmost dew.
　　　　　　　　Ignoto.

This is an unusually skeptical, demystifying praise-poem. Most commendatory verses (and all the others here) create and sustain heightening epideictic fictions about the origins and disposition of the poetry—the Muses in a triumph, the English Orpheus, the supportive, generous patrons, the dedicatees of rare discernment, and so on. However, in Ignoto's conceit, poetry is not high art but craft, a workmanlike thing that can be seen in a shop, judged, bought or not, tasted or not, complete with a shop-sign and proverbially needless garland at the door.[15] The nonverbal, customary sign—the garland over the shop-door instead of on the head of the poet—awards a georgic or commercial laureation. If *The Faerie Queene* is figured as wares, Spenser as the artisan-shopkeeper, readers as buyers, and laureation as a mercantile signal, then commendatory poetry is advertising space. The texts that more usually admit this truth—that poets must eat, that literature operates within economic systems—were complaints to the purse, "go little boke" topoi, letters to patrons, dedicatory supplications and hints. The other CVs and DSs do hint at the anticipated generosity of Elizabeth and others. But this poem makes its main conceit mercantile, and its open theme the problem of knowing how to value (and whether to purchase) Spenser's work. Ignoto's poem finishes the collection with an extended metaphor of the acts of writing, reading, and judging that demystifies the hints and turns away from the loftier images in the preceding six poems.

Ignoto's poem sets poetry out as craft and workmanship rather than as inspired art. Yet it assumes, rather than actually treating, Spenser's good craft and workmanship, and turns its real attention to the reader's problem of evaluating the praises of it. It also speaks what is unspeakable in most commendatory poems: jealousy, mixed motives for praise, salability of poems. And the poem treats in some detail the reader's immediate interpretive problem—that is, the problem of knowing how to evaluate praises like the commendatory verses. Ignoto openly expresses ambivalence about the motivations for praise and about insincere and unnecessary praise. Stanzas 1 and 2 open with the problem of poetic envy: on the one hand, not to praise shows envy, but so does too much praise. Ignoto admits he needs "to free [his] minde from enuie's tuch" in stanza 3. But jealousy is not the only trouble with commendatory poetry. How much of literary praise is merely conventional, just custom emptied of meaning? Ignoto admits further that he writes this praise only from a sense of convention or tradition: "and thus I hang a garland at the dore / Not for to show the goodness of the ware / But such hath beene the custome heretofore." Beyond the problem that customary signage can be detached from the signified of the "goodness of the ware," is not commendation superfluous if the work itself is good? "For when men know the goodness of the wyne / Tis needless for the boast to have a sygne" (lines 11–12). Then, too, how much commendation is excessive? "To labour to commend a piece of work / which no one goes about to discommend" actually raises doubts about it (stanza 2). Ignoto's skeptical, pragmatic commendation, in sum, actually focuses not on *The Faerie Queene* but on the motives behind the Commendatory Verses themselves and on problems in evaluating literary praise.

Our margin writer quietly answers Ignoto's focus and his new economic epideixis with a further revision—an inversion, really—of the value of literary praise and another kind of challenge to the Commendatory Verses. Just as in Ignoto's poem, the focus in the margin-poem is less on *The Faerie Queene* than it is on a revisionary reading of the value of praise. Where Ignoto's stanza 1 asserts that to see such a work and not to praise it is either to lack judgment or to be envious, our margin-writer shows neither envy nor poor judgment. On the other hand, runs Ignoto's stanza 2, no one has dispraised *The Faerie Queene,* so praise would seem unnecessary and would indicate some flaw needing to be covered. No flaw in Spenser, says the margin poem's line 5. Ignoto knows the pitfalls of praise and recognizes envy when he sees it (stanza 3), but *The Faerie Queene* is so great "As that no pen can set it forth too much." This touches on the problem of hyperbole in praise poetry, which he solves with a silent, polyvalent, and thus ambiguous sign, the garland over the shop-door. The margin poet solves the problem of hyperbole by means of scale, raising Spenser's merit of "endlesse prayse" and "immortall light," but only writing a sixain after all. "No pen can set it forth too much"? My pen, implies this margin poet, can hardly set it forth at all. Yet, "Give your hoast his dew," says Ignoto; in this small space, responds the margin writer, I can only give a sixain, but it is worth more than all the rest. Our writer responds to Ignoto's doubts about the value of epideixis by inverting the system, ascribing greater value to small praise. Christianity beats capitalism? Probably not, but after Ignoto's skepticism, small praise raised to greatness at least does not risk hyperbole, raise doubts of jealousy, or hang needless noisy signs above the wine.

WIDOW'S MITES, RHETORICAL AND BIOGRAPHICAL

Is the rhetoric of reevaluation necessary to the writer's actual case or is it simply playful and exceedingly modest? Is the writer's poetic corpus actually small, so that this poem does actually give and display the writer's best, or is this a deft commendatory move highly sensitive to its immediate context? In other words, is the window-persona backed by biography?[16] To assess the degree of biographical fact behind the rhetorical claim we would need to assess the extent and quality of the poetic oeuvre of the writer of this sixain, and to do that would require identifying the author and dating the poem—using biography and historical context to guide literary interpretation. The widow's mite trope and the character of the inscription lead first to the question of gender: does the writer's self-representation as a widow mean that Anonymous is in this case female? Does the unpracticed italic hand[17] reinforce that tantalizing notion?

There is as yet no other evidence of authorship to support the idea that a woman wrote these lines. The poet's self-representation as a widow need not be understood as biographical fact: the widow's mite trope was widely used as an image, in titles, and as a moral topic by sixteenth- and seventeenth-century male writers such as William Hunnis, Tobie Matthew, Richard Waite, Robert Coster, Anthony Batt, Thomas Lawson, and others, as image, in their titles, and as a sermon topic.[18] Many but not all early modern "widow's mite" imprints are overtly religious. Sermons, treatises, praises of the Blessed Virgin Mary, but also discussions of the Commonwealth, of the plague, and of the seven liberal arts take the title "widow's mite," sharing our margin poet's proudly humble rhetorical position.[19] The idea seems to have been to cast one's modest (but, according to the parable, valuable) thoughts into a treasury of ideas about an important topic. To secularize the purpose of the biblical conceit is no surprise in a syncretic age, and like the plague, the Sabbath, or the Commonwealth, *The Faerie Queene* was a topic important enough to receive

a treasury of opinion (the Commendatory Verses) into which a writer
might modestly throw his or her two cents. Clearly, one need not
have been a literal widow to cast a rhetorical widow's mite. And yet
early modern women such as Elizabeth Hincks, Alice Hayes, and
Elizabeth Redford found the image useful, too.[20] For both male and
female writers, the widow's-mite image invokes the parable's relative
reevaluation, though the writerly modesty it conjures was perhaps
especially useful in a female writer's self-presentation.

Personas are not poets. However, if we still wish to pursue the
writer's rhetoric of self-presentation as if it were a biographical lead,
we might look to the Sidney-circle women, and perhaps first to Mary
Sidney Herbert, countess of Pembroke. There are verbal resonances
between this poem and Spenser's dedicatory poem to Mary Sidney
Herbert, found a few pages later in the 1590 *Faerie Queene*:

> Remembraunce of that most Heroicke spirit,
>   The heuens pride, the glory of our daies,
>   Which now triumpheth through immortall merit
>   Of his braue virtues, crownd with lasting baies,
> Of heauenlie blis and euerlasting praies;
>   Who first my Muse did lift out of the flore,
>   To sing his sweet delights in lowlie laies;
>   Bids me most noble lady to adore
> His goodly image liuing euermore,
>   In the diuine resemblaunce of your face;
>   Which with your vertues ye embellish more,
>   And natiue beauty deck with heauenlie grace;
> For his, and for your owne especial sake,
>   Vouchsafe from him this token in good worth to take.

Our margin poem echoes in part several of Spenser's phrases to the
countess: "Heroicke spirit" (1.1), "immortall merit" (1.3), "braue
vertues" (1.4), "lowlie laies" (1.7). Might the margin poem in a way
return the "token" in Spenser's trademark dodecasyllabic final line,
"Vouchsafe from him this token in good worth to take"? The verbal
similarities to our margin poem led me to wonder if Mary Sidney
Herbert, countess of Pembroke, might have written the poem in an
early copy of *The Faerie Queene*—her own return "token," her own
two cents' worth. And the writer's persona as widow resonates with
Mary Sidney Herbert's literal biography, since her husband, the 2nd
earl of Pembroke, died in 1601.[21] But a sixain written in on page

600 is not much of an answer to a sonnet here, late in the Dedicatory Sonnets (DS 15). There is space on the page after Spenser's sonnet to Mary Sidney Herbert into which this poem could easily have been written, had it been intended as an answer poem.[22] Of course the writer of the widow's mite poem does not answer with a hexameter final line and does not in all cases spell the echoing words the same way. Furthermore, Spenser's sonnet is both a dedication to the countess of Pembroke and a tribute to her brother Philip Sidney, a fact—and an elegiac mode—that the widow's mite writer ignores entirely. Other kinds of evidence fall in line against authorship by the Countess: provenance records do not confirm any relation between this copy and Herbert, and paleography actually disproves such enticing speculations. Margaret Hannay and Noel Kinnamon, editors of the works of Herbert, have told me that this careful italic is probably not her hand. Kinnamon explains that the distinctive g and t here are unlike those in examples of Herbert's cursive hand.[23] The margin poem's literary and material features invite but finally do not support speculation about the poem as an answer to Spenser's dedication to Mary Sidney Herbert.[24]

Red Herrings, Dead Ends: Interpretation without Biography?

The desire to pin biography to such a rhetorical position is perhaps irresistible. It was at first for me, and putting a name to the poem seems to be the wish of nearly every scholar with whom I have spoken about this inscribed poem. Although the goal of this essay is not to identify the writer of the widow's mite poem, that persistent desire to read persona as poet, or at least to link biography to literary interpretation, deserves attention because it highlights some of the evidentiary problems of dealing with early modern marginalia. The enticing red herring of Mary Sidney Herbert pursued above shows how several kinds of material and formal evidence may be brought to bear to rule out an attribution of authorship. In trying to identify the writer of the little tribute to Spenser, provenance and paleography are the first steps; who has held this book, and can we compare their hands to this one? We can also try to track the hands of early modern writers of widow's mites, with the idea that a writer already finding this trope a useful piece of rhetoric might also have used it to commend *The Faerie Queene*. In preliminary work I have been able to investigate and rule out a few likely widow's-mite writers, such as William Hunnis and Tobie Matthew.[25] Gabriel Harvey, so closely connected to Spenser and writer of one of the Commendatory Verses, uses highly variable hands, but so far none seems to match.[26] One colleague suggested to me that Spenser himself might have written playful self-commendation in his own margins; the fact that corrections in this same hand also appear in the volume—corrections that exceed those of the printer's errata list—makes this an especially intriguing idea (see figs. 3 and 4), as does Erickson's hunch that Spenser was involved in the creation of the Commendatory Verses.[27] Spenser, as Lee Piepho has recently shown, writes both italic and secretary hands, but neither matches this hand.[28] None of the hands displayed in volumes I and II of Peter Beal's *Index to Literary Manuscripts* matches, even though the "matching" of hands is hardly an exact science, and human handwriting is notoriously variable.[29] Beyond paleography, one can pursue authorship via provenance, stylistics, or allusion, for instance.[30] An inquiry into the circulation in manuscript of the other Commendatory Verses might yield a connection via provenance or paleography. But with so many false leads, one comes to feel like a detective trapped in a bad academic novel. Speculation overtakes investigation, and unknowns accumulate: seventeenth-century owners of the book, its nineteenth-century binder, and women writers of widow's mites are on the long list of suspects not yet completely questioned or not available for questioning.

A further problem with trying to identify the writer either as a woman, a member of the Spenser-Sidney circle, or both—indeed, with trying to identify the writer at all—is that the hand cannot even be dated with certainty. The matter of dating, as usual, has real interpretive consequences. If written sometime between 1590 and, say, 1625, we could understand the poem as part of the actual, primary, literary coterie around *The Faerie Queene*. If written much later than that, the poem would have to be understood as recording a retrospective rather than a contemporary response to *The Faerie Queene*. The poem's imitative mode and allusiveness would in that case participate in the deliberate archaism of eighteenth-, nineteenth-, or even twentieth-century "Spenserianism," and would notably include the deliberate physical imitation of a sixteenth-century hand as well. With the evidence available, there is no way to know whether we are dealing with a contemporaneous response to a major literary event, or with a nostalgic appropriation of an old literary monument. It could be a much later hand (after all, even in 2005 we can imitate an italic hand), although Steven May points out that the secretary

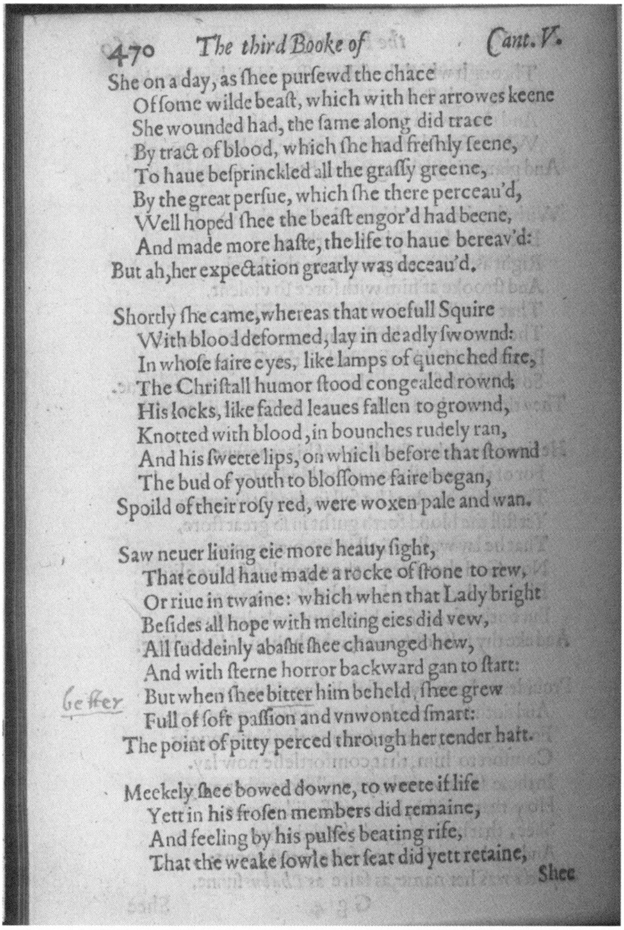

470 *The third Booke of* *Cant. V.*

She on a day, as fhee purfewd the chace
 Of fome wilde beaft, which with her arrowes keene
She wounded had, the fame along did trace
By tract of blood, which fhe had frefhly feene,
To haue befprinckled all the graffy greene,
By the great perfue, which fhe there perceau'd,
Well hoped fhee the beaft engor'd had beene,
 And made more hafte, the life to haue bereav'd:
But ah, her expectation greatly was deceau'd.

Shortly fhe came, whereas that woefull Squire
 With blood deformed, lay in deadly fwownd:
In whofe faire eyes, like lamps of quenched fire,
The Chriftall humor ftood congealed rownd:
His locks, like faded leaues fallen to grownd,
Knotted with blood, in bounches rudely ran,
And his fweete lips, on which before that ftownd
 The bud of youth to bloffome faire began,
Spoild of their rofy red, were woxen pale and wan.

Saw neuer liuing eie more heauy fight,
 That could haue made a rocke of ftone to rew,
Or riue in twaine: which when that Lady bright
Befides all hope with melting eies did vew,
All fuddeinly abafht fhee chaunged hew,
And with fterne horror backward gan to ftart:
But when fhee bitter him beheld, fhee grew
 Full of foft paffion and vnwonted fmart:
The point of pitty perced through her tender hart.

Meekely fhee bowed downe, to weete if life
 Yett in his frofen members did remaine,
And feeling by his pulfes beating rife,
That the weake fowle her feat did yett retaine,
 Shee

Fig. 3. Courtesy of Elaine Smyth, Curator of Special Collections, Hill Memorial Library, Louisiana State University.

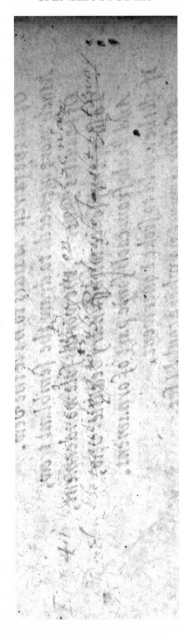

Fig. 4. p. 606 (errata page). Courtesy of Elaine Smyth, Curator of Special Collections, Hill Memorial Library, Louisiana State University.

element of the crossed out S might be the mark of a person accustomed to or most comfortable using secretary—defaulting to secretary, and self-correcting—which would indicate an earlier rather than a later date for this poem.[31] Without more sophisticated science than what is currently available to me, we can only guess at a date for this faded ink.

Uncertainty about dating, authorship, and historical context—and the enjoyable, instructive pursuit of red herrings—may simply be the state we must accept when dealing with many manuscript poems and marginal marks. These marks record individual readers' responses and occasions of active engagement with a text, but it can be difficult to contextualize such occasions accurately or to generalize from such ephemeral particulars. Beyond this one instance, marginal responses to Spenser and to printed paratextual epideixeis promise to reveal literary communities at work and to illuminate their responses to Renaissance systems of poetic valuation. Yet even without that kind of promising general inquiry, even without the support of biography, answers to "what's a poem worth?" are available to us in such anonymous particulars as this little poem. I hope that future researchers will identify and date the hand and explain the author's biographical relation to Spenser and his literary circle. Until then, we can nevertheless clearly understand the rhetorical and poetic relations of this poem to its immediate literary and material context: following Ignoto's skeptical, mercantile-based lead but using an allusive new trope, this poem challenges epideictic systems of literary value by throwing in its clever two cents.

Louisiana State University

NOTES

1.   In the Hill Memorial Library, Baton Rouge, Louisiana. The poem is found at the bottom of p. 600 (folio Pp5[v]). As Anne Lake Prescott points out, this poem was noticed by Ellis, as recorded in "Spenser Allusions in the Sixteenth and Seventeenth Centuries," comp. Ray Heffner, Dorothy E. Mason, Frederick Padelford; ed. William Wells; in *Studies in Philology* 68.5 (1971): 1–172; 69. Thanks to Elaine Smyth, Curator of Special Collections, for encouragement and for expertise in acquisitions and book history, and to Paul Dowling of Liber Antiquus for information on the book itself. Thanks to Professors Margaret Hannay and Noel Kinnamon for expertise and advice about the possible relation of this hand to that of Mary Sidney Herbert, countess of Pembroke. Thanks also to Steven May, Anne Lake Prescott, Georgianna

Ziegler, Heather Wolfe, Jane Donawerth, Nicholas Crawford, and H. R. Woudhuysen for advice, expertise, and encouragement in this inquiry. Thanks likewise to the members of the 2005 Shakespeare Association of America workshop on marginalia: Holly Crocker, workshop leader, William Sherman, William Slights, Janet Starners, and Kellie Robertson. Thanks to Leigh DeNeef and Allen Carroll for challenges issued at the 2005 Southeastern Renaissance Conference about, respectively, the dating of the hand and the gender of the writer.

2. Marx, *Critique of the Gotha Program,* 1875, quoting, probably, Louis Blanc, *Organisation du Travail,* 1840.

3. This copy of the work contains both the seven commendatory poems, here called CV1-CV7, and the dedicatory cancel sections (with seventeen sonnets in all, including the cancel sections, here called DS1-DS17) of *The Faerie Queene.* For more information on the various copies of the work, see F. R. Johnson, *A Critical Bibliography of the Works of Edmund Spenser Printed Before 1700* (Baltimore: Johns Hopkins University Press, 1933), Hiroshi Yamashita, ed., et al., *A Textual Companion to* The Faerie Qveene *1590* (Tokyo: Kenyusha, 1993), and Jean Brink, "Materialistic History of the Publication of Spenser's *Faerie Queene,*" *Review of English Studies* ns 54.213 (2003): 1–26.

4. Erickson, "Spenser and His Friends Stage a Publishing Event: Praise, Play, and Warning in the Commendatory Verses to the 1590 *Faerie Queene,*" *Renaissance Papers* (1997): 13–22. See also L. G. Black's entry in *The Spenser Encyclopedia,* ed. A. C. Hamilton (Toronto: University of Toronto Press, 1990), 291–93; Robert McNamara, "Spenser's Dedicatory Sonnets to the 1590 *Faerie Queene*: an Interpretation of the Blank Sonnet," *Spenser Studies* XVIII (2003): 293–99; James P. Bednarz, "The Collaborator as Thief: Raleigh's (Re)Vision of *The Faerie Queene,*" *ELH* 63.2 (Summer 1996): 279–307; others cited in Erickson. On the Dedicatory Verses, see Erickson's note 5, p. 16.

5. The pentameter sonnet of two quatrains and sestet is followed by the sonnet of seven couplets in poulter's measure (a sort of seven-by-seven square in that each of the seven couplets closes with a seven-beat line).

6. The sixain would later be called the "Venus and Adonis" stanza. Had these been hexameter lines, Harvey's poem would have likewise formed a kind of six-by-six square.

7. Wordplay includes line 3, "this rare dispenser"; line 5, puns on dual meanings of "desert" and "dew" for deserving and due; lines 9–10, punning polyptoton, "fair be the guerdon of your Faery Queen / even of the fairest the world has ever seen." CV6 puns on "tyred."

8. For a slightly different view of the final pairing see Erickson 20–21.

9. CV3's "sacred fury" and Spenser's Muse "masking" in "haughty verse"; in CV5 the Grave Muses parade, yet Spenser is in a role additional to that of poetic receiver—he is a "dispenser" of their and Eliza's gifts. See also CV6. That our margin poem calls on Spenser's "Heroicke Muse" is another point in favor of the partisans of Calliope in the long critical war between those following Josephine Bennett (preferring Clio as Spenser's Muse) and those following Padelford (preferring Calliope). See the Variorum, vol. 1, appendix IX, 506–15 on the Muses of *The Faerie Queene.* (*The Works of Edmund Spenser: A Variorum.* 10 vols. Eds. E. Greenlaw,

C. Osgood, F. Padelford. Baltimore: Johns Hopkins University Press, 1932–1957.)
Note, however, that Clio ennobles the worthies, in one of Spenser's invocations
(Variorum III.3.3–4). For a thorough review of classical and medieval muse traditions
as they relate to this question and to Spenser's Muses in general, see Thomas P.
Roche, Jr., "Spenser's Muse," in *Unfolded Tales,* eds. George Logan and Gordon
Teskey (Ithaca: Cornell University Press, 1989), 162–88.

10.   CV2 (ll. 8–12); CV3, especially the final two lines; CV 4 (ll. 5–6); CV 5
(ll. 5–6).

11.   This is a common feature of Renaissance commendatory poetry: *aemulatio* or
imitation of the author praised as the sincerest form of compliment. Thomas Warton
long ago noted that the first Ralegh sonnet "imitates the manner of the author
whom it compliments" (*Observations on The Faerie Queene of Spenser,* 1754 and 1762;
II.253, cited in Variorum III.305). The printed poems are "Spenserian" in several
senses, not only imitating Spenserian style, as Warton notes, but also alluding to
Spenser and to parts of his work and punning on his name. A. C. Hamilton notes
that CV2 resembles *TFQ* III's proem (Hamilton, ed., *The Faerie Qveene* [London:
Longman, 2001], p. 721). More obviously, CV2 also refers directly to *TFQ* Books
III and II, "Chastitie . . . or Temperaunce" (line 7). Hamilton further notes that
CV4 refers to the *Epithalamium Thamesis.* In another vein, many have noted the pun
on Spenser's name at CV5, line 3, "this rare dispenser." Our margin-poet makes
no puns on Spenser's name but does use syntax and diction that are identifiably
"Spenserian," as note 13 explains.

12.   Harvey's CV3 treats Spenser's generic advance openly: "Collyn I see by thy
new taken taske / Some sacred fury hath enricht thy brayns . . . that liftd thy notes
from Shepheardes unto kinges" (lines 1–5). CV4, though it begins with a lyric
implication (Orpheus), ends with this couplet: "For he hath taught hye drifts in
shepheardes weedes, / And deep conceits now singes in Faeries deedes" (lines 9–10).
Various poems figure Spenser as the English Petrarch, Homer, Orpheus, and Virgil,
one poem adding its comparison to the next and each adding a generic implication
about Spenser's place as the English Poet. Our margin writer does not treat the
developing career of the poet but does glance at Spenser's generic and modal variety
(romance, "Ladies loue"; historiography, "worthies"; epic, "loftie layes" and "Heroicke Muse").

13.   The syntax in this sixain recalls the woven turns of many Spenserian stanzas,
a certain digressive and recursive elaboration of a single thread. The handwritten
poem takes one overall syntactical line: heroic muse, vouchsafe me leave to yield
him endless praise. That line is complicated and interrupted by a parenthetical, a
relative clause, and an expanded preceding indirect object—exactly the kind of
syntax that halts students and makes it better to read *TFQ* slowly. The parenthetical
description of the addressee, the muse, in lines 2–3, ("distyld from Ioue aboue, /
Inspiringe Spenser . . ."), also doubles back to the real subject, Spenser and his
book's style ("loftie layes") and topics ("woorthies and ladies loue"). Line 5 further
complicates the main syntactical line, with a relative clause, "whose vertue fayer
deserues immortal light," elaborating a previous indirect object ("him," line 4). This
recalls what Spenser does in the larger scale, too, putting something in the reader's
view and only explaining it later. Delayed naming and character introductions, as

well as landscapes that only reveal themselves fully after the protagonists are already well in (Bower of Bliss, Busyrane's Castle, etc.), are examples of this Spenserian habit of mind. We are to learn as we go, in the unfolding, and this poem captures in miniature that habit of informational delay or delayed elaboration. A Spenserian syncretism shows up in an easy turn between classical and Christian allusions. To make Heroic Muse/Jove (line 1), and the widow's mite (line 6), the endpoints of the commendation is to contain whole worlds: from divine to human, from grand to modest scales. The metatextual turn found here (the poem drawing attention to itself) is also frequent in Spenser, but like the poem's compression, that trait is common in Renaissance lyric.

At word level, too, certain phrases evoke or allude quietly to Spenser. "Endlesse prayse" recalls the "endlesse worke" itself. Not just the familiar "God help the man so wrapped in errours endlesse traine," but the "Endless monument" etc., and at *FQ* I.xi.7.6, "A worke of labour long and endlesse prayse." "Endlesse" is a favorite word of Spenser (he uses it about seventy times, fifty of those in *TFQ*). Other words in the poem with Spenserian resonance are hard to separate from a general resonance in early modern culture: vouchsafe, virtue, distilled, lofty lays. "Woorthies" and "Immortall light" likewise, though the latter phrase has been seen as a preoccupation of Spenser's that links him to late writers like Milton. Taken individually, none of these words can be read as Spenserian allusion, but when together in this context, they may constitute an echoing response to Spenserian diction. There is enough syntactical and lexical resonance here, I think, to identify a compressed Spenserian style and *aemulatio,* or at very least, a literary attentiveness.

14.   In the physical and formal senses, the handwritten poem looks like a coda or even a final stanza to Ignoto's poem (see fig. 2), and in theme it responds by further revising and reimagining the scene and values of commendation.

15.   Proverbial lines traced at least as far back as the *Pilgrimage of Man,* line 21405, a translation from French, versions of which were reprinted in Renaissance England in 1508, c.1520, 1606, 1612, 1613; see STC 19917.5ff. At this writing, the French original is not definitively traced. See also Tilley W462, who cites Erasmus, *Adagia* 589c; Taverner 1539, Gascoigne 1575, and of course the epilogue to *As You Like It.* See also Lyly's *Euphues* I.181 (1579).

16.   In another vein, does the writer's failure to summon the heroic muse link biography to the chosen genre and scale? Religious genres, but not epic, were considered suitable for women writers, as Kellie Robertson reminded me (personal correspondence, 2004).

17.   As you can see (fig 1.), it is an oddly mixed hand. Heather Wolfe, Curator of Manuscripts at the Folger Library, calls it a "highly individualized, unpracticed italic hand with elements of secretary." The letters are carefully separated from one another, the "t" vertical is distinctive, and the "g" is formed beginning with a clockwise stroke that moves straight to the descender without a reversal of direction. The spacing seems artificial, as if written more slowly or less naturally, with each letter written separately without connectors. Might this be an imitation of the visual form of printed letters?

18.   William Hunnis, *The Poore widowes mite* [bound with *Seuen Sobs of a sorrowfull soule . . .* and other works] (London: Henrie Denham, 1583); the STC shows at least

fifteen entries before 1636. A G. [attributed to Tobie Matthew, recusant Catholic], *The Widdowes Mite cast into the treasure-house of the prayses of our B. Lady . . .* (St. Omer: 1619, with several rpts.). Antonie Batt, *A poore mans mite . . . concerning the rosarie . . .* (London [or Douai?]: 1634 and 1639). Robert Coster, *A Mite cast into the common treasury* (London: 1649). Stephen Jerome, *A Ministers mite cast into the stocke of a weake memory* (London: T. H., 1650). I have not found further information about Richard Farnesworth's mite, supposedly printed in 1653. J. W., *A Mite to the Treasury in consideration of the Common-Wealth* (London: T. Newcomb, 1653). Edward Billing [perhaps Edward Borough], *A Mite of Affection manifested in 31 Proposals . . .* (London: 1659), displaying a less obvious titular allusion to the parable. Richard Waite, *The Widdowes mite cast in to the treasury of the Lord God* ([1663?], London: s.n., 1683), a treatise on redemption. Henry Adis, *A Fannaticks mite cast into the king's treasurie* (1666). Theophile Garencières, *A Mite Cast into the treasury of the famous City of London . . .* (London: 1655 [two editions]; Tho. Ratcliffe, 1666). Thomas Lawson, *A Mite into the treasury, being a word to artists . . .* (London: Andrew Sowle, 1680). There is also *The Widow's Mite cast into the treasury for the repairing of the breaches of the temple . . .*, 1695; written by J. St. N. who will not share his name but who tells us he is 91 years old and "a student in St. Paul's epistles."

19. Most of the writers of religious "widow's mites" are Catholic, with Quakers taking up the theme later in the period.

20. Most examples of women widow's-mite writers occur much later, in the seventeenth century and after. Elizabeth Hincks titles her defense of Quakers *The Poor Widows mite cast into the treasury . . .* (London?: s.n., 1671); Alice Hayes titles her autobiography *A Legacy, or Widow's Mite . . .* (London: I. Sowle, 1723; T Sowle Raylton and Luke Hinde, 1749; Luke Hinde, 1765; rpt. Philadelphia: Andrew Steuart, 1766; London: James Philipps, 1786). Elizabeth Redford defends the Sabbath in a treatise titled *The Widow's Mite, humbly offered, not impos'd . . .* (London: s.n., 1690).

21. Thanks to Margaret Hannay, whose extensive knowledge of Sidney and Herbert biographies corrected and clarified several points here.

22. Robert McNamara argues that this space was an "empty place" left to honor Sidney as empty places were set at banquets honoring fallen comrades.

23. Thanks to Professors Hannay and Kinnamon for their expertise and their kind and speedy responses to my query. Kinnamon writes: "Because surviving examples of Mary Sidney's hand are all cursive, comparison with the hand of the new poem will necessary be inconclusive. This is not to say that she could not have adopted a different hand for a special occasion such as inscribing a set of verses in a treasured volume by an admired poet, but her hand and this one have no common features that could be considered significant. Examples of clear differences include 'I,' 'p,' 'th,' 'd,' and the ampersand. The hand of 'Heroicke Muse,' however, does have some distinctive elements that would be helpful in making an eventual identification. The lowercase 't' is indeed a good example, and so is the surprising final upward and right-curving stroke of lowercast 'g.' But both are quite different from the 't' and 'g' of Mary Sidney's cursive hand. Two other possibly distinctive letters in the new poem are the fully angular 'k' and the frequently 'footed' 'r.' Otherwise, the 'Heroicke muse' hand is fairly generic, particularly with respect to the sinous 'y' and somewhat angular 'w' " (Correspondence, February 2005).

24. Margaret Hannay further suggests that other Sidney women might be likely suspects; were this essay aimed primarily at identifying the poem's author, I should want to see the hands of Phillippa Sidney Hobart, Catherine Sidney Mansell, and Elizabeth Sidney Manners. Lady Mary Wroth's hand it seems to me not to be; see Josephine Roberts, ed., *The Poems of Lady Mary Wroth* (Baton Rouge: Louisiana State University Press, 1993), 77–81; see also Roberts, "The Huntington Manuscript of Lady Mary Wroth's Play, *Loues Victorie,*" *Huntington Library Quarterly* 46 (Winter 1983), 156–74. The crossed-out S recalls some Sidney women's use of that figure in manuscripts, but this one to me looks like a mistake, not a flourish. See Margaret Hannay, *Phillip's Phoenix: Mary Sidney Countess of Pembroke* (New York: Oxford University Press, 1990), 193; Hannay notes that Wroth used the same symbol as the Dowager Countess, which "[emphasized] their identity as Sidneys," 273, note 123. See also Mary Ellen Lamb, *Gender and Authorship in the Sidney Circle* (Madison: University of Wisconsin Press, 1990), especially 194–228 and notes on 268–72. Jane Donawerth suggests Anne Lock, and while the modest tone rings true, the hand does not match the italic hand shown in Susan Felch, ed., *The Collected Works of Anne Vaughan Lock* (Tempe, AZ: ACMRS, 1999). Anna Weamys might be a suspect, as a late continuer or imitator of Spenser-Sidney romance styles; there is no holograph manuscript of her work, according to Patrick C. Cullen, ed., in Anna Weamys, *A Continuation of Sir Philip Sidney's Arcadia* (New York: Oxford University Press, 1994), lxv.

25. Despite William Hunnis's possible biographical connections to Spenser through the court of Elizabeth, it is not his hand and is not written in his poetic style. He was "Gentleman of her Majesty's Chapel" and teacher there. Folger manuscripts X.d.459 (12) and V.a. 307 by Hunnis show a hand unlike this one. Hunnis favored humility topoi, as witnessed by his obsequious New Year's poem to Elizabeth, but his preferred form seems to have been the fourteener. This hand also seems unlike that of recusant Catholic Tobie Matthew, as shown in Folger manuscripts G.b.10 and X.d.141), a conversion narrative.

26. Virginia F. Stern, *Gabriel Harvey: His Life, Marginalia, and Library* (Oxford: Clarendon, 1979). E. Scott, ed., *Letterbook of Gabriel Harvey, edited from MS Sloane 93* (Camden Society, 1884; rpt. NY: Johnson Reprint Corp., 1965).

27. Most of the corrections consist of one or two words written in the margin near the incorrect printed word or words, with the printed works underlined (fig. 3). As Paul Dowling of Liber Antiquus says, "It appears that the reader is making selected corrections as he/she reads. The corrector is clearly not ticking off the corrections on the errata leaf (there are many more that go uncorrected and two of the corrections that are made don't appear in the errata). If we look to a later printed edition for the source, it can be no earlier than the 1609 (since the second correction does not appear in print in either the 1590 errata or the 1956 2nd ed.)" (private correspondence, 2004). I have found two other corrections, on pages 70 and 72 of the book; neither illuminates the case further. There is also some evidence of other corrections lost to us by the trimming and washing of the book, probably in the nineteenth century. On 606 is a long, intriguing correction, barely visible even with electronic enhancements: ". . . Guyon by the way / Reed she traveling . . . Redcrosse knight by th'way" (fig. 4). This clearly is an effort to correct the

famous slip in Book III, Canto ii, stanza 4, and a closer look at the hand and the metrics of the line could tell us more about the corrector and the widow's mite poet, if they are the same person. I have also discovered in this copy two instances of corrected mispagination (88 for 86, 89 for 87 and again, 92 for 90 and 93 for 91; Johnson signals some of these, but the difference here may mean an imposition problem in quire F). On Spenser's involvement in the CVs, Erickson writes: "I would be willing to conjecture that Spenser, Ralegh, and Harvey, perhaps along with others, together fashioned all the Commendatory Verses in much the same way that the mysterious E. K. (probably Spenser and Harvey together) wrote the annotations to the *Shepherdes Calender*" (21). But see Jean Brink for evidence of less Spenserian involvement in the volume than we usually think.

28.   For a sample of Spenser's italic hand and discussion of it, see Lee Piepho, "Edmund Spenser and Neo-Latin Literature: An Autograph Manuscript on Petrus Lotichius and His Poetry," *Studies in Philology* 100.2 (Spring 2003): 123–34; sample images are on pp. 125 and 126. For early opinions, see H. R. Plomer, "Edmund Spenser's Handwriting," rpt. for private circulation from *Modern Philology* 21.2 (Nov. 1923): 201–07. Plomer explains that H. Jenkinson, in *Library* III (1922), 1ff, mentions that a letter in Latin in the Irish state papers in italic may be Spenser's. Plomer says that Grosart in editing Spenser decided that this letter was in Spenser's italic hand; Plomer doubts it and thinks a clerk copied it.

29.   Peter Beal, comp., *Index to English Literary Manuscripts,* vols. I and II (London: Mansell, 1993). An example of the problem: George Chapman's "aboue" and "y" look much like this hand, and his footed "t" might pass, but his "g" is unlike this one in the direction of the stroke. Chapman's hand is in Beal vol. I, pt. 1, p. 193.

30.   Thomas Brooke, a nineteenth-century collector, owned not only this book but several other Spenser works: *Complaints* (1591), *Amoretti and Epithalamion* (1595), *Colin Clouts* (1595), *Prothalamion* (1596). After Brooke's death in 1908 the collection was sold mostly at Sotheby's between 1909 and 1923. The Folger Library holds numerous other Brooke-owned books, none of which has a hand like this one. One might also examine other books bound by Francis Bedford (1799–1883), not necessarily for Bedford's hand, but for the hand of Bedford-connected book-owners. Earlier provenance information would be most helpful. On another tack, see "Spenser Allusions in the Sixteenth and Seventeenth Centuries," comp. Ray Heffner, Dorothy E. Mason, Frederick Padelford; ed. William Wells; in *Studies in Philology* 68.5 (1971): 1–172 and 69.5 (1972): 175–351. Part I (1580–1625) and 2 (1626–1700) contain responses to Spenser by numerous pre-1700 writers, one of whom could be our margin-responder as well. As for stylistics, MacDonald P. Jackson explains and illustrates a method of using online proximity searching to establish authorship, including the use of rhyme words and patterns of rhyming, as well as collocated words. See *Defining Shakespeare: Pericles as a Text Case* (New York: Oxford University Press, 2003), 194ff on online proximity searching, and 95–104 on rhyming words. Thanks to Henry Woudhuysen for this reference.

31.   MLA conference, Washington, DC, December 2005.

KENNETH BORRIS

Sub Rosa: Pastorella's Allegorical Homecoming, and Closure in the 1596 *Faerie Queene*

Pastorella's homecoming at Belgard, which fills half the final canto of the 1596 *Faerie Queene*, should have some climactic importance for both Book VI and Spenser's poem as a whole, but it has appeared relatively insignificant, for most scholarship addressing Book VI published during the last twenty years says little or nothing about it. However, the episode involves an allegory of major interpretive importance, with tropological and anagogical aspects. Pastorella's return to Belgard involves detailed textual correspondences with the formerly well-known Parable of the Prodigal Son, and even repeats some of the parable's diction as in sixteenth-century English Bibles. According to an interpretive consensus extending from patristic exegetes to Elizabethan Protestants, that parable uses family reunion to portray God as a loving parent who cherishes as his children those who are lost to him but return, and restores their heavenly inheritance. As in *The Fowre Hymnes* and the Graces episode of Book VI, Spenser's syncretic and eclectic writings involve some profound engagements with Platonism, and by reviewing comments of Plotinus, Ficino, Leone Ebreo, Castiglione, and Spenser himself, we find the quasi-prodigal allegory of Pastorella's homecoming draws further on some complementary motifs, metaphors, and concepts of Platonic discourse. Melissa effects Pastorella's restoration to her parents as heir of Belgard, and her obvious counterpart in romantic epic would have been Ariosto's

Spenser Studies: A Renaissance Poetry Annual, Volume XXI, Copyright © 2006 by AMS Press, Inc. All rights reserved.

Melissa in the *Orlando furioso*, who signified the restorative power of divine grace according to most of Ariosto's allegorical commentators, including Spenser's contemporary Sir John Harington. These findings much enhance appreciation of the philosophical and theological depth of Book VI and its conclusion of the 1596 *Faerie Queene*. Besides revising our notions of Book VI, Courtesy, and its allegorical development, and thus opening up that book to many new considerations and inquiries, knowledge of Belgard's parabolic and Platonic allegorism reveals new thematic and structural correlations between the ending of Book I and that of the whole *Faerie Queene* in the final published format that Spenser authorized. As when closing Book I, for example, Spenser models the end of Book VI on passages of the Book of Revelation. Reassessment of the Belgard episode thus enables redefinition of closure in the 1596 *Faerie Queene*, and the poem's general structure.

> To lead to the contemplation of divine things and thus awaken the mind with images, as the mystical theologian and the poet do, is a far nobler work than to instruct by demonstration.
> —Torquato Tasso, *Discorsi del poema eroico*[1]

*I*N THE FINAL CANTO OF BOOK VI, its hero Calidore does not resume his quest to vanquish the Blatant Beast until he brings the book's heroine Pastorella, the shepherdess he has just rescued from the Brigands, to the castle of Belgard to convalesce. Once she regains her health he leaves her there while he completes his quest. Meanwhile, finding Pastorella's distinctive birthmark like an unfolding rose upon her breast, the castle's lord and lady, Bellamour and Claribell, determine she is really their daughter lost in infancy. Claribell originally named her for the rosette, but that name remains Belgard's secret (VI.xii.18).[2] Some maintain this episode involves little or no allegorism,[3] and most assume its import is very generally moral, to furnish another courteous exemplar.[4] Others have sought British topical allusions in a few stanzas about Claribell's father (VI.xii.4–6),[5] while some have found "vague . . . parallels" with the Proserpine myth in Pastorella's total story in Book VI, so that it involves an "archetypal pattern of death and rebirth."[6] Nevertheless, although this episode fills half the 1596 *Faerie Queene*'s climactic canto, as if it is important, most scholarship addressing Book VI published during the last twenty years says little or nothing about it, so that it lacks significance in the book's current assessment.[7] Various central features of Pastorella's homecoming invite a new allegoresis that enables extensive commentary throughout, complements the prior readings, opens up the book to further reconsiderations and inquiries, and reveals Spenser's vigorous, wide-ranging, and creative engagement with his culture in concluding the 1596 text.

Although long-lost Pastorella's reunion with her parents clearly alludes to the Parable of the Prodigal Son as I will show, and parables were known as much for their perceived theological meanings as for their stories, such interpretive implications of the Belgard episode have not previously been addressed. However, as in the Belge episode of Book V for example, Spenser had strong commitments to biblical poetics and developing allegorical homologies with biblical narratives.[8] Pastorella's quasi-parabolic homecoming expresses a symbolic reconciliation with God that has tropological and anagogical meanings. Spenser represents the reunion partly according to complementary Christian Platonist notions of the definitive importance of divine beauty and love for humankind that he explicitly articulates in *The Fowre Hymnes*, likewise published in 1596. Melissa effects the reunion, and her allegorical role reconfigures her Ariostan namesake's formerly conventional signification of divine grace. Various critics have already noted the episode's explicit theological engagements, though without addressing the correlative allegory. Pastorella's reunion with her parents, Richard Mallette observes, is "sonorous in the language of salvation," with "echoes of redemption," and "more than any book since the first" in *The Faerie Queene*, "this one is pervaded with the discourses of salvation."[9] We can now appreciate how appropriate indeed those textual features of the reunion are, for they point to and reflect upon the themes of its theological allegorism.

Pastorella's restoration to her lost parents thus has a thematic logic substantial enough to justify its conclusive, twelfth-canto position in both Book VI and in *The Faerie Queene* as published in 1596. The parabolic and Platonic allegory builds on the Graces episode for further adumbration of Courtesy's philosophical and theological implications and contexts. We see too how useful indeed Spenser's *Fowre Hymnes* can be for clarifying the allegorism of at least the 1596 *Faerie Queene*, on account of the *Hymnes*'s relatively explicit doctrinal content, although they have been little used for such purposes as yet. Insofar as Pastorella has been found somewhat analogous to Proserpina, an ancient model of loss and restoration, death and recovered life, that correspondence befits the episode's allegory from the syncretic standpoint of much early modern mythography. The Belgard allegory counterpoises the Beast in the second half of Canto xii, and underwrites the hero's victory over it, which is modelled on the old serpent's defeat in the Book of Revelation. The ending of Redcross and Una's story, likewise involving an only child's restoration to her parents in a book's final canto, has long been read both tropologically and anagogically, and Spenser's closure of the 1596 *Faerie Queene* builds on that paradigm. Spenser not only sought to appropriate priestly roles and authority as Jeffrey Knapp argues,[10] but developed his poetic in accord with formerly common literary assumptions, based partly on Homeric reception and reinforced by Protestant poetics, that poetry at best, and hence heroic poetry in particular, impinges on theology.[11] Such views remained compelling long after Spenser, as for Milton.

Some terminology needs initial clarification. The Belgard allegory involves representation of God, and according to age-old theological traditions all such description is necessarily provisional and inadequate, posited "after a manner of speaking." My argument and its vocabulary take this for granted. Also, my historicized usage of "Platonic" and its cognates refers to the generalized Platonic tradition formerly seen to extend from antiquity into Spenser's time and beyond. Applied to developments of Platonism in early modernity, our present concern to distinguish what we would now call "Neoplatonic" adaptations would be anachronistic in most Spenserian contexts, and so I rarely use the vocabulary of "Neoplatonism" here.[12]

PASTORELLA'S PARABOLIC RETURN

At first glance Pastorella's homecoming at Belgard appears based on a motif germane to pastoral romances and Cinquecento romantic epics, whereby a foundling or noble scion's true parental heritage becomes restored through recognition of some distinctive token.[13] However, Spenser typically redevelops conventional generic repertoires for allegorical purposes in *The Faerie Queene*, and engineers such effects through conflation of a genre's standard imagistic and narrative elements with figurative analogues, or "transformative models."[14] In Book V's Belge episode, for example, the poet transfigures its narrative basis in Ariosto's Olympia episode by combining that with biblical apocalyptic and Protestant historiography.[15] At Belgard the generically apt literary material has similarly undergone structural allegorization through mixture with biblical paradigms that have vehicles analogous to main elements of Spenser's narrative: especially the prodigal's restoration, but also recovery of the lost sheep;

heirdom or inheritance; humankind's exile from the supposed home-land of heaven; and Solomon's spouse.

Such biblical materials were fundamental to Protestant poetics, and to the expressive procedures of Spenser's own poetic, which often effects its allegorical transformations through combination of biblical narratives, motifs, and metaphors with literary ones. Throughout Europe, the parable of prodigal return was a standard model for liter-ary confabulations, as it were, not only in the fashionable dramatic subgenre of "prodigal son plays," but also in chivalric and other romances and pilgrimage allegories of various types.[16] Pastorella's homecoming aligns so closely with the prodigal's that some of Spens-er's diction is identical to the parable's.

The biblical prodigal squanders his inheritance and returns with remorse to his father, who had thought him "lost" and "dead" in "a farre countrey," and gladly celebrates his return (Luke 15:11–31).[17] After Humphrey Tonkin's passing mention of a general correspon-dence between the parable and Pastorella's restoration in 1972, Na-seeb Shaheen observed, and A. C. Hamilton concurred in his *Faerie Queene* of 2001, that Pastorella's mother's reactions to her long-lost child's return reflect the parabolic father's comment upon the prodi-gal's return: "this my sonne was dead, and is aliue againe" (Luke 15:24).[18] Although these insights have not been further pursued inter-pretively or otherwise to date, there are more correlative passages, as well as various convergences of diction, italicized below. The relevant comment of the prodigal's father actually appears twice, for emphasis, in Luke 15:31 as well as 24: "this my sonne was *dead*, and is *aliue againe*: and he was lost, but he is founde." Claribell responds as does the parent of a child "Which hauing thought long *dead*, she fyndes *aliue*" (VI.xi.21). She asks in amazement, "liuest thou my daughter now *againe?*/And art thou yet *aliue*, whom *dead* I long did faine?" (VI.xii.19). As the prodigal is "*founde*" in Luke 15:24 and 31, so Spenser's diction involves the cognate "fyndes." These biblical verses further resonate in the end of Canto xi: though Pastorella "long had lyen *dead*," she is "made *againe aliue*" by Calidore (VI.xi.50). As the biblical father, first seeing the returned prodigal, instantly "*ran* and fel on his necke, and *kissed him*" (Luke 15:20), so Pastorella's mother, upon hearing of her return, immediately "*ran* to the straunger Mayd," and "A thousand times she her embraced nere/With many a ioyfull *kisse*" (VI.xii.19–20). These events evoke the parabolic father's "compassion" (Luke 15:20), and Pastorella's mother's "pitty" (VI.xii.21). After the prodigal's father recognizes and accepts the long-lost son, pronouncing him "aliue againe," they begin "to be merie" (Luke 15:24), and Spenser's story concludes with great "ioy" at Belgard, as Pastorella's father "Acknowledg'd for his owne faire *Pastorell*" (VI.xii.20–22). The parabolic father's visual recognition of his son ensures the latter's filial reacceptance (Luke 15:20); Pastorella's parents see tokens of her identity that ensure hers (VI.xii.15–22).

The most telling allusive indicators are the foregoing cases where the poet's diction twice coincides with three words in two parallel verses of the parable: *dead, againe, aliue* (VI.xi.50.8–9, xii.19.8–9; Luke 15:24, 31). These correspondences are unlikely to be just coincidental. They are each tripartite and hence protracted, even though the parallel segments of Spenserian and biblical discourse are brief. They are repeated. And the contexts are broadly similar anyway. The poet could have used many other words instead, including cognates of these, to describe the same reaction of Pastorella's parents to her restoration. And they need not have thought her dead, as the parabolic father had likewise assumed, only lost. The emphatic reiteration of these particular chains of discourse in Spenser's context, as in the parable, is itself an additional parabolic correspondence. Whereas Spenser's diction thus reflects the current English Protestant conventions for translating the Bible here, the Roman Catholic Rheims New Testament's differs, just as Spenser's readily could have.[19]

Moreover, sixteenth-century writers who sought to evoke or approximate the parable and its theological meaning in their fictions conventionally imitated these two parallel biblical verses, Luke 15:24 and 31. Attesting to the prodigal's finding and revival, hence his symbolic transformation from death to life, these remarks of the biblical father are central to the parable's conclusion narratively, emotionally, and thematically. *Acolastus*, a Neo-Latin dramatization of the parable by Willem de Volder (Gulielmus Gnapheus), was well known in Reformed England, and his conclusion repeats those same two verses, as in the Vulgate: "quia/Hic filius meus iamdudum mortuus/ Erat et reuixit, perierat et inuentus est."[20] In Robert Greene's romance *The Mourning Garment*, an adaptation of the parable published in 1590, prodigal Philador returns and his father remarks, he "was lost, and is found, . . . was *dead* and is *aliue againe*": the same wording of the current English Protestant Bibles reflected also in Spenser's Belgard episode.[21] Continental dramatic and nondramatic writings, such as the prodigal plays of Joris van Lancvelt (Macropedius), Castellano Castellani, and Burkhard Waldis, would furnish further examples.[22] The most committed imitators of the parable tend, like Spenser, to reproduce or evoke the terms in which it renders this defining moment of its narrative.

As Spenser's rendition of the situation somewhat differs from the biblical account, with a mother besides a father, and a lost daughter instead of a wayward son, so this major parabolic archetype was often redeveloped yet still retained recognizable allusive impact. An extended reproduction would have been trite. This parable had already been variously conflated with the pilgrimage theme, for example, to produce many versions of allegory and romance.[23] Book I of *The Faerie Queene* rearticulates that tradition to some extent, and one of its main English precedents, Anne Lake Prescott argues, is Stephen Bateman's chivalric allegory of prodigal pilgrimage, *The Travayled Pylgrime* published in 1569.[24] The prodigal son plays refresh their biblical paradigm partly by varying the familial and narrative circumstances.[25] Greene situates the action primarily in Thessaly and introduces a pastoral subplot. "As far as Greene and his fellow writers strayed from the biblical story" of prodigal restoration, Richard Helgerson observes, "they were aware of it as the ultimate source of their fiction."[26] Greene, for example, declares he has "moralized a divine history" (9:125).

Just as Spenser combines and reconfigures various literary and non-literary motifs and intertexts as a means of writerly wit and resourceful allegorism, his own modifications of the parable befit his style, narrative, and allegory in many ways. His change of the prodigal's sex facilitates closure in Book VI by rounding off the heroine's story, while further enabling, as my conclusion explains, a significant homology with the ending of Book I, where Eden's King and Queen also regain their wandering daughter and sole heir. Since the prodigal's type of former waywardness would be inappropriate to a Spenserian female heroine, the poet reconfigures its symbolism in Pastorella's exile, wound, and imprisonment in Canto xi, likewise standard former tropes for the infirmities of postlapsarian errancy. Thus "weake and wan" when arriving at Belgard, she needs help like the prodigal (VI.xii.11). Addition of the loving maidservant and mother adds warmth, while the new names (Melissa, Claribell, Bellamour, Belgard) further the allegory as I will show later. As the parable addresses the prospects of the soul, so the prodigal's Spenserian feminization befits the theological allegory, for the soul in early modernity was commonly imagined as a young woman, like Alma, and designated with feminine pronouns. Precedents for that included conventional allegoresis of the Song of Songs (as prefaced in the Geneva Bible, for instance); Castiglione's *Il cortegiano*; iconographical handbooks; and, I will show later, Platonic treatises.[27]

Another Spenserian revision of the parable ensures the Pastorella allegory more readily appears to accord with the Thirty-Nine Articles on the roles of grace and free will in salvation. The parabolic father spontaneously extends forgiving welcome when the prodigal arrives;

but the latter had already independently decided to return and repent (Luke 15:17–20). The Geneva comment tries to gloss over that sequence's challenges to Calvinist theology by insisting "God preventeth us [i.e., anticipates human need] . . . before we crye unto him," so that the prodigal's own initial decision may appear previously conditioned by implicit divine intervention. Adjusting the narrative instead, Spenser has Pastorella "brought" to Belgard, so that she herself makes no evident decision to go there (V.xii.3,10). Even in her recognition and reacceptance by her parents, Pastorella is wholly passive, and that reunion depends on the intercessions of Melissa, who partly signifies divine grace as I will show. Likewise, Article Ten, "Of Free Will," declares "the condition of man after the fall of Adam is such, that he cannot turne and prepare himselfe by his owne natural strength . . . to faith and calling upon God, . . . without the grace of God by Christ preventing [i.e., anticipating and predisposing] us."[28] Yet, as Mallette argues for Book VI in general, Spenser still negotiates between Calvinist and "moderate" Protestant positions according more scope to free will, such as Hooker's, so that the relations of providence to human initiative remain mysterious.[29] Pastorella's prior choices, especially her choice of Calidore rather than Coridon, have somehow turned out to conduce her restoration.

Despite some variances on matters of detail, a consensus on the parable's main significance extended from patristic exegetes to Elizabethan Protestants.[30] Its family reunion thus portrays God as a loving father who welcomes as his children those who are lost to him but return, and gathers them into his home as heirs of his heavenly kingdom. The Geneva Bible glosses the parabolic father as God, as do introductory summaries of Luke 15 in some other English Bibles, such as the Great Bible. Erasmus, Calvin, Augustin Marlorat, and John Hooper all advance much the same general interpretation, whereby the parabolic father is a "figure" expressing "the fatherly kindness of God" (Calvin), and the prodigal returning to the father's house "meruellously" sets forth the "condition of a soule restored" (Hooper).[31] In Samuel Gardiner's Elizabethan *Portraiture of the Prodigal*, the son's "*ioyful welcomming home*" tropologically signifies "*the felicitie of the faythfull*," and anagogically "the ioy and happines which we shal bee partakers of in the kingdome of heauen," or the soul's enjoyment of its heavenly patrimony in afterlife (7, 263).[32] Hence Gardiner talks of "our myrth in our fathers house in the life to come" (265). The official Elizabethan "Homily of Repentance, and of True Reconciliation unto God" similarly invokes this parable to urge "returne vnto the Lord," and pray that "after . . . this life, [we] may liue eternally with his Sonne."[33] The Geneva Bible's concluding gloss for the parable relates it to attainment of "life euerlasting" with God. The epilogue for Volder's *Acolastus* insists on this parabolic play's "hidden- . . . mystery" imaging fallen humanity's salvation, and stresses God's love summons all to "rejoice at being restored to our Father's favour" and "partake of that bliss forever" (203).[34]

The Belgard episode's parabolic homologies allegorically restructure its romantic motif of the long-lost child parentally recognized and restored, so that Pastorella's parents provisionally express aspects of God, and her return and restoration image the prospects of human redemption. Her homecoming thus extends the theophany intimated by Spenser's Graces: celestially contextualized mythic divinities, "daughters of sky-ruling Ioue," who partly body forth aspects of divine agency, or "all gifts of grace" (VI.x.13, 15, 22). Calvin allows for certain types of representation of God even in the visual arts,[35] and Spenser's model here is not only biblical but was already current in Protestant literary adaptations. Pastorella's parents are not personifications to be equated with divine attributes, but, rather as in the parable itself, characters whose narrative role to some extent focuses theological and other meanings. While relying on this biblical precedent for accommodating expression of heavenly things to earthly experience, as Milton's Raphael would say, Spenser lessens the parable's meiosis or representational incongruity. The parabolic father performs various actions incommensurate with his divine significance and verging on tapinosis, such as killing the fatted calf and eating, and yet there was no perceived figurative impropriety.[36] Just as Spenser assumes "earthly tong/Cannot describe, nor wit of man can tell" the heavenly New Jerusalem (I.x.55), he presents images bearing on transcendental subjects as provisional approximations. The Belgard allegory involves an apophasis or elliptical poetic of speaking silence, sub rosa, that retracts as much as it says through the interplay of its analogical concinnities with their intrinsic limitations.

The prodigal's shift from apparent death to life when restored to his father epitomizes one of the parable's theological emphases, and Spenser follows it most closely on this point. The poet not only repeats three words of the two relevant parabolic verses in the current English Protestant Bibles, we have seen, but does so twice, and likewise within a brief compass, a couplet in each case (Luke 15:24, 31; VI.xi.50.8–9; xii.19.8–9). He again recurs to that shift in stanza 21 of Canto xii, with similar language, and Pastorella's seeming death dominates Canto xi. Death is a standard biblical and hence theological metaphor for "separation of soule and body" from "Gods grace" or favor, while life or revival often express the contrary state of saving restoration.[37] Both Erasmus and Marlorat, for example, gloss the parable accordingly (fol. cxxiii[b]; 249, 251–52). When Melissa hails Pastorella as the "Lady whom high God did saue" (VI.xii.17), Calidore's beloved typifies the spiritual situation of prodigal revival in the parabolic allegory.

Pastorella's homecoming further evokes the Parable of the Lost Sheep as well as the biblical paradigms of heirdom, exile from the true home or country, and Solomon's spouse. Jointly appearing in Luke 15, the parabolic sheep and prodigal were both applied to reconciliation with God. With her pastoral affinities, Pastorella regained evokes the lost sheep that its owner rejoices to regain. She is also her parents' restored heir who recovers her patrimony. As we are "the children of God," Paul claims, "we *are* also heires, euen the heires of God," hence "made partakers of the Father's treasure" (Rom. 7:16–17 and gloss). We have "an inheritance . . . reserved in heaven," Peter supposes (1 Pet. 1:4), and that belief is often biblically treated elsewhere, as in Ephesians 1. Though born at Belgard, Pastorella was immediately sent abroad and reared by shepherds as ignorant of her true origins as she was herself. Thus "fostred vnder straunge attyre" (VI.xii.6), she has been like the biblical "stranger in a strange land" (Ex. 2:22), estranged from her homeland and patrimony. The narratives of exile in Genesis and Exodus provided types and metaphors representing life in the world as an alienation from presumed heavenly origins and God, to be rectified through return. For Paul Abraham's experience abiding "in a strange countrey," looking for "a city . . . whose buylder and maker is God," typifies the human condition. The faithful, he claims, are like "strangers and pilgremes on the earth" who "seke a countrey from whence they came out," or "citie" that God "hath prepared for them": "a better" and "heauenlie" one that is their proper land or home (Heb. 11:8–16). Spenser named his younger son, born in 1594, Peregrine, from the Latin "peregrinus," "alien, of another country."

As the Song of Solomon characterizes his spouse as "the *onlie daughter* of her mother, and she is *deare* to her that bare her" (6:8–9; my emphasis), Spenserians have long found her paradigmatic for Una in these respects, and yet she corresponds just as well to Pastorella. To Una' s father she is "his onely daughter deare" (I.xii.21). But Spenser dramatizes these biblical verses in several stanzas when Pastorella's "mother of one chylde" regains "her owne daughter, her owne infant deare" (VI.xii.19–21). As the Geneva argument declares, the spouse commonly represented "the faithful soule or . . . Church" as Christ's beloved. Insofar as Pastorella's homecoming relates to prodigal restoration and hence the soul's, her analogy with the spouse, like Una's, is pointedly apt.

The motif of spiritual exile, travel, and return underwriting the symbolism of Pastorella's peregrinations was ubiquitous in medieval and Renaissance culture.[38] Not only applied to allegoresis of travel and quest narratives such as the *Odyssey*, it constituted a structural paradigm of many medieval and early modern texts including Spenser's own Legend of Holiness (e.g., I.x. 60–66). Combination of this motif with parabolic prodigal restoration, as in Pastorella's story, had become a major tradition of allegory and romance, with many exponents including Guillaume de Deguileville, Jean de Courcy, Olivier de la Marche, Jean de Cartigny, John Lydgate, Stephen Hawes, Hernando de Acuña, Stephen Bateman, Lewes Lewkenor, William Goodyear, Nicholas Breton, and Anthony Copley.[39] Pastorella finally comes to reside in beauty's home, Belgard, where love unites with beauty—Bellamour with Claribell—and "ioy" attains its "perfect forme" (VI.xii.21–22). The prodigal's return, Gardiner says like other early modern commentators, partly expresses "the endless and unspeakable ioies . . . in the kingdom of heauen," or "the ioyes of the world to come" (40, 243).

Pastorella's Platonized Homeland

While modeling the allegory of Pastorella's homecoming mainly on parabolic prodigality, Spenser reconfigures the familial context in ways that evoke Renaissance Platonic accounts of divine agency, creation, and heaven in terms of love and beauty. Pastorella springs from *Bell-amour* and Clari-*bell* at *Bel*-gard, hence from conjoined love and beauty.[40] As love and beauty are richly developed concepts in Spenser's thought, with transcendental significance, so these three names defining the nature of Pastorella's restoration—or what she comes home to—are not insignificant. By the mid 1590s, his poetry had already drawn profoundly on Platonic thought for many years.[41] In *Colin Clouts Come Home Againe*, first printed in 1595, and *The Fowre Hymnes*, first printed the same year as Book VI in 1596, Love created the world and its creatures, and creation's "wondrous Paterne" was "perfect Beautie," so that Love and Beauty are the progenitors of humanity.[42] Spenser calls beauty "the great Creatours owne resemblance bright" in *The Faerie Queene* (IV.viii.32), and a "beame . . . sparkled from aboue" in *Colin Clouts* (line 468). Standard readings of the Graces' dance in Book VI assume it involves deep Christian Platonist poetic theology about God's relations with humanity and the cosmos.[43] Whereas these concerns have previously seemed to evaporate after Canto x, they undergo substantial further development in the book's conclusion, as we should expect.

In *The Faerie Queene* and *Fowre Hymnes*, Spenser almost certainly drew on Leone Ebreo's once widely known *Dialoghi d'amore*,[44] and when Leone closes that treatise by anticipating humankind's return to a divine patrimony through beauty and love, his extended metaphor of homecoming broadly correlates with Pastorella's return to her Platonically evocative origins:

> *Philo.* For the supremely beautiful being our father, first beauty our mother, and the highest wisdom our native land whence we are sprung, our good and our happiness consist in returning to that bourn and in being gathered to our parents, rejoicing in sweet sight of and joyous union with them.
>
> *Sophia.* God grant that we . . . are not cut off from such divine joy, but that we may be amongst the elect who attain to ultimate happiness and final beatitude.[45]

In addition to beauty, Spenser's allegory of Pastorella's return stresses love (Bel-*amour*) rather than wisdom, as Marsilio Ficino does in treating this subject.[46] Yet for Leone too, "the true image of the love of God for the beings lower than himself is the love of a father for the child of his body" (253–55). And as Spenser's allegory relates God's nature or creativity to an amorous human couple, Leone declares "his divine essence would not represent the highest form of life did it not reflect in itself the beauty and wisdom of the beloved, the wise lover, and the perfect love of them both," derived "as from the father and mother" (299; cf. 425).[47]

Although Spenser's allegory could well have specific debts to Leone, such ideas and metaphors were widely diffused in Platonic discourse. For third-century Plotinus the soul's homeland is "our country from which we came," that of "our Father," God, where the soul rejoices in attaining supreme beauty and love's fulfillment. "In her natural state," the soul "is in love with God and wants to be united with him; *it is like the noble love of a girl* (παρθένος) *for her noble father* (πατρὸς)."[48] But through embodiment, souls "forget their father, God," and "that they themselves came from that world; just as children who are immediately torn from their parents and brought up far away do not know who they themselves or their parents are." Those in that condition are to be led back to their origin (V.1.1).

Spenser's joyous family reunion, whereby Pastorella regains her forgotten parents and home of Belgard lost in infancy, expresses such spiritual return.

Many analogous passages involving comparable metaphors appear in the writings of Ficino, who translated Plotinus and profoundly influenced Spenser.[49] Ficino published letters in which God is at once "matchless beauty," lover, "source of all joys," and "most tender Father." "Of You alone are we born," Ficino declares, "so have pity on Your children, banished . . . so far from their heavenly country," who "long for . . . our father and country." By returning "may we be made joyful," loving "Your infinite beauty." The soul is indeed God's lost "daughter." Though wanting to find her "father," she at first perceives him as a stranger, and does not know him until he reveals his paternity.[50] For Ficino, that estrangement expresses the soul's alienation from God, through which it has lost knowledge of its origins, and Spenser's narrative of Pastorella as exiled foundling and recovered daughter has comparable significance. In *De amore*, "since the face of a parent is pleasing to children, . . . the face of God the Father" is "most pleasing to souls. The splendor and grace of this face . . . is to be called universal beauty. And the impulse toward that is to be called universal love" (V.4). Hence "love leads souls back to heaven" and "bestows eternal joy" (IV.6). Or as Ficino's renegade disciple Pico della Mirandola declares in his *Commento*, "when the will finally possesses ideal beauty, it is filled with ineffable bliss."[51]

Platonic doctrines of love and beauty also had more popular (as opposed to erudite) diffusions, as in Pierre de la Primaudaye's encyclopedia, *L'Académie française*. God "is the fountain of all true and perfect love" and "there is none so express an image thereof . . . as the love of fathers and mothers towards their children . . . ." After earthly life, the soul "returneth to her first birth" or true heritage, to be welcomed by divine love like a father's or mother's.[52]

The major English literary exponent of Platonism active in the 1590s—Edmund Spenser himself—further shows the currency of basic elements of the Belgard episode's theological allegory in early modern Platonist discourse. Spenser's Platonic philosophizing becomes most explicit in *The Fowre Hymnes*, published in 1596 as was Book VI. While the relatively concentrated Platonism of the first two hymns at least notionally appears to yield to a more conventional Christianity in the latter two, ostensibly written much later, those still frequently evoke writings of Plato, Plotinus, Ficino, and Leone, and still evince Renaissance Platonic interests in conceiving divinity and its relations with humankind rapturously in terms of both love and beauty. Spenser was committed enough to the content of all four hymns that he published them together.

Love and beauty are central means for defining human life and God's nature and agency in Spenser's hymns. Such ideas also inform his Belgard allegory, with some shifts of approach and emphasis. In the first two hymns, Love creates the cosmos according to Beauty's pattern, and earthly beauties reflect their divine source so that lovers may thus again apprehend their heavenly origin's "happie port" in "joyous" delight (*HL*, lines 280–98). Divine creativity involves a "Mother" or paradigm of beauty from whom Love is born (*HB*, lines 8–16). She or "heavens light" is also the "first sourse" of all who partake in beauty, and their "first countries sight" is in heaven (lines 162–67, 190–93). After some heavenly preexistence, souls descend to earthly embodiment "Out of their heauenly bowres" (lines 201–02), and heaven is their first country or homeland in this further Platonic sense. The second two hymns again describe God and divine creativity in terms of love and beauty. God is "that eternall fount of love" or "Lord of Love," as well as beauty's "eternall fountaine" (*HHL*, lines 99, 127; *HHB*, line 21). His nature involves a loving couple's interplay, for Sapience, "The soveraine dearling of the *Deity*," sits "in his bosome" as "his owne Beloved," of "beauty soverayne" (*HHB*, lines 183–85, 241, 228, 217). Human beings come from this amorous source, the "Pallace" of the divinely creative lover and his symbolic beauteous beloved, and are to return to it to find joy in the sight of that beauty (*HHL*, lines 99–119, 274–87; *HHB*, lines 232–75, 295–301).

The Belgard episode has further Platonic significance, for just as "Claribell," "Bellamour," and "Belgard" coincide in "bel," they constitute a tripartite configuration of terms conjointly focusing on beauty and love. As Edgar Wind explains, Renaissance Platonism evinces great "enthusiasm for mystical triads" referring, tacitly or otherwise, to the Trinity; and particularly for ones involving love or beauty.[53] "God governs things," Ficino says, "by the ternary number" (*De amore*, II.2). So many commentators have already referred Spenser's dancing Graces to triadic formulae and philosophical techniques of Renaissance Platonism that Elizabeth J. Bellamy has declared "a critical consensus" that Spenser's Acidalian vision "is, in some general sense, 'Neoplatonic.' "[54] Like Ficino, Michael J. B. Allen observes, Spenser was committed to triadic motifs, partly because "the Platonic interpretation of a myth must see it in terms of movement away from, conversion towards, and movement back into the One."[55] Spenser's Graces express tripartite cosmic cycles of benefit and constitute a triadic structural principle for Book VI as a whole. As Alastair Fowler and Gerald Snare have shown, they have various travesties (such as *De*-sp-*etto*, *De*-f-*etto*, and *De*-c-*etto*), subtypes, and expansions.[56]

The triadic articulation of love and beauty through *Bell-amour*, Clari-*bell*, and *Bel*-gard is another such Platonic device, and though apparently unnoticed in prior criticism, it has conclusive importance for Book VI and the whole 1596 *Faerie Queene*. The quasi-parabolic context reinforces the anagogical implications. This triad interpretively expands Spenser's Graces, and Pastorella's assimilation into it renders her analogous to Spenser's Fourth Grace (VI.x.25–27). Spenserians have already proposed that the Graces in Book VI evoke Platonic analyses of the cosmos in terms of benefits proceeding from and returning to God in a threefold circulation impelled by divine beauty and love, and we now see that the book's conclusion furthers such interpretations. Pastorella's biography involves a three-part cycle of origin at Belgard, movement away, and return. The definitive principles of the episode's allegorized poetic theology are love and beauty, as Spenser's interests in Ficino and Leone, documented in the *Hymnes*, would lead us to expect. Through its love-beauty triad, the Belgard allegory blends the representation of God in the biblical parable of prodigality with early modern Platonic accounts of the operations of triune divinity. Ficino, for example, used the Graces to typify its processes and developed various triadic schemes accordingly, such as *amor, pulchritudo, voluptas* in *De amore*: inasmuch as this circular current "begins in God and attracts to Him, it is called Beauty; inasmuch as emanating to the World it captivates it [sic], it is called Love; inasmuch as returning to its author it joins His work to Him, it is called Pleasure" (II.2; cf. Wind, 36–44). Ficino assumed with John that "God is love" (John 4:16), and with Plato that love, defined as desire for beauty, mediates between mortals and divinity. The theological allegory of Belgard represents humanity's situation in a comparable way.

Platonic tradition afforded many precedents for Spenser's expression of the relations of divinity and humankind through those of Claribell and Bellamour with Pastorella at Belgard, and the poet used those precedents himself in other writings. Portrayal of God could provisionally involve the interactions of lover and beloved, love and beauty, father and mother, while the soul could appear their offspring or daughter who leaves her place of origin or true heritage for earthly life, forgetting them, but can return to enjoy fulfillment of the originary divine love and beauty, or, so to speak, its lost true parents and home. Pastorella's exile from Belgard at birth thus partly expresses the soul's loss of its supposed heavenly patrimony in passing to the world (VI.xii.6–9), while her return to Belgard and reunion with her

parents images recovery of that presumed divine heritage. The soul,
I have already shown, was commonly represented as a young woman,
like Alma, in Spenser's time.

SPENSER'S ANAGOGICAL BELGARD

Claribell and Bellamour's great house anagogically signifies heaven,
or the correlative tropological paradise within, and there are many
metaphoric precedents in the New Testament, varied Christian writings, and the texts we most associate with Renaissance Platonism.
For Jesus, heaven is "my Father's house," for Paul "the household
of God," for La Primaudaye "that house" or "palace" for God's
"children," his "heirs" (John 14:2, Eph. 2:19; pp. 969, 973). As God
deals with his "children" as their "father," Calvin maintains, so God
brings them into his "houshold, and vniteth himselfe to them, that
they may be one together" (3.24.1). A castle had long been a symbol
of "the other world" or paradise within.[57] By naming this symbolic
residence "*Bel*-gard" Spenser Platonically defines heaven and the
soul's return to it according to beauty, as would Leone, Ficino, and
Castiglione's Bembo in *Il cortegiano*, who declares heaven is "the
high mansion place where the heavenly, amiable and right beauty
dwelleth, . . . in the innermost secrets of God" (320–21).[58] Spenser
himself similarly speaks of "the house of God" or God's "wyde Pallace" in *The Fowre Hymnes* (*HB*, line 193, *HL*, line 102), and fills it
with both beauty and love.

In designating the setting for Pastorella's quasi-parabolic and Platonic return, "Belgard" further epitomizes various interconnected
Spenserian notions about the ultimate significance of beauty, the
anticipated beatific vision (the sight of God supposedly enjoyed by
souls in afterlife), and visual perception. Renaissance Platonists typically conceived heaven and the soul's experience of return to it as
the ultimate efflorescence of love conjoined with perfect beauty,
manifested in God's presence. These beliefs somewhat overlapped
with Christian conceptions of the beatific vision and of joy as heav-
en's definitive emotional state.[59] In Spenser's writings the basic meaning of "belgard" is "beautiful look," from the Italian "bel guardo,"
so that Belgard appears dedicated to experience of the beauteous
gaze and figuratively suggests the type or ideal thereof, or scene of
its fulfillment.[60]

Spenser repeatedly refers to Platonic beliefs that the sense of sight
depends on the eyes' emission of rays of light from within the mind,

and that human beauty is a divinely enkindled luminescence most fully realized within.[61] For Spenser, then, the beauteous glance of the belgard radiates transcendentally originated beauty, and vision itself has visionary significance. In *Colin Clouts*, "Beautie" is "the burning lamp of heavens light, / Darting her beames into each feeble mynd" (lines 873–74), and in Spenser's hymn of Beauty, its "immortall beame" shines "in the face" particularly, and thence "darts amorous desyre" (lines 13, 23, 149, 36–60). Evincing beauty's "celestiall ray," women emit "sweet belgards" like "twinckling starres" from their eyes (lines 162–63, 187, 255–57). In Belphoebe's "heauenly face," the "glorious mirrhour of celestiall grace," "many Graces" attend her eyes, "Working belgardes" (II.iii.25). Based partly on assumptions that humankind was created in the image of God, that the image is most physically evinced in the human face, and that human excellences are provisional indications of divinity and the beatific vision, such notions had much early modern authority, reflected in literary texts (as in Spenser's celebrations of Gloriana, the *Amoretti*, and *Fowre Hymnes*) and in philosophical and theological treatises (such as Richard Hooker's *Laws of Ecclesiastical Polity*).[62] Belphoebe's belgards spring from eyes that are "liuing lamps . . . , / Kindled aboue at th'heauenly makers light" (II.iii.23). In *Amoretti* 8, the beloved's eyes are "full" of the maker's "living fire," and through their "beams" "Angels come to lead fraile mindes" towards "heavenly beauty" (lines 1–9). In Spenser's view, a belgard rightly perceived has revelatory import.

In the allegory of Pastorella's return, Belgard itself focuses potential for full perception of beauty. For Plotinus, contemplation of "absolute beauty" is "the ultimate contest" for souls, to be "blessed in seeing" that " 'blessed sight' " (I.6.7). Implying some eye contact, "Belgard" further suggests such a gazing face-to-face. Biblical accounts of the beatific vision define it as a mutual gazing upon God "face to face" that yields divine knowledge, union, and joy (Ex. 33:18–20, Ps. 16:11, 1 Cor.13:12, 1 John 3:1–2). As Hooker defines it, with some Platonic influence, this "intuitive vision of God in the world to come" manifests "that incomprehensible Beauty which shineth in the countenance of Christ," and brings ineffable "endless union" (I.xi.6, cf. iv.1). Ardently anticipating such a spectacle in both *Heauenly Loue* and *Heauenly Beautie*, Spenser declares in the latter, "Faire is the heaven, where happy soules" "still behold the glorious face / Of the divine eternall Maiestie" (lines 78–81). Devotion to "that loving Lord" yields his "*sight*," and that is "celestiall beauties blaze," revealing "Th'Idee of his pure glorie," and kindling "celestiall love / . . . through *sight*" (*HHL*, lines 204, 273, 277–87; my emphasis). That "glorious *sight*," the poet concludes in *Heauenly Beautie*,

confers "All happie joy," to be "written" in the beholder's "inward
ey" (lines 281–87, 295–98; my emphasis).

The loving embraces of Pastorella's final reunion with Bellamour
and Claribell "in ioy" within Belgard (VI.xii.22) prefigure the soul's
final attainment of that vision in union with God, or in Castiglione's
Bembo's phrasing, the "most happy end for our desires" attained in
"the high mansion" of "the heavenly . . . beautie" (320–21). Early
modern Platonic writers such as Ficino, Leone, and Castiglione represented spiritual fulfillment as a satisfaction of human desire for love
and beauty that could only be found in God, so that heaven was to
be experienced as joyous union with ultimate beauty through love,
as in Spenser's *Fowre Hymnes*.[63]

As Spenser presents Belgard, named for the perceived beauty of a
line of vision, it seems much more a condition of being or felt
experience than a physically defined place. Rather than specifying
any concrete features of the castle, Spenser tactfully evokes the grace,
beauty, joy, and love within Bellamour and Claribell's Belgard, and
draws on Platonic and biblical resources such as the Parable of the
Prodigal to express its quality. Hooker comparably claims that, ena-
moured with "the goodness of beauty," the soul in afterlife will be
"perfected with . . . joy, peace, and delight" in God's "sacred pal-
laces" (I.xi.3, iv.1). In Bellamour and Claribell's rule of Belgard prior
to Pastorella's return, "they ioy'd in happinesse together, / . . . in
peace and loue entyre" (VI.xii.10). As the word "ioy" appears frequently in the Belgard episode, so Pastorella's homecoming is especially "full of ioy" (VI.xii.16), and Christian accounts of God,
heaven, and spirituality have traditionally stressed that emotion as in
Psalm 16:11 and Revelation 21:4: in God's presence "is the fulness
of ioye." Almost swooning for "passing [i.e., surpassing] ioy" when
she regains Pastorella, Claribell experiences this passion "*In perfect
forme*" (VI.xii.21; my emphasis). The story of Pastorella closes accordingly as Claribell runs to tell "her loued Lord" the great news:

> Who *ioyning ioy* with her in one accord,
> Acknowledg'd for his owne faire Pastorell.
> There leaue we them *in ioy* . . . .
>
> (VI.xii.22; my emphasis)

Spenser leaves them in this joyous rapture of union, this "ioyning
ioy,"as if that is their continuing state. Correlating with the parable of
prodigality, the reunion anagogically images union with God. "Gods
children," says La Primaudaye, anticipate "the life everlasting" in

"full fruition of God our soveraigne Good, . . . when wee shall be perfectly united unto him by true Love, . . . beholding him face to face," "full of ioy" (490, 489; cf. 973).

PASTORELLA'S ROSY REBIRTH

To effect this joyous reunion, Spenser somewhat modifies the prodigal paradigm. Unlike her biblical counterpart, Pastorella was exiled at birth, and so, in the manner of romance, the poet's recognition scene depends on discovery of a distinctive cachet of belonging. A roseate birthmark upon her breast identifies Belgard's long-lost scion (VI.xii.15). The closest romantic analogues yet known appear in Boiardo's *Orlando innamorato*, where Fiordelisa's birthmark like a mulberry on her breast effects reunion with her parents, and in Tasso's *Il Rinaldo*, where Florindo's, like a scarlet flower ("un fior d'orto vermiglio"), restores him to his father.[64] But Spenser reinterprets the generic convention by reconfiguring it within a quasi-parabolic allegorical context. Van Lancvelt (Macropedius) had already effected some such redefinition in his prodigal play *Asotus*, where an old scar upon the son's breast identifies him (lines 1484–1506). The symbolism of Pastorella's rosy mark is comparable to the biblical mark or secret name that signifies salvation, and to theological discourse about the image of God said to inhere in humankind.

Her token appears "like christall bright, / . . . a litle purple mold, / That like a rose her silken leaues did faire vnfold" (VI.xii.7). Crystal often symbolized purity, the heavenly Jerusalem shines "cleare as cristal" in Revelation 21:11, and Spenser's references to that substance sometimes involve christological wordplay implying derivation from Christ or Christ-likeness.[65] Besides being an attribute of Venus and symbol of love or spiritual love, the rose was associated with heaven,[66] and an insignia of mystery and secrets (as in the expression *sub rosa*). Purple could betoken penitence, sacrifice, martyrdom, and glory. "Trueth shal bud out of the earth," claims Psalm 85, anticipating heavenly fruitions according to the Geneva gloss, and Pastorella's true origin emerges at last through her revealed rosette, restoring her lost patrimony. The proem's "heauenly seedes of bounty soueraine" that were "Planted in earth" may thus appear to come symbolically full circle (VI.pr.3).

In the comparable biblical motif of the saving mark or seal, "they that shalbe saued, are marked,"and so "the heir" of God's patrimony "is sealed vp to life euerlasting" (Geneva argument, Ezek. 9, and gloss, 9:6). The Book of Revelation claims that God's servants are "sealed" or marked (7:3), and "a new name" will be given "to him that overcometh" spiritually, "which no man knoweth saving he that receiveth it," to be written "upon" the bearer like an insignia of divine belonging (2:17, 3:12).[67] When Pastorella was born inscribed with her distinguishing rose, her mother Claribell named her accordingly (VI.xi.18), and that name, which the poet does not divulge, remains sub rosa, the secret of Belgard (VI.xii.18–22). Merely the provisional name conferred by her foster parents during exile, "Pastorella" is not her true name.

Another significant analogue of Pastorella's mark is the divine image, insofar as it appeared, as Calvin explains, the enduring and distinctive insignia of human origin, "*engrauen*" within the mind, or composed of "*marks* of likenes *grauen*" in humanity, so that it evokes reciprocal divine love and reconciliation (1.15.2–3; my emphasis). Hence God accepts as his "children" those "in whome he seeth the markes and features of his owne face" (3.17.5). Using much the same familial metaphors, La Primaudaye stresses the image is the Creator's distinctive mark of lineal affinity in humans that motivates his love, as parent for child (481, 581). Compared to theological understanding of the image, Pastorella's period of exile would correspond to human alienation from God on account of the Fall (said to have degraded and obscured the image); and the birthmark's rediscovery at Belgard (whereby she regains her patrimony) to divine reacceptance and renewal. Associating Pastorella's birthmark with a term he elsewhere applies to the divine image, Spenser calls it a "mold" (VI.xii.17), implying both "mole" and also "mould" in the sense "pattern" (due to its rose-like form). As "the images of God," the poet says, human beings display "The wondrous workemanship of Gods owne mould" (I.x.39, 42). Forming humanity upon a "heauenly patterne" "out of his owne like mould" in *Heauenly Loue*, God beholds himself in that "selfe mould" (lines 108–19, 198).

Just before the prodigal's story in Luke 15, the Parable of the Recovered Coin likewise addresses reconciliation with God, and patristic allegoresis applied it to recovery and renewal of the divine image, signified by the insignia impressed upon the coin regained.[68] Pastorella bears the imprint of her origin at Belgard. A vast rose symbolizes heaven and hence divinity in Dante's *Paradiso*.

The implications of Pastorella's rosette blossom under the presiding influence of Claribell's "handmayd," Melissa. Claribell entrusted her with the babe, born during her parents' imprisonment, so that Pastorella could be "fostred vnder straunge attyre" in the protection of

exile.[69] When exposing the infant in "the emptie fields," Melissa
notes the birthmark, hides to observe what aid appears, and the shepherd Meliboe takes Pastorella home, to rear her as if his own. The
infant Knight of Holiness was likewise exposed in an open field and
found by a ploughman who reared him (I.x.66). When she unwit-
tingly returns to Belgard, Melissa becomes her maidservant, redis-
covers the rosy mark, and informs Claribell, who verifies her lost
daughter's restoration accordingly.

Spenser portrays Melissa's restorative interpretation of the birthmark as a pregnancy of wit, and although correlation of mental conception with physical pregnancy was a common conceit, in this
context it has theological resonance. Perceiving the rose, Melissa
begins "to *cast* / In her *conceiptfull* mynd, that this faire Maid / Was
that same *infant*," thus becomes "*full* of joy," and, deeply "*mou'd*"
by this "*matter*," delivers the news to Claribell in a "*sodaine thro*"
(VI.xii.16–17; my emphasis). Spenser's puns include "cast" (both
"consider" and "give birth") and "thro" (both "emotional parox-
ysm" and "struggle of childbirth").[70] As Hamilton observes, "Pastorella is 'born' again" in effect (685*n*), and that, we can now see, befits
the quasi-parabolic allegory: "except a man be borne againe, he can
not se the kingdome of God," that is, "To entre therein" (John 3:3–7
and gloss; cp. 1 Pet. 1:23). This was a common trope, so that La
Primaudaye urges "we ought to consider the image and similitude
wee have of our eternal nativity in this our mortal birth, and that
birth whereby we are born unto an immortal life" (547). We are to
be "made heirs according to the hope of eternal life," Paul claims,
through "the new birth" (Titus 3:5), and Pastorella is reborn, as it
were, Belgard's heir.

MELISSA'S PROVIDENCE

In assessing Melissa's role, prior Spenser criticism has focused on
quite obscure eponymous women or priestesses in Greco-Roman
myth and religion, and the interpretive results have been relatively
inconsequential as yet.[71] Moreover, the theological allegory of the
Belgard episode has been mostly terra incognita, including its parabolic and Platonic aspects. Yet, just as Melissa is the subcharacter or
symbolic associate of Pastorella's parents, she likewise expresses a
further aspect of divinity, in her case compassion and restorative
care complementing maternal Claribell. Such significations were not

uncommon. Gardiner declares that God responds to prodigality "like vnto a Nurse, who seeing her tender childe venturing to come vnto her, that it shoulde not take a fall, maketh speede and runneth to it" with "mercie" (212–13). Reflected in various textual details, this Spenserian symbolism also has a generic basis in former understandings of Ariosto's Melissa in the *Orlando furioso*, who was commonly said to signify divine grace or providential care.

Melissa's care for Pastorella explicitly posits gracious divine interventions anyway. When exposing the exiled infant, Melissa wonders what "mortall hand, or heauens grace" will help, and when she finds the lost daughter has actually returned to Belgard, she concludes "the heauens" have "graste" Claribell "To saue her chylde," who is thus the "Lady, whom high God did saue" (VI.xii.8, 16, 17). Melissa perceives herself as a contributing agent in a drama of divinely superintended events bringing ultimate saving restoration. Much as some prior characters in *The Faerie Queene* are explicitly means of providence in their restorative interventions, or symbolize divine grace or care, Melissa's allegorical role accords with her perception.

Compassionate Melissa left infant Pastorella's rose "Bedeaw'd with teares" when she was exiled (VI.xii.8), and since dew was formerly thought to fall from the heavens to refresh the earth, it had long figured heavenly blessings and divine aid or grace.[72] Wordplay involving its cognates, analogues, and homonyms resonates throughout the Belgard episode (cf. VI.xii.5.2, 6.5, 7.6, 8.4, 14.9, 15.4, 19.7, 20.9), and this thematic lexical group comprises the dew of nightly moisture in the natural world; a metaphoric counterpart falling from human eyes; and "due" in the senses fully appropriate or timely, as in the "dew time" of Pastorella's birth (VI.xii.6). Spenser uses dew symbolism theologically in various contexts, as in Redcross's battle with the dragon or Arthur's healing of Amoret's wounds (I.xi.33–36, 48–51; IV.viii.20). There may well be sacramental resonance, just as the Elizabethan baptismal rite claims God "didst sanctify . . . all . . . waters to the mystical washing away of sin" (BCP, sig. N6[b]). In a comparable symbolism of mollification, contrition, compassion, and regeneration, Repentance's tears bathe Redcross in "salt water sore, / The filthy blottes of sin to wash away" (I.x.27). The final rediscovery of Pastorella's rosette that Melissa tearily bedewed in her infancy occasions Claribell's "weeping," so that she embraces her daughter "with many a melting tear" (VI.xii.19–20). Pastorella finally turns out to be born in due time, to be duly cared for and dewily anointed Belgard's proper heir.[73] Thus recovering her true identity, and through Melissa's pregnancy of wit, Pastorella may seem "borne anew of water," so to speak, as the baptismal liturgy, echoing John

3:5, claimed all who would "enter into the kingdome of God" must be (BCP, sig. N6ᵇ). The interplay of these words and images relating to "dew" in Canto xii furthers the exploration of time, chance, and fortune in relation to possibilities of divine providence that characterizes Book VI, and proceeds explicitly in this context as well.[74] To describe Calidore's subsequent quelling of the Blatant Beast, the poet twice uses such a term in this canto: "subdew" (VI.xii.arg., 31).

Melissa's allegorization of divine grace or care for humanity had a formerly obvious precedent in romantic epic, for another Melissa conventionally assigned such meaning appears in Ariosto's *Orlando furioso*: a major model, generic paradigm, intertext, and sometimes narrative source of *The Faerie Queene*. However, although Spenser's *Variorum* noted this eponymous Ariostan character's existence (6:265), Spenser studies has not attended to her since, nor to her sixteenth-century reception. Ariosto's romantic epic turns on the saving of Ruggiero from the vices focused in Alcina so that he can become Bradamante's consort and champion Charlemagne's Christian forces against Moslem invaders. Much of Ruggiero's positive development depends on interventions of the wise and benevolent enchantress Melissa, and Ariostans agree that the story involving them, Alcina, and Logistilla is the poem's central allegory. The *Orlando furioso* is so important to *The Faerie Queene*, and Melissa to Ariosto's text, that Spenser's use of her namesake for a crucial restorative role in concluding his heroine Pastorella's story in the climactic canto of Book VI, and in a context explicitly positing divine intervention (VI.xii.16, 17), clearly broaches questions of strategic allusion.

Although temptations of intemperance are not at issue in Spenser's context, unlike Ariosto's, the fundamental roles of both poets' Melissas are pointedly similar. Ariosto's is "benign and wise (benigna e saggia)";[75] Spenser's compassionately good and "trustie," with a percipient "conceiptfull mynd" (VI.xii.7, 16). Both are agents of positive transformation, revealers of truth, advisors, and facilitators of the good. Yet Spenser's is relatively humble, Claribell's dutiful maidservant, and the allegory thus involves a simple domesticity more in keeping with Reformed spirituality than Ariosto's impressive enchantress would be. Spenser's Melissa pointedly evokes and revises the Catholic poet's model. Nevertheless, both Melissas indeed function alike as the deus ex machina, as it were, or agency whose crucial intervention effects the happy outcome, in their respective stories. Hence they can both readily serve as implicit agents of providence or symbolic proxies for divine grace.

Both roles also stress the character's important care for the hero or heroine, and in Natale Conti's explication of ancient names, "Melissa" derives from the Greek μέλειν, "taking care."[76] Many editions of Ariosto's *Orlando* included Lodovico Dolce's verse arguments for each canto, and he links that poem's Melissa with "taking care."[77] Simone Fornari, Ariosto's major cinquecento commentator, observes that, when the poet first divulges Melissa's name, the general context implies that etymology. "This name 'Melissa' expresses in Greek what our language calls 'care and practice [i.e., of that care],' " and so "the poet calls her 'that benign enchantress who always took care' " of Bradamante (vii.39), and says Melissa has " 'more care' " for Ruggiero than he has for himself (vii.42).[78] Melissa carefully draws Ruggiero from Alcina to virtue, and then Ariosto reveals her name (vii.66). When Spenser first names his corresponding character, the context defines her as the agent of care: Claribell appoints "her own handmayd, *that Melissa hight, / . . . to attend her* [i.e., Pastorella] *dewly day and night*" (VI.xii.14; my emphasis). Thus discovering Pastorella's indelible rose, Melissa intercedes with Claribell and Bellamour to restore their lost child.

From 1542 well beyond Spenser's death, editions of the *Orlando furioso* almost always provided allegorical commentary, and the dominant early modern tradition of Ariostan allegoresis from then onward (including Fornari, Thomaso Porcacchi, Clemente Valvassori, Gioseffo Bonomone, and Sir John Harington) correlated Melissa's care of Ruggiero with divine love and grace recovering humanity.[79] In his translated *Orlando* first published in 1591, Harington draws on Bonomone's account to declare Melissa "is to be understood the divine inspiration of the grace of God."[80] Through her help, Ruggiero gains access to Logistilla's idealized realm, which Ariosto explicitly relates to true beauty and good. Just as in Spenser's story of Pastorella's restoration to Belgard, the good outcome depends on Melissa's agency, not Ruggiero's: hence the sixteenth-century interpretive recourse to divine grace supplementing human nature, an obvious hermeneutic move in that cultural context.

Fornari most fully expounds that conventional allegoresis of Ariosto's Melissa. Harington's known consultation of Fornari instances the latter's currency among Ariosto's English cognoscenti, and Fornari's commentary is one of the books that Spenser, given his great interest in Ariosto and in allegorical romantic epic, most likely studied. Melissa, Fornari argues, is an agent of "divine love" and signifies "prevenient grace, which divine love instills in human minds in an instant" (prior to willed assent). Her name reflects that meaning, in his view, for this grace proceeds, he says, "from the *care* of divine love for us mortals" (2:121, 117; my emphasis). Melissa's role instances comfort of "souls, showing to them the love of the divine goodness, so that they would know themselves so loved," and hence seek to "correspond to such love," in a requital like "that which a dear son usually brings to a sweet father" (2:122–23, 141, 143). Fornari's recourse to the familial metaphor, probably informed by the prodigal model, parallels Spenser's Belgard allegory. Grace thus liberates Ruggiero, Fornari continues, "from an empty and obscure prison of death to which he was destined because of the sin of the first man" (2:144). Just before returning to Belgard, Spenser's Pastorella is liberated from an obscure hellish prison where death "doth . . . stalke" at large (VI.xi.16).

"All that follows afterwards, of the discourse of Melissa," Fornari affirms, "is none other than to recommend the greatness of divine love towards mortals" (2:144). Proceeding to Logistilla's realm through Melissa's aid, Ruggiero thus binds himself "to the rock of true felicity," as it were, in "hope of that sweet and highest beatitude of the contemplative life," when "the mind walks in the heavens" and discerns "that vast sea of divine beauty, . . . whence all souls take their being," together with "the most high and burning love for us mortals" (2:172). Ariosto's Melissa herself articulates Platonic doctrine (vii.6), and in general for Fornari, that poet "follows the ideas of Plato, yet not deviating from Christian philosophy" (2:134). This approach to Ariosto would have been profoundly interesting to the author of such writings as *The Fowre Hymnes*.

The story involving Alcina, Melissa, and Logistilla is certainly an allegory at least engaging the matters that Fornari and his counterparts propose. Ariosto's Melissa enables Ruggiero to reach Logistilla's castle ("castello," "castel"; x.52–53), and it is the demesne of "eternal beauty and infinite grace (bellezza eterna ed infinita grazia)" according to the poem's narrator (x.45). The castle images a condition of virtue analogous to and thus prefiguring heaven. Logistilla instills soaring thoughts approaching "the glory of the beatified," Ruggiero is told, while the narrator maintains the substance of her castle's walls seems heavenly and yields true knowledge of the soul (x.47, 58–59). Ruggiero attains it through a series of symbolic events and interventions, most importantly Melissa's. The significance of Spenser's Castle Belgard is analogous to that of Logistilla's castle. Unfolding the latter's Platonic import, Fornari's account evinces clear correspondences with the Belgard allegory in general content, as does Ariosto's own linkage of Logistilla's castle with "bellezza eterna" and beatific approximations. Spenser's usage of the name "Melissa" in conjunction with his character's role of caring intervention, crucial to Pastorella's full restoration to Belgard, allusively correlates the episode with that central Ariostan context and its Cinquecento allegoresis.

While evoking the etymology of care assumed by Dolce, Conti, Fornari, very likely Harington, and probably Ariosto (from the Greek μέλειν), Spenser's Melissa also attends to a notional flower, and so some inter-related Greek meanings of μέλισσά, "bee," "honey," and "poet," may have additional relevance. Spenser's "Melissa" would thus further refer to the bee's formerly well-known symbolic roles whereby it signified, in one sense, the beneficence of inspired poetry and "the right poet," in Sidney's phrase; and in another sense, that of reading "pro bono."[81] Reading "in malo" was contrarily signified by the spider. As a bee extracts honey from flowers, so readers should interpret poems, many urged, so as to yield good, and improve in character. On two "knavish" tales of the *Orlando furioso*, Harington insists "the Bee will pike out honey out of the worst of them."[82]

Besides "dewly" attending Pastorella "day and night" (VI.xii.14), Spenser's Melissa is a benevolently careful interpreter. Through her compassionate attentiveness she discovered the exiled infant's rosy birthmark (VI.xii.7–8), and when grown-up Pastorella appears, Melissa observes she bears that long-remembered mark, deduces she is the same lost daughter, and advises Claribell accordingly. Claribell then verifies "by very certaine signes" that Melissa has not misread the situation (VI.xii.20, 16). While Spenser thus arranges the narrative to approve Melissa's interpretive authority, we cannot confirm her further insistence that, despite the vicissitudes of Pastorella's life, it ultimately evinces "the heauens" and "high God" beneficently working "to saue" her (VI.xii, 16, 17). Reading these events pro bono, Melissa projects her own impulses of nurturing care into the heavens, so that divine love constitutes, in effect, a higher-order Melissa. She functions in part as an internal yet unintentional commentator on the unfolding allegory. The narrator himself promotes her kind of view, as when he explicitly assures readers of divine involvement when Calidore saves Pastorella from the Brigands (VI.xi.36). And in restoring Pastorella to her long-lost parents, Spenser resolves his tale by engineering a coincidence that could seem miraculous, while ensuring readers' emotional investment in wanting the reunion to be true, and thus in approving Melissa's general credibility.

PASTORELLA'S RESTORATION AND THE 1596 *FAERIE QUEENE*'S CLOSURE

Spenser announces in the proem for Book VI that his Courtesy sprang from a theologically conceived "sacred" source, "heauenly seedes of

bountie soueraine" (VI.pr.3). As the poet rejects "outward shows" in
defining true courtesy, its touchstone is profoundly inward: "vertues
seat . . . deepe within the mynd" (VI.pr.4–5). The Courtesy to be
valued differs sharply from conventional understandings of courtesy,
then, and Spenser accords the virtue a philosophical and theological
depth conducive to allegorical treatment. The book's allegory fully
develops these central principles of the proem. Just as Spenser depreci-
ates courtesy from the outset, Book VI seeks to approach Courtesy's
wellsprings through allegorical inquiry and exploration. The allegory
of Belgard that I have traced clarifies much in the book, for Pastorella's homecoming in the climactic canto culminates the presentation
of Courtesy. The tropological and anagogical content addresses inner
resources for pursuing the virtue, the conditions of doing so, and its
ultimate origins, so that the proem's manifest theological interests are
consistent with the poem's ensuing development. The Belgard allegory further exfoliates the Graces' dance as it applies to redemptive
graces. Otherwise appearing incongruous, the clear parallels between
Pastorella's and Una's homecomings are thus clearly apt, and the
allegory counters the ravening Beast by offering an implicit answer.

As in Redcross's or Alma's cases, Pastorella's role, modelled on
the parabolic prodigal's, partly addresses the prospects of the soul in
general. Her tropological and anagogical assimilation to Belgard implies a correlative outcome for Calidore, who brought her back. His
arrival and welcome there allegorically imply some advancement in
the progression through sanctification to glorification.[83] Calidore
considerately stays "Vntill" Pastorella convalesces, then resumes his
quest's responsibilities (VI.xii.13). Her recovery and homecoming at
Belgard enact a symbolic spiritual reinforcement, and that, as well as
Calidore's own visit there, underwrites his subsequent victory over
the Blatant Beast. Spenser accordingly emphasizes that he *must* present
Pastorella's restoration before turning to the quest's outcome:

> But first, ere I doe his aduentures tell,
>   In this exploite, *me needeth to declare*,
>   What did betide to the faire Pastorell,
>   During his absence. . . .
>
>   (VI.xii.14; my emphasis)

The argument for the canto likewise correlates Pastorella's restoration
with Calidore's victory.

In the final cantos of Books I and VI, Spenser leaves his couples
Una and Redcross and Pastorella and Calidore in analogous situations, and we have now found that the Belgard episode involves

comparable theological allegory. Calidore rests at Belgard with his
beloved Pastorella before completing his quest; Redcross rests at liberated Eden with Una before pursuing a further quest he promised
Gloriana (I.xii.18–19). As her parents' "onely daughter, and . . . onely
heyre" like Pastorella (I.xii.21; cf. I.vii.43), Una too recalls Solomon's
bride, who conventionally signified the soul or the Church (Song
Sol. 6:8–9). And Una too becomes a somewhat prodigally wandering
or "Errant damozell" (II.i.19), yet regains her mother and father
partly through her lover's heroic agency, yielding "Great joy"
(I.xii.40–41). Both heroines mourn the loss of their lovers who have
left to fulfill heroic commitments (I.xii.41; VI.xii.14). Redcross
promises to return in six years, after completing his additional quest.
Spenser's wording implies that Calidore is to return to Pastorella after
completing his original quest, with no further heroic enterprises to
delay reunion:

> he bethought
> *To leaue his loue*, now perill being past,
> *With Claribell, whylest* he that monster sought
> Throughout the world, and to destruction brought.
>
> (VI.xii.13; my emphasis)

Spenser tactfully postpones Una and Redcross's enduring union
because it would allegorically imply a final, apocalyptic apotheosis,
and the delay befits the poet's emphases on continuing heroic engagement and the worldly embattlement of virtue. The correlative case
of Calidore and Pastorella involves such considerations. Since Belgard
is more idealized than Una's home on account of the names involved,
the absence of any threat to it, and the more fully developed parabolic
analogy of prodigal restoration (whereby the parents adumbrate aspects of God), the poet becomes yet more discreet here. The possibilities of marriage are left implicit. Moreover, in a narrative analogue
of only seeing through a glass darkly, as it were (I Cor. 13:12),
Pastorella's joyous confirmation as Belgard's true heir remains unknown to Calidore within the bounds of the fiction, as does her secret
name of the rose. If Spenser's Contemplation has some authority in
allegoresis of *The Faerie Queene*, the hero's departure to fulfill obliga-
tions of his virtue would allegorically precondition and indicate future lasting reunion with his beloved, and all that entails (cf.
I.x.55–64). Perhaps for Book VI's heroic couple the five further completed books of *The Faerie Queene*, or their cumulative pattern of
heroic development, somewhat fulfill or render moot the six years

of separation stipulated for Una and Redcross at the end of Book I. Insofar as a central model of the initial book is the medieval and early modern tradition of combined prodigal-pilgrimage allegory, as Prescott argues in relating Book I to Bateman's chivalric *Pylgrime*, that Spenserian train of thought further effloresces in the 1596 installment's closing narrative of Calidore and Pastorella, where their travails come to yield her roseate restoration to Belgard and his corresponding victory. The interpretive realm of Belgard subsumes liberated Eden.

Both these concluding cantos also jointly imitate the old serpent's binding and subsequent escape in the Book of Revelation (Rev. 20:1–3), with Archimago and the Blatant Beast as its surrogates (I.xii.36; VI.xii.34–39). Spenser's diction becomes more biblical in Book VI, where Calidore's "great long chaine" for binding the Beast echoes the Geneva text's "great chaine" for binding the old serpent (VI.xii.34; Rev. 20:1). The poet's comment on the Beast's later escape, "Thenceforth more mischiefe and more scath he wrought / . . . *then he had* done *before*," follows and even quotes part of the Geneva gloss for the old serpent's escape in Revelation 20:3: "after this . . . Satan had greater power *then he had before*" (VI.xii.39; my emphasis).[84]

Since the Book of Revelation had much importance for Spenser, as in Book I and the final cantos of Book V where the Blatant Beast first appears, the Beast's alignment with Revelation 20 in the closing stanzas of the 1596 *Faerie Queene* would not be casual. "S. Calidore," as the title page for Book VI calls him, correlates with the "Angel" who binds the old serpent (Rev. 20:1–3). For Protestants he commonly signified Christ or the divinely appointed apostles, as in the Geneva gloss, and so Calidore's success somewhat recalls them as well as those who "did not worship the beast," and "liued and reigned with Christ," in Revelation 20:1, 4. Then, after a "thousand yeeres," "Satan shalbe losed" from that bondage "for a litle season," corrupt many, but finally be "cast into a lake of fyre . . . , where the beast and the false prophet shalbe tormented . . . euermore" (20:3, 7–10). This is the Second Coming and Last Judgment when "*the boke* of life" opens, revealing the names of the blessed, and the New Jerusalem appears (Rev. 20:11–21:1).

The Beast likewise escapes "*long after*" Calidore's victory (VI.xii.38; my emphasis), and the period of its bondage in Spenser's story is analogous to the millennium of Satan's before he is loosed, in the Book of Revelation. Hence the Beast's subsequent depredations, including attacks on authors and the poet himself, implicitly correspond to Satan's renewed activities after his release, that are to usher in the apocalyptic vindication of his opponents and victims. *The Faerie Queene*'s 1596 addition thus ends upon the prospective threshold of "a new heauen and a new earth" (supposed imminent in much early modern Protestant historiography), "the day of restauracion of all things" (Rev. 21:1 and gloss). While Spenser assures us in Sonnet 80 of the *Amoretti* that *The Faerie Queene* was to be continued, he nonetheless closes Book VI in such a way as to evoke and defer to the anticipated opening of "another book, . . . *the boke* of life" (Rev. 20:22).

In view of the Belgard episode's theological allegory, Spenser's final alignment of the Beast with Revelation 20 becomes much more intelligible, as do the other concluding homologies between Books I and VI. Pastorella's quasi-parabolic restoration to Belgard allegorically anticipates the great "day of restauracion" when, Revelation 21:7 claims, God is to welcome those he acknowledges as his children to their inheritance. Hamilton observes that the two episodes of Canto xii—Pastorella's homecoming and the engagement with the Beast—"are equally matched at 19 stanzas each" (683*n*). The loving restoration and the ravening escaped beast counterpose each other like thesis and antithesis, offered to our assessment.

Much interpretively depends on how and to what extent we contextualize the Beast's escape. From the outset in Book I, *The Faerie Queene*'s quests are always to some extent incomplete or frustrated, expressing the earthly elusiveness of ideal resolutions and perfected virtue.[85] Just as Book V assumes that the world has far declined from a golden age to stone (V.pr.2), postlapsarian social realities are inevitably problematic in Spenser's view, so that he would only have expected the poem's fashionings of readers and models of virtue to have partial and imperfect effects at best.[86] Yet, as closure for a book of *The Faerie Queene*, Spenser's account of the world's refractoriness and sufferings when ending Book VI, lastly including himself and his own writing, is heightened by its terminal position within the whole 1596 edition. On the other hand, Spenser's hero is not bitten or eaten by the Beast (which would have been pessimistic), but instead attains a victory that "long" endures, a point commentators often miss (VI.xii.38). Moreover, sixteenth-century authors quite commonly decried their detractors within their writings, and Spenser's adaptation of that convention here is relatively innovative, poised, and hence detached.[87] Whether we are theists, agnostics, or atheists, if we attend to the local resonance of Revelation 20 on account of that biblical book's paradigmatic role in much of *The Faerie Queene*, and the central importance of Protestant apocalyptic historiography in Elizabethan culture, the 1596 *Faerie Queene* ends by rebuking the world and projecting transcendental egress. For Protestants the Book of Revelation was a main basis not only of polemic, but also of faith in ultimate vindication despite present reverses. In that view, the true Church and its adherents were bound to suffer; but that very abuse paradoxically identified them as Truth's advocates whom God would reward at last.[88] If we further attend to the quasi-parabolic implications of Pastorella's homecoming, we find that Spenser proceeds to engage the Beast in Canto xii only by first allegorizing such an apotheosis, by way of a vehicle emotionally appealing enough to promote assent. Even literally, the Belgard story instances how happy endings can serendipitously unfold beyond all our expectations. The attendant allegory endues this outcome of romantic wish-fulfillment with the ideological foundation of a justificatory theodicy.

Yet because Spenser's textual counterweights to the Beast's final rampage are largely allusive, allegorical, and implicit, readers may also downplay or disregard them, in which case there would seem little to oppose the Beast. Whereas the poet's basic theological positions are relatively clear in Book I, as in the introductory stanza of Canto x, by Book VI he had come to avoid such overt didacticism and leave readers more to their own devices in reckoning with his still darker conceits. Allegory etymologically means "speaking other,"[89] and Spenser's faery allegorism increasingly became an ironic mask enabling him to address different readers differently while nonetheless shaping the parameters of discourse, and dividing hermeneutic sheep from goats. His final epigram, "do you my rimes keep better measure, / And seeke to please, that now is counted wisemens threasure," contextually implies verbally ironic sarcasm of opportunists and his detractors, who have been subsumed in the Beast.[90] The standard reader response theories of Spenser's time ranked readers evaluatively. Literary fiction, Sidney maintained, was rightly to be used "but as an imaginative groundplot of a profitable invention" (103). In Leone's, Conti's, Harington's, and Abraham Fraunce's hierarchies of readership, apprehension of the literal story was merely basic, whereas higher capacities perceived the moral sense, and some, beyond that, the greater philosophico-theological senses.[91] Yet others would incorrigibly tend to extract ill, like the spider that, by gleaning venom rather than honey from flowers, typified reading "in malo," contrary to the bee.[92] Spenser himself refers to that commonplace in his dedication to *The Fowre Hymnes* (690). Prior to 1590, he had similarly written, "let *Grill* be *Grill*, and haue his hoggish mind" (II.xii.87).

Appearing in the 1596 *Faerie Queene*'s final canto, shortly after Colin Clout's self-reflexive appearance, Spenser's deployment of "Melissa" under the sign of the rose seems a symbolic insignia of his

poetic. The right poet's goal, Sidney claims, befits "the ending end
of all earthly learning," to "draw us to as high a perfection as our
degenerate souls, made worse by their clayey lodgings, can be capable
of" (82–83). A higher-order analogue of Melissa's own pro bono
reading, which seeks to rectify loss and bring truth to light, the Belgard allegory accords with such aims. Its theodicy offers to answer,
finesse, or redefine the challenges implicitly posed by Pastorella's
initial predicament and later dangers, and by the Beast's present attacks. Melissa's reactions to Pastorella's loss and return provide a
textual exemplar for positive responses, while associating the pro
bono model with Spenser's text and creativity by evoking the herme-
neutically symbolic bee. The splendid affirmative images of the
Graces' fleeting fictional theophany, Pastorella's rescue in Canto xi,
and her homecoming assert the power of poetry to effect beneficent
revelation—though not to Momus, Zoilus, "Stoicke censours," or
the Beast. Spenser had already announced at the start of the 1596
addition, "To such therefore I do not sing at all" (IV.pr. 4).

McGill University

APPENDIX: THE ALLEGORISM OF PASTORELLA'S
ENIGMATIC ORIGIN (VI.xii.4–6)

In just three stanzas beginning the Belgard episode, Spenser outlines
the original circumstances of Pastorella's parentage, birth, and exile.
Though paternally intended to marry the Prince of Picteland, Claribell fell in love with and secretly wed Bellamour instead. Discovering
that, her enraged father imprisoned each of them separately, yet Bellamour still somehow impregnated Claribell. Fearing her father might
wrathfully kill the baby, she had her maidservant Melissa arrange that
it be "fostred vnder straunge attyre," the shepherd Meliboe bore it
away to raise as his own in pastoral obscurity, and Belgard's heir
seemed lost (VI.xii.4–6). Until the end of her story, Pastorella does
not even know that the shepherd and his wife were not really her
parents. As Richard Neuse observes in *The Spenser Encyclopedia*, the
poet presents "Pastorella's identity . . . with deliberate mystification," as a "riddle . . . , and the story of her parentage surely serves
the same purpose."[93] I have shown that central features of the Belgard
episode strongly invite theoretical allegoresis, if we allow for the

importance of the correlation cultural contexts in Spenser's intellectual and literary formation. Pastorella's mysterious origin, identity, and exile complement the episode's allegory of the soul's restoration. Since the passage's brevity makes interpretation much more speculative, I reserve it for this appendix.

Since not all parts of an allegorical narrative were necessarily expected to do more than help establish the vehicle,[94] the story of Claribell and Bellamour's early difficulties in stanzas four to six might simply set up conditions for Pastorella's exile and return in order to launch the ensuing tropological and anagogical allegory. Or these stanzas could modulate into a local allegory of a topical or political kind, for comparable shifts of allegorical subject occur in prior episodes of *The Faerie Queene*. Prompted by Spenser's reference to the Prince of Picteland, some critics have already suggested such applications here, and yet, as Neuse objects, their accounts include no counterparts for Pastorella, despite her centrality here.[95] Neuse thus topically focuses on relating Pastorella to Queen Elizabeth, and her parents to Elizabeth's. However, he too leaves main elements unexplained, such as how Anne Boleyn would connect to any historical counterpart of a princely Pict. As yet, no topical proposal readily fits enough of the passage's details (including, most importantly, the birth and exile of an infant who returns to her original parents) to appear authoritative.

Otherwise, either in lieu of topical reference or polysemously supplementing it, these stanzas most likely introduce the tropological and anagogical allegory of the Belgard episode with a "dark conceit" of poetic theology. Such subject matter was to be expected in serious literature, particularly in the variants of heroic poetry, on account of the strongly allegorical early modern reception of the major ancient epics.[96] Both the topical and theological applications here would involve the trope "enigma," in George Puttenham's terms, to speak covertly "by way of riddle."[97] I will explore the theological possibilities. Whereas the prior topical readings each allegorize a few details of the passage and ignore the others, so that they may seem arbitrarily selective, I seek to apply a more stringent standard, as in my prior publications on portions of Spenser's "continued allegory" as he called it in the *Letter to Ralegh*. The claims of a given allegoresis to textual development and relevance strengthen to the extent it is answerable to and interpretively opens up the text, so that it had best account for all the main features of the passage at issue and illuminate much else there besides, including its symbolism, wordplay, and intertextualities.

In the passage outlining the conditions of Pastorella's birth, the expression of allegorized poetic theology would mainly depend on three apparent structural analogies. First, Claribell clearly marries beneath the princely height of her prospects in wedding Sir Bellamour (VI.xii.4), and this social instance of the reconciliation of height with relative lowliness would provide a figurative model for the creative union of beauty with love in general.[98] Second, as Claribell's father opposes the couple's marriage and punishes it by imprisoning them, so this contretemps would express some notional conflict within the godhead (as it may be described provisionally). Yet a definitive paradox is involved, for her father's severity, the cause of the couple's objection, nevertheless leads to a creative union of beauty and love, and finally a joyous reconciliation. The rule of the punitive father ends with his death and the succession of Claribell and Bellamour at Belgard, which initiates, in effect, a new dispensation. Third, the circumstances relating to Pastorella's origins—such as her degraded birth in prison, exile from Belgard, loss of her patrimony, subsequent sufferings, and need to return—would reflect upon the human condition. In the Belgard episode's quasi-parabolic allegory of return, her role relates to human spiritual restoration. All three of these posited structural analogies have clear precedents in sixteenth-century Platonism and Christian theology.

In treating the union of beauty with love as a problematic reconciliation of high and low, as Claribell socially descends to love Bellamour, the allegory would engage a central problem of Renaissance Platonist theory of love and beauty. If love is the desire for beauty, as Socrates maintains in Plato's *Symposium*, then beauty is by definition beyond love's attainment, for through a desire we seek what is lacking, not what is already enjoyed. So how could the goal of love so defined, union with beauty, be fulfilled? Beauty would ever transcend love. How could the beloved, by definition superior, requite love? And how, Christian Platonists wondered, could God love creation, or creation spring, as they liked to suppose, from divine love and beauty? These are fundamental issues of Leone Ebreo's long *Dialoghi d'amore*, for example, wherein Philo the lover seeks union with his beloved beauty, Sophia, who remains elusive (e.g., 181). They are also reflected in numerous literary writings of the time, such as Maurice Scève's *Délie*, Sidney's *Astrophil and Stella* (star-lover and star), his Arcadian account of Philisides and Mira, and Drayton's *Idea*, not to speak of Spenser's own texts.[99] The allegory of Claribell and Bellamour's relationship appears to effect resolution through analogy with the Christian principle of extraordinary, self-abnegating love. Claribell chooses a socially inferior match with Bellamour, despite consequently heavy costs for her, loses her social advantages, and becomes a wretched prisoner, all for love. In *Heauenly Loue*, likewise published in 1596, Spenser says that Christ became an "abiect thrall" for love of humankind (lines 134–40). In Arthur's recapitulation of Christ's harrowing of hell in Book I, he undertakes the noxious descent into Orgoglio's filthy dungeon to liberate Redcross, for "Entire affection hateth nicer hands" (I.vii.40).

Moreover, by positing a conflict whereby Claribell's father opposes and severely punishes her union with Bellamour, and by resolving that conflict through the couple's eventual succession, Spenser's account of Pastorella's parentage corresponds to various paradigms of Christian theology evident elsewhere in his writings. The most obvious analogy is the rigor of the Law and resultant so-called "bondage" yielding to the regime of Grace. The prescriptive rule of Claribell's punitive father yields to hers and her consort's, associated with beauty and love. Also comparable is the allegorical tradition of the four daughters of God, who represents Justice, Truth, Mercy, and Peace as his sometimes conflicting daughters. Justice argues for condemnation of fallen humanity, for example, but Mercy for forgiveness and redemption.[100] Elements of human experience and behavior, including anger and curses, were often used provisionally for symbolic description of God's nature.[101] For Marsilio Ficino in *De amore*, divine creation involves both "the reign of the tyrant Necessity" and "the rule of Love" (V.11). Portrayal of God in diverse and sometimes conflicting aspects is certainly Spenserian, for the representations of deity or divine agency in *The Fowre Hymnes* include, among others, the "eternall fount of loue and grace"; the dreaded lord who "bruseth all his foes to dust"; and female Sapience (*HHL*, line 99; *HHB*, lines 145–56). *The Faerie Queene* too evinces such a diversity. We could compare, for example, the Graces in Book VI; the transcendental representations of Gloriana, who partly symbolizes divine glory,[102] and whose imagery is much like Sapience's; Contemplation's vision of the New Jerusalem (I.ix.46–47, 53); and equity's interplay with the divine virtue of justice, expressed through that of Isis with Osiris (V.vii.1–3, 22). In the Belgard story, this particular passage would thus allegorically engage much the same theological problem as Calvin does when he observes that the Bible attributes a "seeming of contrarietie" to God, both "angrie and bent against" humanity and yet loving, and that this is a provisional mode of expression addressing the needs of human capacities in their weakness. Citing Augustine, Calvin concludes that God both hated and loved fallen humanity in an incomprehensibly loving manner.[103] Spenser sharply contrasts the punitive Lord "renoued / For ... might," whose response to Pastorella is dreaded (VI.xii.4, 6), with the "loued Lord," Bellamour (VI.xii.23), with whom she finally joins in joy.

The biblical resonances of Claribell's father's title, "the Lord of Many Islands," complement this reading. Lacking any narrative rationale or verisimilar development, his appellation is conspicuously irrelevant, in Harry Berger's phrase, and hence interpretively provocative. The physical setting of Belgard in this Lord's domains involves nothing maritime, nor any islands, nor does Spenser bother to specify Calidore and Pastorella's means of reaching it.[104] However, Jehovah often appears a mighty overlord of "isles" or "islands" in sixteenth-century English translations of the Old Testament. Thus they render the complex Hebrew word 'iyim, which has various senses including countries, lands, peoples, or lands of the gentiles, senses particularly apparent in the Psalms and Isaiah. The "ysles" will be "astonished" by God's wrath (Ezek. 26:15–21), and "the Lord will be terrible," for "he wil consume all the gods of the earth, and euerie man shal worship him . . . , euen all the ysles of the heathen" (Zeph. 2:11). Various biblical contexts attribute great power to "the Lord" by hailing his dominion over far-flung islands that praise him and await his law (e.g., Isa. 41:1–5; 42:4, 10–12; 49:1; 51:5). Familiar in Spenser's culture, this biblical significance of "islands" would have been especially activated in conjunction with "Lord."

In one sense, Claribell's great father's effort to marry her to the *Prince* of Picteland helps define her contrary espousal of *Sir* Bellamour (VI.xii.6) as one of relative social lowliness, thus paradigmatically reconciling high and low as we have seen. In another, it could have further indicated her father's apparent harshness. "Pictland" and Picts were often associated with barbarism,[105] much as Claribell finds this prince repugnantly "forrein" (VI.xii.4). An incidental compliment to England may be involved. By specifying Pictland, which referred to parts of Scotland, and locating it "nere" Belgard (VI.xii.4), the poet may imply England's inclusion in Belgard's domains, and hence in its prefigurations of anagogical joy. A somewhat comparable tradition associated England with the classical paradise, the Isles of the Blessed or Fortunate Isles.[106] Or, if we consider the standard early modern etymology of "Pict," painted or adorned,[107] Claribell's father's plans for a prestigious union would figuratively imply dissemination of beauty through representative expression, "making," or creation in some sense. According to Thomas Cooper, "pingo," the formerly standard root of "Pict," means not only "to paint," but also "to draw out the shape and fourme of a thynge." The Platonic "wondrous Paterne" of beauty is variously depicted throughout creation in the poet's *Hymne in Honour of Beautie*. Here at Belgard, however, a match of beauty ensues in which love is paramount in that union's effects, whatever the costs and sacrifices: an outcome comparable to Spenser's following hymns, *Heauenly Loue* and *Heauenly Beautie*.

In any case, stanzas four to six evince a broad and apparently structural analogy with former theological notions of the human condition. Pastorella, the focus of an allegory of spiritual restoration in the episode, is conceived and born "in dongeon deepe," in a state of captivity, and exiled from Belgard, all on account of the altercation between the Lord of Many Islands and her parents. States of captivity, bondage, and exile had age-old metaphoric applications to humanity's supposed subjection to original sin resulting from the Fall, much as Spenser has Orgoglio imprison Redcross (I.viii.1, 37–41). Pastorella's imprisoned or captive state at birth and subsequent exile provide a proleptic epitome anticipating the motif's full development in her captivity portrayed in the Brigands' dens. The conditions of her birth also suggest an analogy to "the child of wrath" or "heir of wrath," phrases and notions common in sixteenth-century Christian discourse.[108] The Lord of Many Islands wreaks "great rage" upon Pastorella's parents, she is conceived and born in that predicament, and her mother, dreading that Lord will thus "slay" infant Pastorella, secretly sends her into exile (VI.xii.5–6). From a Pauline standpoint, we are "by nature the children of wrath," or "by birth" according to the Geneva Bible's gloss, through Adam's line (Eph. 2:3). Hence, Spenser's contemporary Thomas Wilson explains, "all men . . . by nature and birth" are subject to "the just anger of God against sin," and on their own account deserve death, for "the wages of sin is death" (Rom. 6:23).[109]

The Elizabethan baptismal rites focus some main theological metaphors comparable to Spenser's passage. There, a "child" or "infant" is "born in original sin, and in the wrath of God," and thus alienated from her or his divine progenitor, but through regeneration is "delivered from . . . wrath," "made heir" of "the kingdom" of "the heavenly father," and received as "his own child" and "inheritor" (BCP, sigs. O1ᵛ-O2ᵛ, N6ʳ, N8ᵛ). Born in degradation and wrath yet soon "Bedeaw'd" by Melissa in a discreet analogue of baptism or divine grace in general (VI.xii.8), infant Pastorella passes through the "troublesome world" beyond Belgard (in the baptismal rite's phrase, BCP, sig. N6ᵛ), to be reconciled at last with her ultimate origin and become Belgard's heir. The parabola of her representative life anagogically effects the result projected for the future of infants in the Elizabethan liturgy.

It is intriguing that infant Pastorella's plight implies some unorthodoxy about the originary taint or flaw. Her birth in prison and subsequent exile express a primal degradation and alienation defining the conditions of her subsequent life, and in that way comparable to the doctrine of original sin. Since she is an infant, her predicament, unlike that of her parabolic counterpart the prodigal son, cannot be directly her fault. Nor, as a collectively inherited model of guilt would require, does some clear fault of her parents cause her jeopardy, even though it arises from their altercation with the Lord of Many Islands. Since Claribell and Bellamour focus aspects of God in the theological allegory as the episode's parabolic allusion indicates, and constitute part of the Platonic Belgard-Bellamour-Claribell triad as I have also shown, they cannot readily serve as analogues of a human transgression to be inherited as with Adam and Eve. And in any case they cannot readily be blamed, for the Lord of Many Islands behaves "cruelly" and "Without compassion," without due regard for the importance of love (VI.xii.5). Instead, in keeping with Spenser's derivations of humanity from divine love and beauty in various creation myths in *Colin Clouts* and *The Fowre Hymnes*, Claribell and Bellamour, as Pastorella's parents, allegorize that origin. If the episode's general theological allegory includes the details of Pastorella's birth, as seems probable, the originary flaw or fault in which Pastorella is implicated signifies "something in the nature of things" for which she is not responsible, nor any other human agency. In the allegory it rather seems to arise from some humanly apparent "contrariety" in the godhead, as Calvin calls it, or perhaps from inherent limitations of the materials or process of creation in uniting high and low, so that suffering and loss result, requiring sacrifice and compassion to be rectified. Thus high and low creatively unite as do Claribell and Bellamour, the allegory implies, and restoration finally occurs as for Pastorella.

Whereas Milton seems adamant about human responsibility for involvement in sin and suffering in *Paradise Lost* ("whose fault? / Whose but his own? Ingrate," Milton's Father says of Adam).[110] Spenser is much more exploratory in these stanzas, justifying his contextual turn to enigma or yet darker conceit, and here again there seems Platonic influence in a broad sense. Neoplatonism's emanationist doctrines make responsibility for any flaws in the universe difficult to segregate from a presumed Creator, while its notions of the soul's preexistence entail a debilitating "fall" into matter if there is to be any human earthly embodiment at all. So if earthly life were divinely ordained, as in Genesis, human responsibility for ostensible sin would become problematic. Insofar as Pastorella's birth at Belgard corresponds to the soul's presumed heavenly genesis, her "fostering vnder straunge attyre" may reflect the soul's shift to earthly embodiment, the guise of flesh, as it were, described in *The Fowre Hymnes*

(*HB*, lines 106–47). Yet the allegory also has Christian affinities in emphasizing love, and an ultimately positive degradation, sacrifice, and suffering, not only on Pastorella's part, but also on Claribell and Bellamour's. In any case, Spenser's representation of God and divine agency in the Belgard episode is provisional, just as they have multiple symbolic correlates. Besides Claribell's father, Claribell, her spouse, and their dispute with her father, there are Melissa; the water symbolism of dew and compassionate tears; Belgard itself; the final "ioyning ioy" there, enjoyed "In perfect forme" (VI.xi.21–22); the favorable providential interventions attributed to the heavens; and the insignia of the unfolding rose.

Notes

1. Tasso, *Discourses on the Heroic Poem*, trans. Mariella Cavalchini and Irene Samuel (Oxford: Clarendon, 1973), 32.

2. Spenser, *The Faerie Queene*, ed. A. C. Hamilton et al., 2nd rev. ed. (Harlow, U.K.: Longman, 2001).

3. See, e.g., Maria R. Rohr Philmus, "*The Faerie Queene* and Renaissance Poetics: Another Look at Book VI as 'Conclusion' to the Poem," *English Studies* 76 (1995): 497–519; Derek B. Alwes, " 'Who knowes not Colin Clout?': Spenser's Self-Advertisement in *The Faerie Queene*, Book 6," *Modern Philology* 88 (1990–91): 26–42; Margaret P. Hannay, " 'My Sheep are Thoughts': Self-Reflexive Pastoral in *The Faerie Queene*, Book VI, and the *New Arcadia*," *Spenser Studies* IX (1991): 137–59.

4. As Pastorella turns out to be a lord and lady's lost daughter, so pastoral and courtly values combine to yield a higher standard of Courtesy and social conduct, through which pastoral values unite with the culture, refinement, and resources of an exemplary court. Pastorella herself comes to epitomize that standard. See, e.g., Humphrey Tonkin, *Spenser's Courteous Pastoral: Book Six of the "Faerie Queene"* (Oxford: Clarendon, 1972), Index, s.v. "Pastorella, rescue and return."

5. Cf. Richard Neuse, "Pastorella," in *The Spenser Encyclopedia*, ed. A. C. Hamilton et al. (Toronto: University of Toronto Press, 1990), 533. Hereafter designated *SE*. Spenser's "deliberate mystification" in the relevant stanzas, Neuse indicates, renders such interpretations quite speculative. See my appendix, "The Allegorism of Pastorella's Enigmatic Origin (VI.xii.4–6)."

6. Alice Fox Blitch, "Proserpina Preserved: Book VI of the *Faerie Queene*," *SEL* 13 (1973): 15–30 (quoting 22, 29). See also Tonkin, 216, 310–15; Douglas Brooks-Davies, "mysteries," in *SE*, 485–87.

7. See, e.g., Douglas A. Northrop, "The Uncertainty of Courtesy in Book VI of *The Faerie Queene*," *Spenser Studies* XIV (2000): 215–32; Joan Fitzpatrick, "Pastoral Idylls and Lawless Rebels: Sexual Politics in Books 5 and 6 of Spenser's *Faerie Queene*," *Explorations in Renaissance Culture* 25 (1999): 87–111; John Breen, "Edmund Spenser's Exile and the Poetics of Pastoral," *Cahiers Elisabéthains* 53 (1998):

27–41; Bruce Danner, "Courteous *Virtù* in Spenser's Book 6 of *The Faerie Queene*," *SEL* 38 (1998): 1–18; Andrew Hadfield, *Edmund Spenser's Irish Experience: Wilde Fruit and Salvage Soyl* (Oxford: Clarendon, 1997), ch. 5; Jeffrey B. Morris, "To (Re)fashion a Gentleman: Ralegh's Disgrace in Spenser's Legend of Courtesy," *Studies in Philology* 94 (1997): 38–58; Darryl J. Gless, *Interpretation and Theology in Spenser* (Cambridge: Cambridge University Press, 1994); Margaret P. Hannay, " 'The Triall of True Curtesie': Teaching Book 6 as Pastoral Romance," in *Approaches to Teaching Spenser's "Faerie Queene,"* eds. David Lee Miller and Alexander Dunlop (New York: MLA, 1994), 172–80; also Hannay's " 'My Sheep are Thoughts' ": 137–59; Michael Steppat, "Social Change and Gender Decorum: Renaissance Courtesy," in *The Crisis of Courtesy: Studies in the Conduct-Book in Britain, 1600–1900,* ed. Jacques Carré (New York: Brill, 1994), 27–40; Eva Gold, "The Queen and the Book in Book 6 of *The Faerie Queene*," *South Atlantic Review* 57.4 (1992): 1–19; Robert E. Stillman, "Spenserian Autonomy and the Trial of New Historicism: Book Six of *The Faerie Queene*," *English Literary Renaissance* 22 (1992): 299–314; Debra Belt, "Hostile Audiences and the Courteous Reader in *The Faerie Queene,* Book VI," *Spenser Studies* IX (1991): 107–35; Michael Tratner, " 'The thing S. Paul ment by . . . the courteousness that he spake of': Religious Sources for Book VI of *The Faerie Queene*," *Spenser Studies* VIII (1990): 147–74; John D. Bernard, *Ceremonies of Innocence: Pastoralism in the Poetry of Edmund Spenser* (Cambridge: Cambridge University Press, 1989); Sean Kane, *Spenser's Moral Allegory* (Toronto: University of Toronto Press, 1989), ch. 6; George E. Rowe, "Privacy, Vision, and Gender in Spenser's Legend of Courtesy," *Modern Language Quarterly* 50 (1989): 309–36.

   8.   Cf. Kenneth Borris, *Spenser's Poetics of Prophecy in "The Faerie Queene" V* (Victoria: University of Victoria Press, 1991), chs. 1–3.

   9.   Mallette, *Spenser and the Discourses of Reformation England* (Lincoln: University of Nebraska Press, 1997), 169. See also, e.g., Tonkin, Index, s.v. "Graces" and "Pastorella, rescue and return."

   10.   Knapp, "Spenser the Priest," *Representations* 81 (2003): 61–78.

   11.   Tasso, 33. Cf. Kenneth Borris, *Allegory and Epic in English Renaissance Literature: Heroic Form in Sidney, Spenser, and Milton* (Cambridge: Cambridge University Press, 2000), chs. 1, 3; Robert Lamberton, *Homer the Theologian: Neoplatonist Allegorical Reading and the Growth of Epic Tradition* (Berkeley: University of California Press, 1986); Bernard Weinberg, *A History of Literary Criticism in the Italian Renaissance,* 2 vols. (Chicago: University of Chicago Press, 1961), Index, s.v. "Theology."

   12.   Cf. Jon A. Quitslund, "Platonism," in *SE,* 546. Also Michael J. B. Allen, "Ficino, Marsilio," in *SE,* 305; Quitslund, *Spenser's Supreme Fiction: Platonic Natural Philosophy and "The Faerie Queene"* (Toronto: University of Toronto Press, 2001), 11–13.

   13.   Cf. Variorum commentary, in Spenser, Vol. 6 of *Works,* ed. Edwin Greenlaw et al. (Baltimore: Johns Hopkins University Press, 1938), 260–62, 371–72. Cited parenthetically in my text hereafter.

   14.   See Borris, *Allegory and Epic,* ch. 2.

   15.   Cf. Borris, *Poetics of Prophecy,* 11, chs. 1–3.

   16.   Cf. Alan R. Young, *The English Prodigal Son Plays: A Theatrical Fashion of the Sixteenth and Seventeenth Centuries* (Salzburg: University of Salzburg, 1979); Siegfried

Wenzel, " 'The Pilgrimage of Life' as a Late Medieval Genre," *Mediaeval Studies* 35 (1973): 370–88.

17. *Geneva Bible*, introd. Lloyd E. Berry (Geneva, 1560; facsim. rpt. Madison: University of Wisconsin Press, 1969). Cited throughout unless otherwise noted.

18. Tonkin, 147; Shaheen, *Biblical References in "The Faerie Queene"* (Memphis: Memphis State University Press, 1976), 168, 210; Hamilton, ed., *Faerie Queene*, 685*n*.

19. In successive sixteenth-century English Protestant Bibles, the parable's text seems somewhat derived from their English predecessors. Much like the Geneva, the Bishops' Bible states, "this my sonne was *dead*, and is *aliue againe*: he was lost, and is founde"; he "was *dead*, and is *aliue againe*: and was lost, and is founde" (Luke 15:24, 32; London, 1585, STC 2143). Likewise William Tyndale's, Miles Coverdale's, "Thomas Matthew's" (i.e., John Rogers's), and Richard Taverner's further Protestant versions (except Taverner substitutes "reuiued" for "aliue again" in one of the two passages), and the Great Bible. Cf. *The New Testament*, trans. Tyndale (London, 1535), STC 2830; *The Whole Bible*, trans. Coverdale (London, 1550), STC 2080; *The Bible*, trans. "Matthew" (London, 1551), STC 2083; *The Most Sacred Bible*, trans. Taverner (London, 1539), STC 2067; Great Bible (London, 1549), STC 2049. Following the Vulgate instead, the Roman Catholic Rheims New Testament of 1582 has "reuiued" instead of "alive again" in both cases (STC 2884).

20. *Acolastus*, ed. W. E. D. Atkinson (London, Ont.: University of Western Ontario Press, 1964), V.v.79–81. Cited parenthetically in my text hereafter. Of Reformed sympathies, Volder visited England in the early 1560s, and this play had forty-seven editions by 1585, including translations into English, German, and French. English performance venues included Trinity College, Cambridge, in 1560–61, and it influenced dramatic and nondramatic writings by John Lyly, Thomas Nashe, Robert Greene, and Ben Jonson among others.

21. Greene, *The Mourning Garment*, in *Life and Complete Works*, ed. Alexander B. Grosart, 15 vols. (London, 1881–86), 9:212; emphasis mine. Cited parenthetically in my text hereafter.

22. Cf. *Georgius Macropedius' "Asotus,"* ed., trans. H. P. M. Puttiger (Nieuwkoop: De Graaf, 1988), lines 1689–90, 1829–30; first printed in 1537. Castellani, *Rappresentazione del figliuol prodigo*, in *Rappresentazioni dei Secoli XIV, XV e XVI*, ed. Alessandro D'Ancona, vol. I (Florence, 1872), 384–85; first printed c. 1500. Waldis, *Der Parabell vom verlornen Sohn*, in *Die Schaubühne im Dienste der Reformation*, ed. Arnold E. Berger, vol. I (Leipzig: Reclam, 1935), lines 1304–06, 1362–65, 1434–37; first printed in 1527.

23. Cf. Wenzel; also Edgar Schell, *Strangers and Pilgrims: From "The Castle of Perseverance" to "King Lear"* (Chicago: University of Chicago Press, 1983), 13–24.

24. Prescott, "Spenser's Chivalric Restoration: From Bateman's *Travayled Pylgrime* to the Redcrosse Knight," *Studies in Philology* 86 (1989): 166–97. Cf. Dorothy Atkinson Evans, "Introduction," in Jean Cartigny, *The Wandering Knight*, trans. William Goodyear, ed. Evans (Seattle: University of Washington Press, 1951), xxix-xlii.

25. The anonymous interlude *Nice Wanton*, printed in 1560, includes a mother and her prodigal daughter, Dalila. In *The Glass of Government*, printed in 1575,

George Gascoigne doubles the parable's main characters for variation. Ravisius Textor's prodigal comedy *Juvenis, Pater, et Uxor* focuses on bad marriage, while his *De Filio Prodigo* features new personifications and moralizing.

26. Helgerson, *The Elizabethan Prodigals* (Berkeley: University of California Press, 1976), 98.

27. Cf., e.g., Castiglione, *Book of the Courtier*, trans. Sir Thomas Hoby (London: Dent, 1928), 313. Cited parenthetically in my text hereafter. Cesare Ripa, *Iconologia* (Padua: Pietro Paolo Tozzi, 1611), 23–24.

28. Article Ten, in Thomas Rogers, *The English Creed* (London, 1585), STC 21226, 33. Cf. *OED*, 2nd ed., s.v. "prevent" v. 4 (theological).

29. Cf. Mallette, 169–200.

30. Stephen L. Wailes surveys patristic and medieval interpretations in *Medieval Allegories of Jesus' Parables* (Berkeley: University of California Press, 1987), 236–45.

31. Erasmus, *The First Tome or Volume of the Paraphrase . . . upon the Newe Testamente*, trans. Nicholas Udall et al. (London, 1548, facsim. rpt. Delmar, NY: Scholars', 1975), fols. cxxii[b], cxxi[a]. Calvin, *A Harmonie upon the Three Evangelists*, trans. E. P. (London, 1584), STC 2962, 494, 493. Marlorat, *Exposition of the Holy Gospel after S. Mark and Luke*, trans. Thomas Timme (London, 1583), STC 17405, 247, 249. Hooper, *Certeine Comfortable Expositions* (London, 1580), STC 13743, fols. 53[a-b]. Erasmus and Marlorat cited parenthetically in my text hereafter.

32. Gardiner, *Portraiture of the Prodigal Sonne* (London, 1599), STC 11579, 7, 263. Cited parenthetically in my text hereafter.

33. *Certaine Sermons or Homilies Appointed to Be Read in Churches*, eds. Mary Ellen Rickey and Thomas B. Stroup, 2 vols. in 1 (London, 1623; facsim. rpt. Gainesville, FL.: Scholars', 1968), 257, 263.

34. Van Lancvelt (or Macropedius) provides his similar *Asotus* such an expository prologue and epilogue.

35. Cf. Calvin, *The Institution of Christian Religion*, trans. Thomas Norton (London, 1599), STC 4423, 1.5.2, 1.11.2. Cited parenthetically in my text hereafter.

36. On tapinosis, negative poetics, and Spenserian poetic theology, cf. Carol V. Kaske, *Spenser and Biblical Poetics* (Ithaca: Cornell University Press, 1999), 174–82. Also Edgar Wind, *Pagan Mysteries in the Renaissance*, rev. ed. (London: Faber, 1968), Introduction. Cited parenthetically in my text hereafter.

37. Cf. Thomas Wilson, *A Christian Dictionary* (London, 1616), STC 25787, 113–16, 345–48.

38. Cf. Samuel C. Chew, *The Pilgrimage of Life* (New Haven: Yale University Press, 1962), chs. 6–7; Gerhart B. Ladner, *"Homo Viator:* Mediaeval Ideas on Alienation and Order," *Speculum* 42 (1967): 233–59; Kenneth Borris and M. Morgan Holmes, "Geoffrey Whitney's *Choice of Emblemes*: Anglo-Dutch Politics and the Order of Ideal Repatriation," *Emblematica* 8.1 (1994): 108–11, 120–23.

39. Cf. Wenzel; Schell, 13–24; Prescott, "Spenser's Chivalric Restoration."

40. "Bellamour" suggests "beauteous love" (French "bel" and "amour"); or "love of beauty" (Latin "bella" and French "amour"), for he loves Clari-*bel* and lives in *Bel*-gard; or "belamour," loved one, as he is "loued" himself (VI.xii.22; *OED*, 2nd ed., sb. 1).

41. Convincingly dated from at least 1580 by Jon Quitslund, "Spenser's *Amoretti VIII* and Platonic Commentaries on Petrarch," *JWCI* 36 (1973): 256–76.

42.   *Loue*, lines 57–112; *Heauenly Loue*, lines 99–119; *Beauty*, lines 29–49. *Colin Clouts*, lines 835–86. In Spenser's *Shorter Poems*, ed. William A. Oram et al. (New Haven: Yale University Press, 1989). Used for Spenser's shorter poems hereafter, cited parenthetically. *HL, HB, HHL*, and *HHB* designate particular hymns. Quitslund treats Platonic beauty's Spenserian importance in "beauty," *SE*, 81–82.

43.   See, e.g., James Nohrnberg, *The Analogy of "The Faerie Queene"* (Princeton: Princeton University Press, 1976), 461–69, 699–700; Lila Geller, "The Acidalian Vision: Spenser's Graces in Book VI of *The Faerie Queene*," *Review of English Studies* n.s. 23 (1972): 267–77; Tonkin, 228–29, 232–36, 257–62, 275–77.

44.   Cf. Ellrodt, *Neoplatonism in the Poetry of Spenser* (Geneva: Droz, 1960), ch. 11; Quitslund, *Supreme Fiction*, 195–96, ch. 7.

45.   Leone Ebreo, *The Philosophy of Love (Dialoghi d'amore)*, trans. F. Friedeberg-Seeley and Jean H. Barnes (London: Soncino, 1937), 427; cited parenthetically in my text hereafter. Compare Leone, *Dialoghi d'amore*, ed. Santino Caramella (Bari: Laterza, 1929), 357–58.

46.   Besides emphasizing heavenly beauty, Ficino insists "what restores us to heaven is not knowledge of God but love." *Commentary on Plato's Symposium on Love (De amore)*, trans. Sears Jayne (Dallas, TX: Spring, 1985), 79 (IV.6). Cited parenthetically in my text hereafter.

47.   Compare also Guy Le Fèvre de la Boderie (1541–1598), on whom see Ellrodt, 114–15.

48.   Plotinus, *Enneads*, trans. A. H. Armstrong, I.6.8, VI.9.9; my emphasis. Cited parenthetically in my text hereafter. Unless stating otherwise, I cite all Greek and Roman texts from the Loeb series.

49.   Cf., e.g., Ellrodt, 118, 135, 139; Quitslund, *Supreme Fiction*, 97, 195–96, ch. 7; commentary on Spenser's *Hymnes* in *Shorter Poems*; Allen, "Ficino," in *SE*, 305–07.

50.   Ficino, Volume I of *Letters*, trans. various (London: Shepheard—Walwyn, 1975), Book I, Letters 4, 116.

51.   Pico, *Commentary on a Canzone of Beniveni*, trans. Sears Jayne (New York: Lang, 1984), Book II, ch. 16. Relative to Ficino's *De amore*, Pico's *Commento* was rare, and the Platonism of Spenser's Belgard allegory appears far closer to Ficino's thought.

52.   La Primaudaye, *The French Academie*, trans. T. Bowes, R. Dolman, W. P. (London, 1618), STC 15241, 480. Cited parenthetically in my text hereafter. Cp. Guy le Fèvre de la Boderie, as in Ellrodt, 114–15.

53.   Wind, ch. 3, Appendix 2. Cf. David W. Burchmore, "Triamond, Agape, and the Fates: Neoplatonic Cosmology in Spenser's Legend of Friendship," *Spenser Studies* V (1985): 45–64.

54.   Quoting Bellamy, "Colin and Orphic Interpretation: Reading Neoplatonically on Spenser's Acidale," *Comparative Literature Studies* 27.3 (1990): 172–92. See, e.g., Allen, "Ficino," in *SE*; Nohrnberg, 461–69, 699–700; Geller: 267–77; Tonkin, 228–29, 232–33, 235–36, 257–62, 275–77.

55.   Allen, "Ficino," in *SE*, 306.

56.   Alastair Fowler, "Emanations of Glory: Neoplatonic Order in Spenser's *Faerie Queene*," in *A Theatre for Spenserians*, eds. Judith M. Kennedy and James A. Reither (Toronto: University of Toronto Press, 1973), 53–82, and *Spenser and the Numbers*

of Time (London: Routledge, 1964), Index, s.v. "Triad"; Gerald Snare, "The Poetics of Vision: Patterns of Grace and Courtesy in *The Faerie Queene* VI," *Renaissance Papers* (1974): 1–8, and "Spenser's Fourth Grace," *Journal of the Warburg and Courtauld Institutes* 34 (1971): 350–55.

57. Cf. Roberta Cornelius, *The Figurative Castle* (Bryn Mawr, PA: Bryn Mawr College Press, 1930); Howard Rollin Patch, *The Other World* (1950; rpt. New York: Octagon, 1970), Index, s.v. "Castle."

58. A fortress of "Perfect Beauty," associated partly with divine Beauty and paradise, appears in the Platonizing English court entertainment *The Four Foster Children of Desire* presented in 1581. Cf. *Entertainments for Elizabeth I*, ed. Jean Wilson (Woodbridge, UK: Brewer, 1980), 61–85.

59. Compare, e.g., Francesco Patrizi, *The Philosophy of Love*, trans. Daniela Pastina and John W. Crayton (Philadelphia, PA.: Xlibris, 2003), 59–60.

60. Since the first *OED* example of "belgard" in English is Spenserian, and the other examples are all from Spenserian poets, Spenser may well have introduced "belgard" into English, as a "Spenserism." In any case, in his poetry it constitutes a technical term informed by Platonic concepts, as I subsequently explain. That is one reason (among many) why "Belgard" as a place-name in Spenser's usage does not merely reiterate the former fashion for giving similar names to estates or mansions.

61. Cf. *Timaeus*, 44B-46C; Ficino, *De amore*, VII.4; Conti, *Mythologies: A Select Translation*, trans. Anthony DiMatteo (New York: Garland, 1994), 234.

62. Cf. Hooker, *Laws*, in *Works*, ed. John Keble, 7th rev. ed., 3 vols. (Oxford: Clarendon, 1888), 1.4.1 (1: 212–213). Cited parenthetically in my text hereafter.

63. Compare, e.g., Ficino, *De amore*, II.2.

64. Cf. *Variorum*, 260–62. Boiardo, *Orlando innamorato*, in Vol. 1, Part 2, of his *Opere*, ed. Antonia Tissoni Benvenuti and Cristina Montagnani, 2 vols. (Milan: Ricciardi, 1999), 2.27.28–29. Tasso, *Rinaldo*, ed. Michael Sherberg (Ravenna: Longo, 1990), xi.89–90.

65. E.g., Fidelia's "Christall face," I.x.12. Referring to Christ, Spenser says "in thy brest his blessed image beare" (*HHL*, line 259): indeed where Pastorella, the "Lady whom high God did saue," has her "christall" mark (VI.xii.7,17).

66. On rose symbolism, cf. Don Cameron Allen, *Image and Meaning: Metaphoric Traditions in Renaissance Poetry*, rev. ed. (Baltimore: Johns Hopkins University Press, 1968), ch. 6.

67. Cf. Wilson, s.v. "new name," 397–98, 771–72. The elect who stand with the Lamb in Revelation 14 have "his Father's Name writen in their forheads" (Rev. 14:1), "the mark of their election" (Geneva gloss).

68. Cf. Aquinas, Vol. 5 of *Catena Aurea*, trans. Thomas Dudley Ryder (Oxford, 1874), 528. Also Wailes, 234–36.

69. On the allegory of Pastorella's parents' biography, see my appendix, "The Allegorism of Pastorella's Enigmatic Origin (VI.xii.4–6)."

70. *OED*, 2nd ed., s.v. "cast," v. VII 42, III 20b; "throe," sb. 1a, 1b.

71. Though not "the nurse and goddess of childbirth" as Hamilton claims (*Faerie Queene*, 685*n*), a nymph named Melissa nurtured infant Zeus when his devouring father Cronus threatened him, and she fed him honey, or bees did. Spenser's fable of Pastorella might thus suggest the fostering of a divinely originated nature. In some

versions, Melissa herself became a bee, as Charles Estienne reports in his dictionary of proper names; or, as Lactantius observes, "Melissa was appointed . . . the first priestess of the Great Mother," Rhea or Cybele and their analogues, "which is why those in charge of the Great Mother cult are still called Melissas." Estienne, *Dictionarium historicum, geographicum, poeticum* (Geneva: J. Stoer, 1596), s.v. "Melissa"; Lactantius, *Divine Institutes*, trans. Sister Mary Francis McDonald (Washington, DC: Catholic University of America Press, 1964), I.22 (91). Compare, e.g., Virgil, *Georgics*, 4.149–52, 219–21; Columella, *Res rustica*, 9.11.2–3; Diodorus Siculus, 5.70.1–5. Porphyry says the priestesses of Demeter or Ceres were called *Melissae* or bee women, and some have claimed Spenser's "Melissa" may have such resonance (cf. Blitch). But Porphyry also uses bees to image the progress of souls, who were called "bees," he says. Porphyry, *On the Cave of the Nymphs*, trans. Robert Lamberton (Barrytown, NY: Station Hill, 1983), 30–32 (sections 16–19).

72. The Elizabethan Book of Common Prayer, e.g., asks God to "sende downe" "thy grace," and "powre . . . the continuall dewe of thy blessing" (London, 1573), STC 16303, sig. B4ᵇ. Cited parenthetically in my text hereafter, as BCP. Compare Gen. 27:28, 39; Ps. 133.3: Hos. 14.5. Cf., e.g., John Fisher, *The English Works*, ed. John E. B. Mayor (London: EETS, 1876), 176; Filippo Picinelli, *Mondo simbolico* (Venice: Paolo Baglioni, 1678), 2.11 ("Rugiada").

73. Compare Pastorella's tearful bedewings with biblical anointing, symbolizing divine favour, healing, or compassion, as in, e.g., 2 Cor. 1:21, Ps. 45:7; and with Arthur's ointment, I.ix.19, IV.viii.20.

74. Cf. Kenneth Borris, "Fortune, Occasion, and the Allegory of the Quest in Book Six of *The Faerie Queene*," *Spenser Studies* VII (1987): 123–45.

75. Ariosto, *Orlando furioso*, in *Opere*, ed. Giuliano Innamorati (Bologna: Zanichelli, 1967), vii.39. Cited parenthetically in my text hereafter.

76. "Melissa. A skillful bee, that is, from 'taking care' (Melissa. Apis callida scilicet, ἀπὸ τοῦ μέλειν à curando)." Conti, "Nominum . . . Explicatio," in his *Mythologiae* (Venice: Comin da Trino, 1567), s.v. "Melissa" (337).

77. Dolce, "Argomento" prefacing Canto vii, in Ariosto, *Orlando furioso* (Venice: Domenico & Gio. Battista Guerra fratelli, 1570).

78. Fornari, *La spositione sopra l'Orlando furioso di Ludovico Ariosto*, 2 vols. (Florence: Torrentino, 1549), 2:117–18. Compare 2:196: "La diligentia si vide nell' intercedere, che fe Melissa, laqual suona cura nel propria nome." Cited parenthetically in my text hereafter. Likewise associating Melissa with "care," Sir John Harington's translation says she "took no little care" of Ruggiero, and Bradamante commends him to Melissa's "care." Harington, trans., *Orlando Furioso*, by Ludovico Ariosto, ed. Robert McNulty (Oxford: Clarendon, 1972), vii.38, 43.

79. Cf. Anonymous, in Richard B. Zacha, trans., "The Allegories to the 1542 *Orlando furioso*," *Allegorica*, 1 (1976): 170–71. Similarly Thomaso Porcacchi, "Allegorie" for Canto vii, in Ariosto *Orlando furioso* (Venice: Domenico & Gio. Battista Guerra fratelli, 1570); Clemente Valvassori, "Allegorie" for Cantos iii, vii, and viii, in Ariosto, *Orlando furioso* (Venice: per Gio. Andrea Valvassori, 1567); Gioseffo Bonomone, "Allegoria" in Ariosto, *Orlando furioso* (Venice: Francesco de Franceschi e compagni, 1584), sig. ★★7ᵃ; Fornari 2:117, 121. Orazio Toscanella differently relates Melissa to reason or continence, and Giuseppe Horologgio to prudence. Toscanella,

"Allegoria" prefacing comment on Canto vii, in his *Bellezze del Furioso* (Venice: P. de i Franceschi, 1574), 77, 86. Horologgio, "Allegorie" prefacing Cantos vii and viii, in Ariosto, *Orlando furioso* (Venice: per Gio. Varisco, 1566).

80. Harington, "A Briefe and Summarie Allegorie of *Orlando Furioso*," in Ariosto, *Orlando*, ed. McNulty, 560. Cp. Bonomone above.

81. Sidney, *A Defence of Poetry*, in his *Miscellaneous Prose*, eds. Katherine Duncan-Jones and Jan van Dorsten (Oxford: Clarendon, 1973), 80–81. Cited parenthetically in my text hereafter. On "μέλισσά" and "poet," cf. Plato, *Ion*, 534A-C; Hesiod, *Theogony*, 74–115; Callimachus, *Hymn to Apollo*, 105–13; Horace, *Odes*, 4.2.27–32; Lucretius, *De rerum natura*, 3.1–13; Varro, *Res rusticae*, 3.16.17. Cf. Frederick Williams, *Callimachus, "Hymn to Apollo": A Commentary* (Oxford: Clarendon, 1978), 93.

82. Harington, 513. Cf. Plutarch, *How a Man May Become Aware of His Progress in Virtue*, 79C-D. Similarly his *How the Young Man Should Study Poetry*, 32E-F, and St. Basil, *To Young Men, on How They Might Derive Profit from Pagan Literature*, 4.7–10. Compare Arthur Golding, "Preface to the Reader," in *Ovid's "Metamorphoses*," ed. Madeleine Forey, trans. Golding (Baltimore: Johns Hopkins University Press, 2001), 27; Ficino, *Letters*, 4.22; Hadrianus Junius, *Emblemata* (Antwerp, 1565), Emblem 33; Joachim Camerarius, *Symbolorum et Emblematum*, 4 vols. (Nurnberg, 1590–1604), I, Emblem 67, III, Emblems 91, 92; Geoffrey Whitney, *A Choice of Emblemes* (Leiden, 1586), 51.

83. Cf. Barbara Kiefer Lewalski, *Protestant Poetics and the Seventeenth-Century Religious Lyric* (Princeton: Princeton University Press, 1979), 16–18.

84. Cf. Borris, "Allegory of the Quest in Book Six": 135–36. However, the Beast relates much more to Elizabethan apocalypticism than I then realized (1987), prior to my research for *Poetics of Prophecy* (1991).

85. Redcross slays the Dragon, but Archimago escapes on the old serpent's model (I.xii.36, II.i.1). Guyon destroys the Bower and binds Acrasia, but Grill remains incorrigible, symbolizing Acrasia's continuing unruliness (II.xii.86–87). Britomart dispels Busyrane's sorceries, but her future husband Artegall, the object of her personal quest of Chastity, is to die young, assassinated (III.iii.28). Artegall frees Irena from Grantorto, but cannot complete that work (V.xii.27).

86. Cf. Borris, *Allegory and Epic*, 179–80.

87. Cf. H. S. Bennett, *English Books and Readers, 1558 to 1603* (Cambridge: Cambridge University Press, 1965), 5–10, 29; *English Books and Readers, 1475 to 1557* (Cambridge: Cambridge University Press, 1952), 50–51; Belt: 109–111.

88. Cf. Borris, *Poetics of Prophecy*, 37, 43–47.

89. Jon Whitman, *Allegory: The Dynamics of an Ancient and Medieval Technique* (Oxford: Clarendon, 1987), Appendix I.

90. The poet's comment is not to be taken literally, for he would in that case have deleted the sharp rebuke of a mighty peer with which he opens the 1596 installment: "Such ones ill iudge of loue, that cannot loue," with "frosen hearts" (IV.pr.1–2).

91. Cf. Leone, 112–14; Conti, *Mythologies*, 322; Harington, "Preface," in Ariosto's *Orlando*, 5–6; Fraunce, *The Third Part of the Countesse of Pembrokes Yuychurch*, ed. Gerald Snare (Northridge: California State University Press, 1975), 8–9.

92. Cf., e.g., Golding, 27. Because Spenser recognizes some readers are incorrigible when concluding Book VI, Philmus claims he must thus reject the formerly standard

"Sidneian" type of morally instrumental, pedagogical literary theory there (511–17). But sixteenth-century poetics commonly assumed, like Golding, that some would read "in malo," and yet others could be influenced otherwise. Sidney too would have taken that for granted, just as there are incorrigible characters in his *Arcadias*, such as Cecropia.

93.   Neuse, "Pastorella," in *SE*, 533.

94.   Cf. Ficino, citing Augustine, *De amore*, IV.2 (72–73); Conti, *Mythologies* (trans. DiMatteo), 50.

95.   Neuse, "Pastorella," in *SE*, 533.

96.   Cf. Borris, *Allegory and Epic*, chs. 1, 3; Weinberg, Index, s.v. "Theology."

97.   Puttenham, *The Arte of English Poesie* (London: Richard Field, 1589), STC 20519, 156–57.

98.   Also, secondarily, a figurative model for the union of soul and flesh, as Anne Lake Prescott advises me.

99.   On the currency of these concerns in early modern philosophy and literature, cf. T. Anthony Perry, *Erotic Spirituality: The Integrative Tradition from Leone Ebreo to John Donne* (University, AL: University of Alabama Press, 1980), e.g., 16, 18, 28, 45–46.

100.   See Hope Traver, *The Four Daughters of God* (Bryn Mawr, PA: Bryn Mawr College Press, 1907).

101.   Cf., e.g., Pseudo-Dionysius, *The Mystical Theology*, ch. 3, in his *Divine Names and Mystical Theology*, trans. John D. Jones (Milwaukee, WI: Marquette University Press, 1980), 217.

102.   Cf. Susanne L. Wofford, "*The Faerie Queene*, Books I–III," in *The Cambridge Companion to Spenser*, ed. Andrew Hadfield (Cambridge: Cambridge University Press, 2001), 109–12; Jeffrey P. Fruen, " 'True Glorious Type': The Place of Gloriana in *The Faerie Queene*," *Spenser Studies* VII (1987): 147–73.

103.   Calvin, *Institution*, 2.16.1–4 (131–33), trans. Norton. Cf. Augustine, *Tractates on the Gospel of John 55–111*, trans. John W. Rettig (Washington, DC: Catholic University of America Press, 1994), 110.6.

104.   An introductory epic simile compares the narrator's progress to a ship's (VI.xii.1), but that is a comparative excursus not part of Pastorella's story itself.

105.   Compare II.x.63, IV.xi.36. See, e.g., William Camden, *Britain*, trans. Philemon Holland (London, 1637), 30. The Picts were commonly considered descendents of the Scythians, former types of barbarity.

106.   "The fortunate islands and Elysian fields in the common opinion of nearly all the major authors of antiquity were in that region of the British isles between western Britain and Thule." Conti, *Mythologies*, 178, trans. DiMatteo. Cf. Josephine Waters Bennett, "Britain Among the Fortunate Isles," *Studies in Philology* 53 (1956): 114–40.

107.   Because the ancient Picts painted or tattooed their bodies. Cf., e.g., William Camden, *Remains Concerning Britain*, ed. R. D. Dunn (Toronto: University of Toronto Press, 1984), 14; Thomas Cooper, *Thesaurus linguae Romanae et Britannicae* (London, 1565), STC 5686, s. v. "pingo," "pictus."

108.   Compare, e.g., Calvin, *Institution*, 2.16.2.

109. Wilson, s.v. "children of wrath," 681. Similarly Calvin, *Institution*, 2.16.3: "wee all haue in vs that, which is woorthie of the hatred of God" and "deserueth Gods indignation," so that "we haue purchased death to our selues" (trans. Norton). 110. *Paradise Lost*, ed. Alastair Fowler, 2nd ed. (London: Longman, 1998), III.96–97.

MATTHEW WOODCOCK

Spenser and Olaus Magnus: A Reassessment

At several points in *A View of the Present State of Ireland* Spenser cites a work by the Swedish Catholic prelate Olaus Magnus, the *Historia de gentibus septentrionalibus* or "Description of the Northern Peoples" (Rome, 1555). Olaus's *Historia* rarely features in discussion of Spenser's use of sources, though it was clearly one of a number of texts he uses when constructing his depiction of Irish customs and tracing their origins in Scythian culture. This essay introduces Olaus's life and work, and its relevance to Spenser, before reassessing earlier attempts at tracing his influence in *The Faerie Queene*. Focus then turns to the specific citations of the *Historia* made in the *View* and to the kind of text that Spenser believes he draws upon, in particular how he appears to read or remember Olaus's work as offering a form of cultural or ethnological history of the Scythians. Understanding how Spenser read Olaus's work—and possibly that of his brother Johannes Magnus—is thus fundamental to our comprehension of how he uses the Scythians to characterize Irish barbarity.

*W*HILE SURVEYING SPENSER'S IMITATIONS of chivalric romance the eighteenth-century commentator Thomas Warton makes the following observation on studying the poet's sources:

We feel a sort of malicious triumph in detecting the latent and obscure source from whence an original author has drawn some celebrated description: yet this, it must be granted, soon gives way to the rapture that naturally results from contemplating the chemical energy of true genius, which can produce so noble a transmutation; and whose virtues are not less efficacious and vivifying in their nature than those of the miraculous water here displayed by Spenser.[1]

Editors and critics ever since have no doubt experienced both triumph and rapture in attempting to place Spenser in context by tracing the potentially vast range of things that he could have read and used, and exploring what this reveals both about his methods of composition and his ideological background. This essay introduces and examines one work that Spenser explicitly signals that he has read, a curious, encyclopaedic text called the *Historia de gentibus septentrionalibus*, written by the sixteenth-century Swedish Catholic prelate Olaus Magnus and published by the author in Rome in 1555.[2] The title is usually translated as *A Description of the Northern Peoples*, for the text is certainly not limited to Scandinavian history and encompasses geography, natural history, folklore, ethnography, religion, commerce and the arts of war. The *Historia* is rarely mentioned in the standard authorities on Spenser's sources, despite the fact that it is cited repeatedly in Spenser's treatise *A View of the Present State of Ireland*.[3] For this reason—and because the context and form of the *Historia* have great bearing upon how Spenser read the text—I shall briefly introduce Olaus and his book, together with the background to its production and reception, before exploring how Spenser uses it in his work. Initially I will consider some of the points in Spenser's poetry where we might experience moments akin to Warton's sense of "triumph" in tracing allusions to Olaus, then move on to examine in more detail Spenser's explicit citations of and borrowings from Olaus in the *View*. This essay is also interested in Spenser's reading practices and the kind of text he thought he was reading when using the *Historia*, and it concludes by arguing that for all the immediate differences in purpose and context between the *Historia* and the *View*, both works present a practical employment of ethnography as part of their overall argument.

Olaus Magnus was born in Linköping, Sweden in 1490 and was educated at home and then at German universities until 1517, when he was appointed as a canon at Uppsala. In 1518 he was sent as a sub-collector for the papal legate to raise money for the papacy in the far north of Sweden, an experience which furnished him with much of the firsthand evidence he cites when outlining the customs and superstitions of the Lapps. Olaus was in Stockholm by 1520, and from this point onwards his life and career, together with that of his older brother Johannes, would forever be shaped by a number of momentous events in the history of the Swedish church and nation. Ever since the inter-Nordic Kalmar Union in 1397 there had been a form of joint sovereignty among Sweden, Denmark, and Norway, an uneasy power balance in which Sweden came under increasing political control from Denmark and periodically erupted into a series of revolutions during the fifteenth century. By the early sixteenth century the Danish king Christian II had largely succeeded in bringing the country to heel, and after a bloody struggle was crowned king of Sweden in 1520. Soon after, Christian consolidated his position by dispatching any remaining supporters of Swedish separatism during the so-called Stockholm "bloodbath." Christian's rule was short-lived and the rebellion, headed by Gustav Eriksson Vasa, led to the eventual defeat of Danish loyalists in 1523 and to Gustav's election as king the same year. Both to manage the debts incurred during his "liberation" campaigns and to consolidate the crown's existing position, Gustav soon looked to the church as a source of revenue. Persuaded by the political expedience of Lutheran arguments regarding royal supremacy and the equation of church property with national property, Gustav initiated a series of ecclesiastical reforms culminating in the Västerås settlement of 1527 that confiscated all church tithes, placed all diocesan property under royal control and gave the nobility administration of monastic estates.[4] The received narrative of Swedish independence thus closely associates liberation from Danish tyranny with the establishment of the Lutheran church in Sweden.

In the year of Gustav's election, Olaus left for Rome to confirm the appointment of his brother Johannes as Archbishop of Uppsala; he was never to return again to Sweden. During the 1520s and 30s the Magnus brothers traveled widely in Europe, spending a significant amount of time in Gdansk, with Olaus serving as secretary to Johannes. In 1529 Gustav invited the brothers to return to Sweden, though their objection to the Västerås settlement and the Reformation in Sweden made such a move untenable. For refusing to return, from 1530 their income was cut off and their property confiscated. From 1538 to 1540 the brothers were based in Venice, where in 1539 Olaus published his *Carta Marina*, a great map of Scandinavia, Iceland, and the Baltic regions, the commentary for which ultimately formed the basis for the *Historia*.[5] In 1541 the brothers moved to Rome, where Olaus continued work on the *Historia* and, on Johannes's death in 1544, succeeded his brother as archbishop. Establishing a press in the hospice of St. Bridget in Rome, Olaus edited and produced several of his brother's works and published his own *Historia* two years before his death in 1557.

It is important to place the Magnus brothers' publications into a Counter-Reformation context. Olaus had attended the Tridentine Council from 1545–52, and had earlier petitioned Pope Paul III not only to condemn Gustav's religious reforms but to go as far as to support an armed intervention in Sweden to restore the country to the Catholic faith.[6] The Magnuses' works, including the *Historia*, were part of a concerted political and textual project aimed at fostering international interest in the Northern nations and using the Swedes' glorious origins and history as an exemplary model with which contemporary moral back-sliding at home could be redressed. Ethnic self-consciousness was persistently presented as the key to reclaiming Sweden for the Catholic Church. A central preoccupation in the Magnuses' reformist project was the idea that the Swedes were directly descended from the ancient Goths and that this ennobling heritage should form the basis of the country's future greatness.[7] Such claims were backed by the production of simple etymological evidence, as Olaus's most recent editor and translator explains: "The tribal name of the 'Götar,' the people of the provinces of Västergötland and Östergötland, was regularly latinized as 'Gothi,' and their identity with the famous Goths, who had finally broken Rome and succeeded to her empire, was self-evident."[8] Incorporating earlier myths and historical accounts of the ancient Goths, Johannes Magnus in his 1554 *Historia de omnibus Gothorum Sveonumque regibus (History of the Gothic and Swedish Kings)* sought to demonstrate the Swedes' glorious past by reconstructing a line of royal descent that stretched from Magog, son of Japhet and grandson of Noah, via two hundred and thirty kings down to Gustav Vasa. By professing to reveal the enlightened history of the Goths Johannes began to rehabilitate myths of Northern tribal barbarity that were used by Italian humanists to constitute the ideal of Roman civility.[9] Johannes's work offered his countrymen a corrective exemplar; as he writes, "I saw that my fatherland's noble and resplendent magnates had thoroughly forgotten the old Goths' extraordinary uprightness, yes, had since fallen away from the virtues of their forefathers to what was less honorable and even into manifest vice."[10]

Johannes's mythical genealogy of the Goths and Swedes is taken up in Olaus's *Historia*, where classical and medieval sources on the

Goths are frequently fused with accounts of contemporary Swedish customs. Olaus repeatedly identifies traces of the Goths in the present-day Northern nations, and he muses upon ancient monuments, standing stones, and Gothic inscriptions (*Historia*, 1:29–31). A document found in Perugia and given to Johannes in 1538, in which runic script sets out Gothic laws akin to those practiced in contemporary Gotland, is excitedly cited as proof of continuity between past and present (*Historia*, 14:25). However, the *ubi sunt* laments as he recalls the ruins of the Gothic palaces at Årnäs and Skara are a poignant reminder of the degenerate state in which the country now lay under Gustav Vasa and the Lutheran church (*Historia*, 2:21). In book sixteen of the *Historia*, when Olaus is at his most scathing toward the present state of the Swedish church and nation, he uses evocation of the past as a means to admonish his contemporaries: "In particular the princes of the northern lands will need to feel no less contrition because, contemptuous of their ancestors' peaceable instructions and pious customs, they have allowed teachers of error to come in and gratify their ears" (*Historia*, 16:32).

The early part of Johannes's *Historia*, detailing the first descendents of Magog, was translated into English and incorporated into George North's *Description of Swedland, Gotland, and Finland*, published in 1561, a copy of which was owned and annotated by Spenser's friend Gabriel Harvey.[11] In the same year, when Gustav Vasa's son Erik XIV was wooing Elizabeth I, copies of both Olaus's and Johannes's histories were sent to England to Lord Burghley in an attempt to stress the antiquity of the Vasa line and assert the cultural heritage of Sweden. In so doing, Erik might thus demonstrate his worthiness as a suitor of a great royal house. The suit, of course, failed, but Erik's sister Cecilia visited Elizabeth in 1565, and on departing the following year she left behind Helena Snakenborg as the beloved companion of William Parr, Marquess of Northampton. Helena eventually married Parr in May 1571, though the marriage was short-lived, as the marquess died in October the same year. Helena's second husband was Sir Thomas Gorges, through whom she becomes the dedicatee of Spenser's elegy to her sister-in-law in the pastoral *Daphnaïda*.[12] Helena is also celebrated in *Colin Clouts Come Home Againe* in the figure of Mansilia.[13]

The conscious construction of an ennobling lineage or a myth of origin is a commonplace both of medieval and early modern panegyric technique, and the Magnuses' collective project offers a further analogue to those works of Italian, French, and Portuguese national epic that deploy the genealogy topos and contrive a mythical heritage for their ruling dynasty.[14] The Gothic genealogy promoted by the

Magnus brothers is, of course, not unlike Spenser's own interest in mythical history. Despite his scepticism toward such practices in one manuscript of the *View*, the construction of a mythical genealogy for the Tudors that stretched back to Arthurian Britain and beyond was a key building block both within Spenser's epic project and in his argument concerning English dominion in Ireland.[15] The Magnuses and subsequent Swedish historiographers did for the Goths what Tudor mythographers had long been doing for the Britons. The Goths' descent from Noah's line and their progressive history of increasing ennoblement actually bears a greater structural resemblance to the kinds of universal history imitated in Spenser's fairy chronicle "*Antiquitee of Faery* lond" (II.x.70–76) than it does to episodes chronicling British history. The interweaving of figures from Biblical, classical and native mythology that Spenser would have found in universal histories, such as that which John Bale appends to his *Scriptorum Illustrium maioris Brytanniae catalogus* (1557), certainly appears to have been the most likely source for the "*Antiquitee*."[16] It should be noted that Spenser does not choose to use Olaus as a source of Gothic history nor to adopt the ennobling image of the Goths at those points where they are mentioned in the *View*, compared to a "mountaine floudd," or in "The Ruines of Rome," described as "th'earths new Giant brood."[17] Spenser's perception of the Goths as barbarous is entirely consonant with how he read Olaus's *Historia* as a whole.

So exactly what kind of text is the *Historia*? Olaus says in the dedication that he writes in response to a request for further knowledge about the Northern nations voiced by a fellow prelate, Adolf von Schaumberg, while at the Council of Trent:

> you enquired of me at one point about the lands of the North: what huge and amazing variety of objects and peoples lay there, what wondrous features unknown to foreign nations; how the men and innumerable creatures in the North, numbed by the constant merciless cold, managed to withstand the harshness of the elements and the cruelty of the climate they have to live with; from what resources life was sustained, and in what way the frozen earth produced anything to favour them.
>
> (*Historia*, Dedication)

In reality, work began on the *Historia* from the early 1540s, but Olaus's list of topics offers a succinct summary of matters covered and speaks crucially of his desire to address the widespread lack of

Europe, the North was particularly associated with paganism and superstition and indeed fashioned as the abode of Satan himself, a connection still exploited (albeit quite subtly) in Spenser's depiction of Archimago (II.iii.19, lines 1–5) and in James VI's Lowlander characterization of Highland barbarity in his treatise *Daemonologie* (1597).[21] Olaus in his preface challenges the biblical authority for the infernal nature of the North (Jeremiah 1:14, "Out of the north an evil shall break forth") by encouraging us to consider an alternate sentence, "Out of the north cometh golden splendour" from Job 37:22. Olaus thus introduces a central preoccupation of his text: the sense of potential possessed by the Northern nations and the desirability of regeneration—specifically spiritual regeneration—in those lands.[22] Olaus devotes the whole of book three to the discovery, confrontation, and correction of superstitions and errors concerning northern *mirabilia*. However, his approach throughout the *Historia* is to excite *admiratio* by making intriguing references to the many different ways in which the North might be considered "otherworldly" and through, as Kurt Johannesson writes, "a clever alternation between what was frightening and wonderful, what was well known and what had never before been observed or experienced."[23] The *Historia*'s concluding sentiment is that one should not denounce that which is new and has previously been undiscovered (*Historia*, 22:22), echoing Spenser's preemptive response to skeptical readers found in the Proem to Book II of *The Faerie Queene*. Olaus's book was designed as an eclectic, though purposive, work of practical ethnography, but that did not stop it from being used as a compendium of Scandinavian folklore. Ironically, the *Historia* soon became a sourcebook reaffirming and reviving interest in myths of the wondrous North.[24] Septentrionalism, like orientalism, it would appear, is hard to dislodge.

Following its initial printing at Rome in 1555, the *Historia* went through six editions by 1669 and was translated into Italian (1565) and German (1567). It was also revised in a shorter, user-friendly edition by Cornelius Scribonius and published at Antwerp in 1558. The "epitome" edition omitted most of Olaus's use of classical authorities and removed material deemed irrelevant to the discussion of northern matters, and was itself translated into French (1560–61), Italian (1561), Dutch (1562) and English (1658).[25] The *Historia* was widely read and frequently drawn upon within literary evocations of northern mythology in works by Torquato Tasso, Thomas Nashe, John Milton, and Robert Burton.[26]

Spenser cites Olaus directly in the *View* when discussing Irish customs and myths of origin, and in doing so was certainly one of the first writers in English actively to incorporate elements of the *Historia* into their own work.[27] He may well have used Harvey's heavily annotated copy, acquired in 1578.[28] As several critics have already observed, Spenser appears to have used Olaus while writing *The Faerie Queene*, particularly for matters relating to the monstrous and the martial. The list of sea-monsters Guyon encounters on the voyage to the Bower of Bliss (II.xii.22–25) includes several creatures identified and illustrated by Olaus in his fanciful treatment of northern sea-monsters (*Historia*, 21:14)—the Ziffius ("xiphia" in Olaus) and Monoceroses ("unicorn-fish").[29] (Milton also makes use of this book of the *Historia* on several occasions for his depiction of Hell.[30]) Michael West suggests that Olaus's chapters (and accompanying woodcuts) on the swimming of armored infantrymen (*Historia*, 10:25–29) lie behind Artegall's ability to swim while wearing full armor following his drop from Pollente's bridge in V.ii.16:

> For Artegall in swimming skilfull was,
> And durst the depth of any water sownd.
> So ought each Knight, that vse of perill has,
> In swimming be expert through waters force to pas.[31]

Like Pollente's courser (V.ii.13), the horses of the Götar were equally able to swim and fight in water (*Historia*, 10:23). Similar use of tactical marvels found in Olaus is evident in the Souldan episode in V.viii.28–43, where Arthur engages in an allegorical iteration of the English defeat of the Spanish Armada. Here the Souldan's "embatteld cart" or chariot, armed with "yron wheeles and hookes," evokes the scythed chariots and armored battle-wagons of the Goths and Swedes (*Historia*, 9:2–3, 12).[32] As Olaus suggests, the most vulnerable point of such machines is the horses and Arthur exploits this weakness ultimately to defeat the Souldan (V.viii.37–38). Finally, the weapon wielded by Grantorto in his battle with Artegall, "an huge Poleaxe . . . , / Whose steale was yron studded, but not long" (V.xii.14), can be found at several points among descriptions of Swedish and Gothic weaponry in Olaus's *Historia*: "the natives carry poles enhanced with four-fold barbs of iron (called polyxor in the vernacular) with which they drag a man down from his steed" (*Historia*, 7:14).[33] Thomas Herron interprets Spenser's use of Olaus in the descriptions of Grantorto and the Souldan as part of coherent strategy to identify both characters with images of specifically Irish villainy,

to "Rodoricke" is not to be found in Olaus Magnus. There are two ways round this misattribution, neither of which are pursued satisfactorily by modern editors. The first is to identify "Rodoricke" with the Scythian King Roderick who led the Picts to Britain and Ireland, the story of whom could be found in the work of Geoffrey of Monmouth, Edmund Campion, and Raphael Holinshed.[40] Roderick sought refuge for his people among the Irish and, when refused, sailed to Scotland where he fought against and was slain by King Marius. Marius nevertheless allowed Roderick's followers to settle in the Scots borders. Alternatively, the direction to Olaus Magnus for this passage of the *View* could actually be a misattributed allusion to Johannes Magnus's *Historia de omnibus Gothorum Sveonumque regibus.* Rodorick ("Rodericus") is the twenty-eighth king of the Goths identified and described by Johannes.[41] Spenser's reference may be based on the association between the Goths and Swedes and the Scythians made in the early parts of Johannes's *Historia*, which clearly informs subsequent citations of Olaus's *Historia* in the *View*, as discussed below. Drawing on the standard early authorities on Gothic history, Cassiodorus, Jordanes, the Babylonian "history" of pseudo-Berosus, and the more recent scholarship of Albert Krantz, Johannes asserts that following the deluge Noah settled in the area we now call Finland and were known as Scythians.[42] From here Noah's progeny through Magog spread to Scandinavia, where they became known as the Goths or Getae (the name derived in some sources from Magog's son Gog or Gother), and they eventually ranged across the whole of central and eastern Europe.[43] According to Johannes there is thus a Scythian and Gothic ancestry to all of the various early nations, such as the Parthians, Cimmerians, and Dacians, that the northern hordes conquered.[44] There is little sense of a consistent distinction made between Scythian and Goth in Johannes's *Historia*, but he repeatedly stresses that the Scythians are the most ancient of nations: "Scythica gens antiquissima."[45]

The key issue in Irenius's "rippinge vp of Ancestries" is the supposed Scythian origins of Irish culture. Contrary to the contrivances of Johannes and his sources, the Scythians were a nomadic people situated in a broad region stretching from the Danube to the Chinese borders who flourished from the eighth to the fourth centuries B.C.[46] For classical authorities the Scythians represented the epitome of barbarity, the antithesis of the Athenian *polis* that was employed as part of a binary fashioning process in order to constitute Athenian civility. Book 4 of Herodotus's *Histories* establishes the principal features of the Scythian model of barbarity, outlining their nomadic lifestyle, savage practices in battle, cruelty toward the slain, and the extreme cold climate of their lands.[47] St. Paul also associates the Scythians with barbarism in Colossians 3:11. The savage Scythian stereotype was utilized repeatedly within the classical and medieval tradition of encyclopedists and epitomisers, largely without question or qualification and, as is common in much early anthropological and ethnological thought, usually with little sensitivity to temporal and spatial specificity.[48] One of the principal conduits for the Herodotan Scythian stereotype for Spenser's period was Joannes Boemus's *Omnium Gentium Mores, Leges, et Ritus* (1520), a collection of manners and customs of different ethnic groups, which again made little suggestion of any time having elapsed between Herodotus's observations and the sixteenth century.[49] Spenser cites Boemus on several occasions, sometimes in conjunction with Olaus, and for the ethnological tradition with which he works in the *View*, the Scythian remains the epitome of barbarity and is represented as such by many of the authorities cited in his treatise.[50]

Spenser is as dedicated to demonstrating the Scythian roots of perceived Irish barbarity as he is to asserting (and constructing) British claims to Ireland. As Andrew Hadfield notes, both of the authorities used by Spenser as evidence for ancient claims that Ireland was British—Diodorus Sicilius and Strabo—also made explicit connections between the Irish and Scythians.[51] Giraldus Cambrensis develops this association in his seminal treatment of Irish origins and customs that forms the basis for similar claims elaborated in numerous Elizabethan treatises and histories including William Camden's *Britannia*.[52] The Scythian model shaped early modern colonizers' preconceptions of a barbaric society and, as Nicholas Canny writes, when the English came to Ireland they soon found features in Gaelic life to fit this model, misreading Irish Catholicism as pagan superstition in need of strict reform.[53] As in European responses to Amerindians, the culturally unfamiliar had to be fitted into an existing, established pattern in order to make sense of what was encountered.[54] As several critics observe, what distinguishes the *View* in particular from contemporary literature on reform in Ireland, is the way in which the ethnographic argument, and conception of the Irish as primitive when measured against the early Britons, provides justification for using force during the civilizing process that Spenser goes on to propose.[55] Thus, Spenser's argument proceeds, one kind of impediment to reform in Ireland are certain customs that derive from the Scythian ancestry, customs that may be compared to those presented in several specific authorities detailing practices and actions ascribed to the Scythians. Origins are used to introduce customs that in turn adduce

when describing the Irish broad swords and broad shields, particularly the wicker construction of the latter (*Prose*, 106). Both items are found among the extensive weaponry used by warriors of the northern nations, which he interprets as being Scythian (*Historia*, 8:23, 13:49 [swords]; 9:13–14 [shields]). There are also several points in the *View* where descriptions of Irish customs and characteristics resemble those practiced by Spenser's "Scythians," for example the excessive lamentation for the dead (*Prose*, 105), the drinking of blood (*Prose*, 108), and their lycanthropic abilities (*Prose*, 109).[61] Ultimately Spenser's use of Olaus is similar to that of his employment of George Buchanan. Following the etymological link of Scots and Scyths discussed above, Spenser draws on Buchanan's *History of Scotland* (1582) to provide extra information about Scythian practices, including the war-cry "Ferragh," broad-swords, and short bows, to support his case for Irish barbarity (*Prose*, 106). Again there is a selective construction of the Scythian here "by which," concludes Irenius, "it maye allmoste infallible be gathered togeather with other Circumstances that the Irishe are verye *Scottes* or *Scythes* originallye thoughe si thens intermingled with manye other nacions repayringe and ioyninge vnto them" (*Prose*, 107).

As I have attempted to demonstrate, Spenser's use of Olaus is founded upon a fundamental misconception of the *Historia* that may to some degree result from a misremembering following an initial reading. If Spenser used Harvey's copy of Olaus he could have done so at any point from 1578 onward, and there are occasions where—if he was not writing with the book beside him—memorial inaccuracies occur, as they do occasionally when Spenser cites Diodorus and Strabo.[62] Referring to Irish short bows and short, bearded arrows as "verye *Scythyan* as ye maye reade in the same *Olaus*" (*Prose*, 106) Spenser clearly recalls the numerous references made in the *Historia* to the northern nations' archery skills and equipment, though nowhere does one find the kind of specific details cited here.[63] Demonstrating that Spenser read or recalled the *Historia* to be a Scythian history may also explain why Spenser believes he has a much greater range of practices and examples that could be drawn upon to prove that "the Irishe are auncientlye reduced from the *Scythyans*" (*Prose*, 109). One can do little more than conjecture, based on the constitutive role that the Scythians play in the legends concerning Irish origins, that the *Historia* would also have supplied material for the promised work on the "Antiquities of Ireland" Eudoxus mentions at the *View*'s close.

It would, of course, be wrong to suggest that Spenser and Olaus are writing exactly the same kind of text. There are great differences in the purpose and structure of both authors' works and, again, we can only speculate on how Spenser would have reacted to Olaus's Counter-Reformation agenda. Similarities, however, can be drawn between the rather liminal positions in which both authors' writing are situated. They both have a particularly ambiguous conception of, and relationship to, where they consider "home"; both are instrumental in maintaining and reformulating enduring myths about their homelands, though do so from a distanced, seemingly exiled perspective.[64] In particular, both the *View* and the *Historia* articulate their authors' liminal situations through their preoccupation with various forms of degeneration. Commentators have long observed that Spenser's *View* distinguishes between the virtue and potential of the Irish landscape and the degenerate (and degenerative) condition of its indigenous culture.[65] At several points there are extended excurses where Irenius praises this "moste bewtifull and swete Countrie" (*Prose*, 62, 155) and the treatise's latter portion provides a detailed geopolitical account of the country's resources broken down by province.[66] As Patricia Coughlan writes, Spenser fashions the Irish landscape not as the original haunt of barbarity but a place degenerated from a state of order.[67] This sense of doubleness between land and people is reflected in *The Faerie Queene* in the presentation of Grantorto as the "great wrong" occupying Irena's kingdom. Myths of ancient British dominion in Ireland and the Scythian heritage of the present indigenous occupants thus function in concert to support New English proposals for reconquest. Degeneration is also a dominant theme in Olaus's *Historia*, though here it is the Lutherans who are to blame. They are cast as an occupying force within the country Olaus loves, the country he sees as a great, lost resource. Indeed, the Magnus brothers' whole project was designed to demonstrate how significant a province the Catholic Church had lost in Sweden and to formulate proposals for its reclamation.[68] The *Historia* provides innumerable examples of the natural and spiritual resources of the northern nations, in particular for the latter the virtuous Lapps who show huge potential for conversion to Christianity (*Historia*, 4:17–18), a task for which Olaus offers his services. Olaus represents Lutheranism as an incendiary force consuming the people, land, and king (*Historia*, 12:22). Lutherans are responsible for the growing state of licentiousness in the North, the mockery of tradition and ceremony, and the decline of charitable culture (*Historia*, 13:50; 14:5; 16:12). For Olaus, identification with the heroic tradition of Gothic and Swedish heroes offered a corrective to ongoing degeneracy, and he takes pains to form close associations between adherence to the

C. Judson, *The Life of Edmund Spenser* (Baltimore: Johns Hopkins University Press, 1945), 147, 152, reveals that there may have been very little contact between Helena and Spenser, and that the praise is prompted by the fact that Arthur Gorges was one of Raleigh's kinsmen. See also Ethel Seaton, *Literary Relations of England and Scandinavia in the Seventeenth Century* (Oxford: Clarendon Press, 1935), 60–62.

13. Oram, ed., 545, lines 508–15.

14. Thomas H. Cain, *Praise in The Faerie Queene* (Lincoln: University of Nebraska Press, 1978), 125.

15. Spenser's most skeptical statement towards the British legends is in the Public Record Office manuscript of the *View*; see *Spenser's Prose Works*, ed. Rudolf Gottfried in *The Works of Edmund Spenser: A Variorum Edition*, ed. Edwin Greenlaw et al., 11 vols. (Baltimore: Johns Hopkins University Press, 1932–57), XI, 82n, 85–6n. All references to the *View* are taken from this edition (hereafter cited parenthetically as *Prose*).

16. *The Faerie Queene*, ed. A. C. Hamilton, 2nd edn (London: Longman, 2001). All references to the poem are taken from this edition and cited parenthetically in the text. See Woodcock, *Fairy in The Faerie Queene: Renaissance Elf-Fashioning and Elizabethan Myth-making* (Aldershot: Ashgate, 2004), 133–34. On Spenser's use of similar kinds of universal history, see Bart Van Es, *Spenser's Forms of History* (Oxford: Oxford University Press, 2002), 112–16.

17. *Prose*, 91, 93; Oram, ed., 392, line 149.

18. On Olaus's sourcing, see *Historia*, l–lv.

19. *Historia*, 8:32–33.

20. R. I. Page, "Lapland Sorcerors," *Saga-Book* XVI: 2–3 (1963–4): 215–32; Ernest J. Moyne, *Raising the Wind: The Legend of Lapland and Finland Wizards in Literature* (Newark: Prentice Hall, 1981). See also Seaton, 275–96; Frank Lestringant, "Une altérité venue du froid: démons et merveilles d'Olaus Magnus (1539–1555)," in Kathryn Banks and Philip Ford, eds., *Self and Other in Sixteenth-Century France: Proceedings of the Seventh Cambridge French Renaissance Colloquium 7–9 July 2001* (Cambridge: Cambridge University Press, 2004), 45–70. Shakespeare alludes to the ability to control the winds magically in *Macbeth*, I.3, lines 10–16.

21. Lawrence Normand and Gareth Roberts, *Witchcraft in Early Modern Scotland: James VI's* Daemonology *and the Northern Berwick Witches* (Exeter: Exeter University Press, 2000), 414.

22. Olaus returns to this theme when he augments and publishes his brother's ecclesiastical history, *Historia pontificum metropolitanae ecclesiae Upsaliensis* (Rome, 1557), to include Johannes's own role in the regenerative process.

23. Johannesson, 188.

24. Seaton, 279.

25. *Historia*, lxx–lxxi. The English epitome was translated by one "J. S." as *A Compendious History of the Goths, Swedes, and Vandals, and Other Northern Nations* (London, 1658).

26. Torquato Tasso uses it for his play *Il re Torrismondo* (1587), see Louise George Clubb, "The Arts of Genre: *Torrismondo* and *Hamlet*," *English Literary History* 47 (1980): 657–69. Olaus makes a single passing reference to Prince Hamlet that is entirely derived from Saxo (*Historia*, 22:2), though Julie Maxwell recently argued

that Shakespeare may have drawn upon a version of the Amleth story found in Johannes Magnus's *Historia de omnibus Gothorum Sveonumque regibus* that was appended to Olaus's *Historia* in the 1567 edition posthumously printed in Basle as *Historia Olai Magni*; see "Counter-Reformation Versions of Saxo: A New Source for *Hamlet?*" *Renaissance Quarterly* 57 (2004): 518–60. Thomas Nashe, in *Terrors of the Night* (1594), alludes to how winds may be bought and sold in northern lands enclosed within three knots tied in a magic thread, another of the "delusions" identified by Olaus of the pagan Finns (3:16); see Nashe, *Works*, ed. R. B. McKerrow, rev. ed. F. P. Wilson, 5 vols. (Oxford: Blackwell, 1958–66), I, 359–60.

27.   Seaton, 206. See, however, David Powel, *The Historie of Cambria, now called Wales* (London, 1584), sig. E4^r, who directs readers to Olaus and Johannes Magnus for further information on Swedish history when discussing Scandinavian incursions in Britain during the ninth century.

28.   Stern, 229. Harvey's copy is now in a private collection.

29.   Madeleine Doran, "On Elizabethan 'Credulity': With Some Questions Concerning the Use of the Marvelous in Literature," *Journal of the History of Ideas* 1 (1940): 174–75. Spenser also drew here upon the works of Conrad Gesner and Sebastian Muenster; see Seaton, 328; Cathleen Hoeniger, "natural history," in *Spenser Encyclopedia*, 501. Maxwell, 548, notes that Muenster incorporated some of Olaus's unpublished material about the north into his *Cosmographia universalis* (1544).

30.   John E. Hankins, "Milton and Olaus Magnus," in D. Cameron Allen, ed., *Studies in Honor of T. W. Baldwin* (Urbana: University of Illinois Press, 1958), 205–07, 210, reveals that Milton owned and used the 1558 epitome edition of Olaus.

31.   Michael West, "Spenser, Everard Digby, and the Renaissance Art of Swimming," *Renaissance Quarterly* 26 (1973): 20–21.

32.   Michael West, "Spenser's Art of War: Chivalric Allegory, Military Technology, and the Elizabethan Mock-Heroic Sensibility," *Renaissance Quarterly* 41 (1988): 672–73. Spenser, like Olaus, may also be drawing upon descriptions of Sisera's chariots from Judges 4:1–3.

33.   See also Olaus, Historia, 8:10; David Haley, "Gothic Armaments and King Hamlet's Poleaxe," *Shakespeare Quarterly* 29 (1978): 410–11. Haley goes on to construct a convincing philological argument (in part using Olaus and Spenser) asserting that "sleaded pollax" in the First Quarto of *Hamlet*, I.i, line 63, should read "studded poleaxe." See also Maxwell, 538–43.

34.   Thomas Herron, "The Spanish Armada, Ireland, and Spenser's *The Faerie Queene*," *New Hibernia Review* 6 (2002): 95–97.

35.   See Saxo Grammaticus, *The History of the Danes, Books I–IX*, ed. Hilda Ellis Davidson, trans. Peter Foote, 2 vols in 1. (Cambridge: Brewer, 1996), I, 69–75.

36.   Willy Maley, *Salvaging Spenser: Colonialism, Culture and Identity* (Basingstoke: Macmillan, 1997), 139–42, discusses the Scot-Scyth identification.

37.   Andrew Hadfield, "British and Scythian: Tudor Representations of Irish Origins," *Irish Historical Studies* 28 (1993): 395–98; Richard McCabe, *Spenser's Monstrous Regiment: Elizabethan Ireland and the Poetics of Difference* (Oxford: Oxford University Press, 2002), 144–45. See also Roland Smith, "Spenser, Holinshed, and the *Leabhar Gabhála*," *Journal of English and Germanic Philology* 43 (1944): 390–401. On Spenser's difficulty in distancing British claims of dominion in Ireland from those of Spain,

67. Coughlan, 55–56.
68. *Historia*, xxxviii.
69. See Hodgen, 162–206.
70. Herron, 96–97.
71. On reading in Spenser, see Anne Ferry, *The Art of Naming* (Chicago: University of Chicago Press, 1988), chapter 1.

JUDITH H. ANDERSON

Patience and Passion in Shakespeare and Milton

The ancient topos *agere et pati*, to do and to suffer, to aggress and to be patient, is conceptually a catalyst in major plays by Shakespeare and major poetic writings by Milton. Patience itself, as a combination of passion and passivity, has a transformative role in *King Lear* and a critical role in *Othello*, as well. In Milton's poems after his loss of sight, however, the traditional binarism of patient endurance and assertive action fully yields to an original, unifying vision. This is true in his Sonnet XIX: "When I consider how my light is spent," in *Paradise Lost*, and in *Paradise Regained*, both of which oppose war and violence. In *Samson Agonistes*, however, Milton starkly reasserts the realities of history and personal situation. These make a difference that challenges and modifies his earlier unifying vision, while not entirely rejecting it.

*I*N *KING LEAR* AND *OTHELLO*, WHEN Shakespeare's anguished protagonists memorably invoke patience, they do so with an unwitting irony that plays on the linguistic genealogy of this virtue, on its combination of passion and passivity. More than a half century later, Milton's poetry recalls the centrality and complexity of Shakespeare's engagement with patience but goes beyond it to render the traditional significance of this virtue dynamic and revisionary. In the unifying insight of the blind poet, patience becomes action, rather than simply giving way to action or being replaced by it. The traditional binarism of passive endurance and assertive action yields to a vision that is both unifying and originally nuanced. This is true at

Spenser Studies: A Renaissance Poetry Annual, Volume XXI, Copyright © 2006 by AMS Press, Inc. All rights reserved.

courageous. But simply put, would medieval and early modern readers have considered the Passion of Jesus feminine? I honestly think
this jury still out.

Turning to patience in Shakespeare's dramas, my purpose is not
exhaustively to survey the topos *agere et pati* but to select representative passages that are particularly suggestive in relation to Milton's
later poetry, that written after the loss of his eyesight. Patience in
Shakespeare's *Winter's Tale*, while monumental, for example, is not
to my purpose as immediately and fully pertinent as is the relation
of patience to action in *King Lear* and *Othello*.[5] In *King Lear*, on the
threshold of Lear's impetuous withdrawal into the storm, his pivotal
speech "O, reason not the need!" moves from an effort to justify a
need of the external trappings of status to the sudden recognition
that his true need is internal: what he needs is patience, understood
as emotional control, endurance, and even penitential suffering, although this last meaning is far from his fully conscious admission
(II.iv.264). His recognition is partial and momentary, almost immediately giving way to self-pity, anger, and irrational futility. Toward
the end of this speech, Lear talks mainly to himself, and his only
choice of action has been reduced to not weeping. Where earlier he
pleaded, "O, let me not be mad, not mad, sweet heaven . . . Keep
me in temper, I would not be mad," now he ends his speech with
the recognition, "O Fool, I shall go mad" (I.v.46–47, II.iv.286). His
statement is at once declarative and promissory. That is, he seems to
welcome the madness, to let it take him. His need of patience has
passed into passion, imminently to be understood as the wrenching
excess and anguish of the raging storm on the blasted heath.

In some sense, *King Lear* is Shakespeare's passion play, and what
impels the old king into its central act begins with his half-compre-
hended outcry "patience, patience I need!" (II.iv.271). What is significant here for Milton's use of the same topos is the proximity,
perhaps the continuity, of patience and action, *pati et agere*. In this
scene, sufferance and passion are not merely successive, although they
are so purely in terms of plot. In a more interpretative, more metadra-
matic sense, they are continuous, *beginning* to blend together. Lear's
desired but unachieved sufferance in the speech becomes instead his
passion, or suffering, on the heath. Yet there is still succession here,
rather than union, and it is impulsive rather than fully conscious
and deliberate.

In *Othello*, patience plays a less central, transformative role than in
King Lear, but this word occurs with remarkable verbal frequency
throughout the play, and it is significantly featured in Othello's tormented and crucial speech during his only extensive interview with

Desdemona alone before the scene of her murder. Othello first invokes patience as an antidote to the emotions attendant on his pain, wounded pride, and humiliation at Desdemona's imagined infidelity. Seeming to allude to biblical Job and speaking primarily, if not exclusively, to and for himself, he declares that he would have found a drop of patience had he only to deal with the raining of "sores and shames" on his "bare head" or with hopeless captivity or, in an image of submersion, with poverty up to his very lips. He adds that he could even have borne fixation as a figure of public scorn and continues,

> But there, where I have garner'd up my heart,
> Where either I must live or bear no life;
> The fountain from the which my current runs
> Or else dries up: to be discarded thence!
> Or keep it as a cestern for foul toads
> To knot and gender in! Turn thy complexion there,
> Patience, thou young and rose-lipp'd cherubin—
> Ay, here look, grim as hell!
>
> (IV.ii.47–64)

By personifying Patience, Othello enacts the erotically and pathologically charged internal debate he is conducting with himself about whether to suffer Desdemona's supposed offense or to avenge it. On the one hand, personification serves to externalize and distance patience and, on the other, to make his interior debate more real to him. His feelings are conflicted to the extent that he still needs to justify his merciless plan to himself—irrevocably to tell himself that Patience herself looks grim, in effect assenting to vengeance. Patience, distractingly young and rose-lipped, is required to become fiendishly fierce and merciless, a self-canceling perversion, or turning, of this virtue (not to mention Desdemona) into its opposite vice *Ira*, traditionally, as here, associated both with rage and the devil. In Othello's monologue, female virtue and male devil, inside and outside, restraint and passion, Desdemona and Othello irrationally coalesce. Othello's labial obsession, recalling his earlier outcry—"Pish! Noses, ears, and lips"—further intimates his disintegrating, dismembering, dehumanizing vision (IV.i.42). As patience turns into destructive passion, his speech verges on the surreal. Othello's speech is the negative obverse of Lear's impetuous flight into the storm, but it is again a conjoining of patience with passion that exposes their emotional and conceptual linkage, if only making them one perversely.

"sensefull"—at once sensually-oriented and at least superficially sensi-
ble—in ways that link it to the honeyed words of Spenser's Despair.[13]
The poet's harsh criticisms of Belial's sensefullness, timorousness, and
sloth, and thus inclusively to his mere passivity—"Thus *sitting*, thus
consulting, . . . [though] in *Arms*"—appropriately lead us to expect
values at once more active *and* more interior in what the poem finally
endorses (164: my emphasis).

Another, essentially relevant passage in *Paradise Lost* highlights the
action of standing, simultaneously combining it with the endurance
and passivity that belong to patience. In this instance I conceive
passivity in the grammatical sense of *pati* in which the subject is acted
upon, rather than being the initiator of action. This passage occurs
during the War in Heaven when the angels wearing God's armor
take the hits of the diabolical cannon. The result is that

> none on their feet might *stand*,
> Though *standing* else as Rocks, but down they fell
> By thousands, Angel on Arch-Angel rowl'd;
> The sooner for their Arms.
>
> (VI.592–95; my emphasis)

The armor is materially confining, and because of it the interiorly
unfallen Angels physically fall, in effect illustrating the impact of Satanic invention on matter. Standing here is also clearly active and
agential, *agere*, and, indeed, it is significantly *opposed* to armor that is
martial like the armor in Ephesians earlier cited.[14] Standing is at once
interior *and* an action. The verb and its essence, act and being, are
one.

Paradise Regained, of course, is in good part a study of patience that
is modeled on the Book of Job, as Barbara Lewalski has demonstrated.[15] I want only to look at the climax of the poem, the Son's
stand on the highest pinnacle of the Temple, where Satan scornfully
challenges him: "There stand, if thou wilt stand; to stand upright /
Will ask thee skill" (IV.551–52). The taunting continues, "Now
shew thy Progeny; if not to stand, / Cast thyself down; safely if Son
of God," and it concludes with the devil's quoting scripture to evidence God's care for his Son. The climax comes in the Son's reply
and its immediate sequel: "To whom thus Jesus: also it is written, /
Tempt not the Lord thy God, he said and stood. / But Satan smitten
with amazement fell . . . " (561–63). Throughout, Satan has in mind
a stance that is physical, and his punning use of words with moral,
ethical, and spiritual valence in Milton's lexicon, such as "upright"

or "stand" itself, characteristically and reductively twists their meaning. The Son's response atop the pinnacle restores a proper *balance*
(to invoke an appropriate pun) between physical and spiritual, outer
and inner, and action and passion. More exactly, it achieves a balanced synthesis of them. His reply is an imperative, yet one dependent on scripture: "Tempt not." More inclusively, his response is at
once a physical and a spiritual act, standing, as well as a speech-act;
it is potent but motionless, conclusive but unaggressive, at once simple and climactic.[16] It leads to Satan's self-destructive fall, which in
contrast is neither freely active nor purely passive. Where Satan is
neither in control nor not, the Son is both free subject and patient
object. The Son's ambiguous—literally doubled—invocation of "the
Lord thy God," at once grasps the potency of his own identity and
accepts the suffering, the passive endurance, of his Passion.

While admiring the thoughtful detail of Fish's recent reading of
the pinnacle scene, once again I wish to address it in the interest
of clarification and distinction, since my own understanding, while
different ("imperative," "potent," "climactic," above), might on
quick reading seem similar. I see Milton's Son as a very human figure,
as well as one divine, and his moment atop the temple as a realization
at once internal and external, a kind of focusing *on and in* his figure
of the sort of doubled projection found in Spenserian allegory: the
narrative of Redcrosse and Sans Joy, Redcrosse and Orgoglio, Redcrosse and Despair. This is not merely a reiteration, a "jumping up
and down in one place" of the sort Fish envisions; it is a realization,
simultaneously subjective *and* objective, interior and embodied, and
one not achieved before in this way or to this climactic extent.[17]

Analyzing the "Nativity Ode," Fish observes that the pagan deities
are vanquished "not because of something the babe does (in the sense
called for in this poem), but because of something he is" (321).
Overlooking the parenthesis, which Fish's larger claims of consis-
tency similarly overlook, I want to focus on the questionable distinction for this divinity of doing and being. If the babe is God in some
derived yet truly agential sense, his *esse*, which is his being, is itself
an act. *Esse* is a verb, and it is also God's being, whether in traditional
philosophy or in the Bible: "I am who am." This is my point. The
options Fish offers the Son in the pinnacle scene are Satan's pernicious
alternatives, as earlier "the immolation of his own will" rather than
his freedom to obey, or not, the more traditional expectation in
Christology (336).[18] Specifically, these options are to stand upright
and prove he is divine, to fall and prove he is merely human, or to
cast himself down in a willful test of scripture (383). The third option
is absurd at this point, if not for a desperate Satan. The other two

personal, not general, application. The Philistine victims seem to have vanished from the "Holocaust" in the phoenix simile, and, with a more terrible irony than Milton could ever have imagined, Samson's tribesmen do not recognize themselves in the destruction. If they think themselves reborn in a worldly, tribal sense in Samson's sacrifice, they have failed adequately to associate themselves with its suffering. Instead, they translate and aestheticize it, along with Manoa's monumentalizing of Samson. The contrast between the perspective of the dragon–simile, which is that of the slaughterhouse, and that of the phoenix–simile, fundamentally lonely, worldly, and ironically distanced from the historical Redemption, sadly and fundamentally compromises the scope and character of Samson's heroism. To my mind, this is Samson's tragedy, and in Milton's play it is at once unflinching and wrenching.

While similarity of interior achievement signals essential value in *Paradise Regained* and *Samson*, outward expression and fully historical realization call that value radically in doubt.[21] Throughout the major poems, Milton presses at the relation of the great binaries, at whose base the immaterial realm—psyche, form, and figure—relates to flesh, matter, and history, or else fails to do so satisfactorily. Within his 1671 volume, in the historical figure of the god–man, this relation first gloriously satisfies, and thereafter in *Samson*, alive historically before Jesus but graphically, poetically, and Miltonically placed after him, it simply does not. At the outset of this essay, I referred to the unifying insight of the blind poet, in which patience truly becomes action. Milton's printed gesture in his last major poetic volume realistically qualifies this claim.[22] Not relinquishing the achievement of interior value a whit, this volume starkly reasserts the realities of history and personal situation within it. These make a real difference, which must be faced, confronted, and acknowledged.

Milton's volume of 1671, double insofar as it contains both *Paradise Regained* and Samson Agonistes, eerily recalls the split reference of Spenser's fifth and sixth books, as well as of his Mutability Cantos, even as Spenser's final statements recalled Chaucer's. Spenser's endings in the fifth and sixth books and the Cantos witness the difference between idealizing fiction and history: Arthur's triumph in Belge's land and Artegall's failure (or aborted efforts) in Irena's land and his subsequent pursuit by the Blatant Beast; Calidore's similarly artificial triumph and the poet's vulnerability to the same Beast; the lingering loveliness of this world within its renunciation at the end of the Cantos. In the multiple views, especially the epic comparisons, hence perspectives, at the end of *Samson*, we are offered only choices for reading, or interpreting, Samson's story, as we are in Spenser's final statements. In *Samson,* if we stop with the Chorus and Manoa, our choices are justifiable vengeance, traditional heroism, or tribal redemption, with the additional possibility of a typological dimension for the New Testament reader—all arguably positive, albeit with strongly ironic qualifications. But I doubt Milton does not expect us also to recognize the brutality with respect to "tame villatic Fowl" of Samson's final action, an action righteous within itself, criminal outside itself, and above all both severely and sympathetically compromised by comparison with the Son's achievement in *Paradise Regained.* Both Milton's other major poems, *Paradise Lost* and *Paradise Regained,* openly oppose war, militarism, and violence. I would not expect less of Milton in *Samson Agonistes,* particularly since I honestly suspect, as have others, that in the volume of 1671 he is measuring himself against Samson and the Son, at once as pertains to the period before 1660, and to its aftermath.

Indiana University

NOTES

1.   See *Anger's Past: The Social Uses of an Emotion in the Middle Ages,* ed. Barbara H. Rosenwein (Ithaca: Cornell University Press, 1998), esp. Rosenwein's introduction, 1–6 and conclusion, 233–47; Lester K. Little, "Anger in Monastic Curses," 9–35; and Gerd Althoff, "*Ira Regis*: Prolegomena to a History of Royal Anger," 59–74. Also, William V. Harris, *Restraining Rage: The Ideology of Anger Control in Classical Antiquity* (Cambridge: Harvard University Press, 2001).

2.   *Gender and Heroism in Early Modern English Literature* (Chicago: University of Chicago Press, 2002), xii; my next sentence is based on Rose's pages 89–90, 96–99. Thanks to Jennifer Vaught for calling Rose's argument to my attention.

3.   *The Riverside Shakespeare,* ed. G. Blakemore Evans et al., 2nd ed. (Boston: Houghton Mifflin, 1997): II.ii.550–87. Subsequent reference is to this edition of Shakespeare, unless otherwise noted.

4.   See Georgia Ronan Crampton, *The Condition of Creatures: Suffering and Action in Chaucer and Spenser* (New Haven: Yale University Press, 1974), chap. 1. Also William Lily, *A Shorte Introduction of Grammar* (New York: Scholars' Facsimiles and Reprints, 1943): "Verbum . . . esse aliquid, ageréue, aut pati significat" (C.ii.ʹ). I have elaborated on Crampton's binaries, adding Lily and extending act and potency to form and matter. For Crampton's conclusions regarding Spenser and Chaucer, which my first sentence in this paragraph invokes, see page 201. Her discussion of individual texts of both poets is inevitably more nuanced than her conclusion.

5.   Another example of monumental patience is to be found in Queen Katherine in *Henry VIII.* But even in such a comedy as *Twelfth Night* it makes an appearance

12.   Milton's connection of patience with fortitude is traditional, although its extent is not: e.g., see Etienne Gilson, *The Christian Philosophy of St. Thomas Aquinas* (New York: Random House, 1956), 285–95, esp. 294: "Like magnificence . . . [patience for Aquinas] is a secondary virtue attached to the principal virtue of fortitude. By fortitude, we hold firm against fear. By patience, we support grief." Milton identifies the two virtues more closely and values patience more highly.

13.   The pun occurs memorably in *The Faerie Queene*, VI.ix.26; for discussion of Melibee's use of it and its link to Spenser's Despair, see my *Growth of a Personal Voice: "Piers Plowman" and "The Faerie Queene"* (New Haven: Yale University Press, 1976), 178–79.

14.   Relevant annotation here ranges widely, though none has my particular focus: cf. Arnold Stein, *Answerable Style* (Minneapolis: University of Minnesota Press, 1953), 17–37; Catherine Gimelli Martin, *The Ruins of Allegory: "Paradise Lost" and the Metamorphosis of Epic Convention* (Durham: Duke University Press, 1998), 325 and chap. 5.

15.   Barbara Lewalski's entire discussion of *Paradise Regained* remains an indispensable point of reference: *Milton's Brief Epic: The Genre, Meaning, and Art of "Paradise Regained"* (Providence: Brown University Press, 1966). Cf. Silver, 26–44. In a provocative discussion of negative (apophatic) theology in *Paradise Regained,* Regina Schwartz challenges the emphasis on the unfolding or discovery of the Son's identity in the poem to be found in Lewalski's and many other subsequent readings. In contrast to the view I take, she considers the Son's role *radically passive:* "Redemption and *Paradise Regained,*" *Milton Studies* 42 (2002): 26–49, here esp. 38. Medieval studies of the psychology of Christ in the Hypostatic Union, not only those in the Dominican Tradition of Aquinas but those in the Franciscan tradition of Duns Scotus, both of whom Milton had read, make it unlikely that he did not think about the psychological relation of Jesus to the Godhead, disinclined as he might have been to speculate freely about it in prose. The humanity of Jesus within Milton's presumed subordinationism (or variant thereof) makes this consideration more likely. Anyone doubting it should look again at *Paradise Regained*, I.192, "Thought following thought," and even more at the metaphor in I.197–98, "O what a multitude of thoughts at once / Awakn'd in me *swarm*" (my emphasis). Milton appears willing to engage Christ's psychology here and to do so provocatively. For a persuasive consideration of Milton's acquaintance with Duns Scotus (though not specifically with his Christology), see John Peter Rumrich, *A New Preface to Paradise Lost* (Pittsburgh: University of Pittsburgh Press, 1987), 148–65.

16.   Cf. Silver, 28: "the words—'Tempt not the Lord thy God'—here express the value of attitude over action, the implied over the demonstrable, the groundlessness of faith over mythic spectacle." To my reading, this view is too binary, too much involved in the either/or that Jesus, Word made flesh, must finally surmount.

17.   For the quotation, see note 11.

18.   My terms attempt both to observe Milton's distinction between God and his Son and the very special relation between them. In *Christian Doctrine,* I.v, Milton concludes that "God imparted to the Son as much as he wished of the divine nature, and indeed of the divine substance also." He then adds, "do not take *substance* to mean total essence," thus at once connecting and distinguishing their natures in a

way that rejects traditional Trinitarianism: *Complete Prose Works of John Milton*, VI, ed. Maurice Kelley, trans. John Carey (New Haven: Yale University Press, 1973), 211. Milton's distinction limits the extent of the divine essence imparted but does not preclude its realization, its agency, its existential mode.

19.   Derek N. C. Wood affords a comprehensive review of approaches to *Samson Agonistes*: *"Exiled from Light": Divine Law, Morality, and Violence in Milton's "Samson Agonistes"* (Toronto: University of Toronto Press, 2001). Wood reads Samson as "the example not to be imitated" (191); his is "the tragedy of fallen humanity, of the stunted and darkened moral consciousness of the fallen human spirit" (164–65). My own view, as argued, is less negative. For another, highly provocative review of recent readings of *Samson,* see Feisal G. Mohamed, "Confronting Religious Violence: Milton's *Samson Agonistes,*" *PMLA* 120 (2005): 327–40. Mohamed argues especially against Fish's separation of the question of Samson's regeneration from his slaughter of the Philistines; instead, "Milton shows us a hero of faith achieving the saintly militarism ["spiritually justified militarism": 333] described by [Henry] Lawrence and [Henry] Vane" (336). For Mohamed, our facing the "religious extremism and political radicalism" evident at times in Milton's writing can lead us to "interrogate the coding of high Western culture as fundamentally rational and nonviolent" and the privileging of "the freedoms of the elect above those of the marginal" (337).

20.   Noting that Samson's head inclines in prayer or meditation immediately prior to his pulling down the pillars, Fish observes that Samson is unlikely to have vengeance in mind (420). With Fish, I see a split between Samson's interior state and the violence of his final action that is everywhere evident at the end of the play.

21.   Cf. Achsah Guibbory, *The Map of Time: Seventeenth-Century English Literature and Ideas of Pattern in History* (Urbana: University of Illinois Press, 1986), 203: "In *Samson Agonistes,* and indeed in all the major poems published late in Milton's life, only the individual actually fulfills the ideal of progress Milton had entertained for England."

22.   I have discounted the (re)publication of *Paradise Lost,* albeit in twelve books, in 1674, the year of Milton's death.

GLEANINGS

BARBARA BRUMBAUGH

Edgar's Wolves as "Romish" Wolves; John Bale, Before Sidney and Spenser

Both Philip Sidney and Edmund Spenser link comments on royal policies that eradicated wolves from England to remarks on allegorically "papist wolves. This brief article notes that several decades prior to Sidney or Spenser another ardent English Protestant, John Bale, directly connected references to these two varieties of wolves. The article also speculates that Bale's harshly negative assessment of King Edgar, the monarch usually credited with eliminating wolves from England, might illuminate *one* reason why Sidney, unlike Spenser, avoids explicitly recognizing Edgar's responsibility for freeing his land from these dangerous beasts. Finally, the article discusses Bale's negative treatment of Rome's legendary founders, Romulus and Remus, who were said to have been suckled by a she-wolf, to elucidate how this myth lent additional resonance to Protestant references to "papists" as wolves and to the Church of Rome as the Whore of Babylon.

*E*DMUND SPENSER AND—ACCORDING to an interpretation offered in a recent article[1]—Sir Philip Sidney combine references to monarchical policies that eliminated literal wolves from England and to allegorically "papist" wolves, although Spenser, like most contemporary historians but unlike Sidney, specifically credits the "Saxon" King Edgar with instituting the policies that freed England from the beasts.[2] Spenser's references appear in the "September" eclogue of his *Shepheardes Calendar*, while Sidney's, the recent rereading argues,

Spenser Studies: A Renaissance Poetry Annual, Volume XXI, Copyright © 2006 by AMS Press, Inc. All rights reserved.

occur during a discourse with which he entertained Philip Camerarius and other distinguished dinner companions in Nuremberg in
the Spring of 1577, when he was serving as an ambassador to Emperor
Rudolph II and other German princes for Queen Elizabeth. The
dinner tale, the article argues, refers allegorically to the removal of
"papist" clergy from England during the reigns of Henry VIII and
Edward VI, employing conventions and symbolism recurrent in Protestant hunting dialogues "to galvanize his audience's support for ac-
tivist Protestant political policies."[3] The article does not, however,
note any examples of Protestants prior to Sidney and Spenser who
connect the two varieties of wolves.

Several decades before either Sidney or Spenser, though, John
Bale, considered by some "the most influential English Protestant
author of his time,"[4] noted Edgar's policies leading to the extermination of wolves in Wales, then, in the sentence immediately following,
referred to the allegorical variety of the animals. The comments appear (in a context discussed below) in *The Actes of English Votaryes*,
Bale's "*chronique scandaleuse*" of English monasticism."[5] In addition to
providing an early precedent of a Protestant writer who links references to the elimination of literal wolves from England or Wales to
"papist" wolves, Bale's treatment of King Edgar *might* shed light
upon an *additional* reason why Sidney avoided explicitly crediting
that Saxon king with freeing England from wolves, although the
rationale suggested in the previous article (wanting to prompt his
audience to apply the dinner tale to contemporary circumstances)
still seems the most immediately pertinent, especially since Sidney
avoids direct references not only to Edgar himself but also to any
specific dates.

Bale's overall treatment of King Edgar is extremely negative. According to Bale, "the Chronicles reporte" that this Saxon king "was
ever a great whore master and a Tyraunte" (K6ᵛ).[6] Bale faults King
Edgar for allowing himself to be manipulated and controlled by Dunstan, archbishop of Canterbury, whom Bale castigates at length for
having "had oft times much a do with devils and with women," for
tyrannizing over a series of English kings, and for being "the first
that in this realm compelled" monks and nuns "to vow chastity and
to kepe claustrale obedience, against the fre doctrine of Saint paul"
(J4ᵛ, K5ʳ). Bale relates that King Edgar had "had a do wyth a yong
maid called Wilfrith" (K6ᵛ), who—Dunstan claimed to Edgar—"was
a professed Nonne," although, according to Bale, "the Chronicles
all agre . . . was no Nonne, but a wench sojornant in" the nunery of
Wilfrith (K7ᵛ, K6ᵛ). As punishment for his relations with Wilfrith,
Dunstan sentenced Edgar to seven years of penance, during which

time he was deprived of his crown, and required him to construct "the great nondrye of Shaftesbury" and twelve monasteries and to agree to "the utter condempnation of priestes mariage through out al hys realme" (K6ᵛ). According to Bale, Dunstan's "victory" caused priests in England to be expelled "by hepes from the cathedrall churches and colledges with theyr wives and children," to be replaced by monks, who would display "prodigious lechery" (K8ʳ).

By the time that he had completed the seven years of penance required by Dunstan, King Edgar, in Bale's interpretation, had "bec[o]me altogether the dum image of the beast" prophesied in Revelation 13 (L1ᵛ).[7] Thus, at the instigation of church officials, Edgar in 969 convened a general council in London that "fully enacted, and established for a law ever to endure, that al canons of cathedral churches, colligeners, persones, Curates, vicars, priests, deacons, subdeacons shuld ether live chast, that is to say, become Sodomites . . . or else be suspended from al spiritual jurisdiction" (L1ᵛ-L2ʳ). Bale therefore condemns King Edgar not only for failings that would have been regarded as marks of bad kingship by theorists from a broad range of time periods and religious leanings—for example, tyranny and moral laxity, as well as "sorcery" and "[n]ecromancye" (J4ᵛ)—but also for characteristics that would have made him especially unattractive to ardent early Protestants—such as allowing himself to be subjugated by and subservient to the papacy and other agents of the Church of Rome[8] and, consequently, promoting the spread of monasticism and, of particular importance to Bale, prohibiting marriage for priests and other church incumbents.[9]

Bale acknowledges that King Edgar, by requiring a tribute of 300 wolves per year from Wales, "destroyed al the wolves in that land" (L3ʳ⁻ᵛ). Yet because Edgar had allowed himself to be dominated by Dunstan and the papacy, Bale immediately contrasts the king's extermination of the literal wolves with his fostering of the allegorically "papist" wolves of the Protestant hunting dialogues (and of the narratives by Sidney and Spenser referred to above):

> But within his own land, the fearce gredye wolves that devoured Christes flock. Act xx. and the wilye foxes that destroyed the swete vineyards of the Lord. Cant. 2. he left untouched yea, rather he set them up, maintaind them, and fed them at hys owne table with most wicked Jesebel. 3. Re. 18. [?I Kings 18:3–4] for in his time they obtain more than xl great monasteries (L3ᵛ).[10]

Although I am certainly not making a source argument, and Bale's *Actes* had, at any rate, been in print for decades before Sidney's ambassadorial tale, it is interesting to recall that the historian William Whitlock[11] (*c.* 1520–1584) supposedly claimed that Philip's father, Sir Henry Sidney, gained possession of many of the manuscripts and books that Bale left behind in Ireland when he was forced to flee the land to begin his second exile shortly after Mary Tudor's accession to the throne in 1553.[12]

In *The Actes of English Votaryes* Bale mentions another connection between Rome (and by extension the Church of Rome) and wolves that lent added resonance to Protestant designations of "papists" as wolves and of the Church of Rome as the Whore of Bablylon. Rome's founders, the "bloudy bretherne" Romulus and Remus, according to traditional accounts (as Bale dismissively observes "[a]fter the mindes of Virgil, Ovid, and such other fabulouse Poetes"), of course, "receyved their fyrst nurryshment of a she wolffe." For Bale, the twins' being suckled by a she-wolf aptly signifies "the wonderfull tyranny whiche should folowe in that great cytie Rome" (Part 2, A3[r-v]).

Bale further associates Rome with both wolves and "whoredom" by referring to an alternate legend about Romulus and Remus's upbringing. Although Bale does not cite him, Livy observes that the alternate, historicizing account was intended to present a "rational" explanation for the origins of the legends of the brothers' being suckled by a wolf. The rationalizing account relies upon the fact that the Roman word *lupa* can mean either she-wolf or prostitute.[13] According to Livy's version of this legend, Faustulus, "chief herdsman" of the king of Alba, after finding the baby brothers being licked by a wolf, took them to his sheepfold to be raised by his wife, Larentia. Thus, some "fancy that the shepherds used to call Larentia 'She-wolf' because of her sexual promiscuity and that this was how the miraculous tale originated."[14] Bale's differing version of an alternative, rationalizing account of the brothers' nurturing associates not only Rome but also the papacy with whoredom (and with Augustine's City of Man) and well illustrates his harshly negative view of the city and its legendary founders:

Other authours reporte, that they were firste nurced of an harlot called *Lupa*, notte farre from the floude of Tiber, where as the Romyshe Pope holdeth nowe his palace, of whome all brothell houses, stewes, or places where such filthynesse is wrought, have theyr names, and are called to this hour *Lupanaria.* Romulus thus preserved by a thefe called *Faustulus*, nurryshed by a

wolfe, and broughte up by an whore, gyven also of hym selfe
to outragyouse lechery, covetyse, and ambycyon, became suche
a traytour to hys owne stocke, as in the ende most cruelly slew
hys naturall brother Remus, to establyshe hys greate buylded
cytie in the wyckednesse of cursed Cayn.

(Part Two, A3ᵛ)

Bale additionally claims that Rome's founders "had an whore to their
mother," Rhea Ilia, who, after becoming pregnant while serving as
a Vestal virgin, alleged that the boys were sired by the god Mars.[15]
According to Bale, Rhea Ilia, as "a professed nonne to Venus, committed whoredome both ways, that is to say, both in soule and in
body," for she both "served the ydolles" and, while "undre the vowe
of chastite [,] . . . dallyed besydes in the darke" (Part Two, A3ʳ).

For Bale, the dual meanings of *lupa* germanely signified the spiritual "whoredom" of Romish "wolves," whether "papist" or
"pagan."

Auburn University

NOTES

1.   Barbara Brumbaugh, " 'Under the Pretty Tales of Wolves and Sheep': Sidney's
Ambassadorial Table Talk and Protestant Hunting Dialogues," *Spenser Studies* XVI
(2000): 273–90. A very useful historical account of the "biblical and ecclesiastical
pastoral" imagery underlying both Sidney and Spenser's tales and the Protestant
hunting dialogues is Patrick Collinson's "Shepherds, Sheepdogs, and Hirelings: The
Pastoral Ministry in Post-Reformation England," in W. J. Sheils and Diana Wood,
eds., *The Ministry: Clerical and Lay*, Studies in Church History 26 (Oxford: Basil
Blackwell, 1989), 185–220; quotation from 185. The article on Sidney's "table talk"
notes Sidney's praise in *Leicester's Commonwealth* of his uncle Leicester as a "valian[t]
do[g]," a usage that demonstrates "Sidney's undoubted familiarity with the dog
metaphor for those entrusted with protecting the 'sheep' of the congregation from
the 'wolves' that threaten their safety, as well as the fact that the metaphor need not
be negative when the dogs are not 'dumb' " (Brumbaugh, 281). The article does
not, however, mention that Leicester represented himself as a dog reluctantly leaving
off guarding sheep on a medal he had issued to commemorate his departure from
the Netherlands after Queen Elizabeth recalled him. The front of the medal portrays
Leicester's "bust and titles." The back depicts "a guard dog walking away from a
flock of sheep. Some watched him sorrowfully; others had their heads buried in the
grass. The legend runs *non gregem sed ingratos invitus desero*: 'I reluctantly leave not
the flock, but the ungrateful ones' " (Derek Wilson, *Sweet Robin: A Biography of*

Robert Dudley, Earl of Leicester 1533–1588 [1981; London: Allison & Bushby, 1997], 297. Photos of both sides of the medal appear as figures 8a and 8b on page 148 of Wilson's book.

2. Brumbaugh, 283.

3. Brumbaugh, 273. The article argues that Sidney may have deliberately avoided referring explicitly to King Edgar or to specific dates in order to increase the likelihood that fellow diners would interpret his references to the wise kingly policies that eliminated "wolves" from England in this allegorical sense.

4. John N. King, *English Reformation Literature: The Tudor Origins of the Protestant Tradition* (Princeton: Princeton University Press, 1982), 56. See the index to King's book for much helpful discussion of Bale's career and works. King (58–61) also describes and responds to Bale's contemporary reputation and influence among his Protestant admirers and his later notoriety as "Bilious Bale" (an epithet first assigned to him by Thomas Fuller), arguing that the "later hostility results, at least in part, from anachronistic application of the literary canons of succeeding generations" (60). Another work that cites many earlier studies on Bale and that offers "a more balanced look at what he achieved in his own lifetime, as well as his later impact" (137) is Peter Happé's *John Bale*, Twayne's English Authors Series 520 (New York: Twayne, 1996).

5. May McKisack, *Medieval History in the Tudor Age* (Oxford: Oxford University Press, 1971), 13. Although Bale originally projected four parts for this history of the English Church, he completed only Parts 1 and 2 (Happé, 52).

6. *The Actes of Englysh Votaryes* (1560; facsimile reprint, Amsterdam: Theatrum Orbis Terrarum; Norwood, NJ: Walter J. Johnson, 1979). Unless otherwise noted, citations (which are given parenthetically) are from Part 1 of this work. In quotations from the work, modernized usage has been adapted for i/j u/v and w, and contractions have been expanded.

7. Bale's comments on Rev. 13 in his full-length commentary on that biblical book elucidate his interpretation of the "dum image of the beast." In Rev. 13:11–12 a beast arises "out of the earth, which had two hornes like the Lambe, but he spake like the dragon. And he . . . caused the earth, and them which dwel therein, to worship the first beast, whose deadlie wounde was healed." The first beast, described in Rev. 13:1, "rise[s] out of the sea, having seven heads, and ten hornes. . . . ." One of these heads seems "as it *were* wounded to death, but his deadlie wounde was healed" (Rev. 13:3). In verse 14 the second beast commands the inhabitants of the earth "that they shulde make the image of the beast, which had the wounde of a sworde, & did live" (*The Geneva Bible* [1560; Madison: University of Wisconsin Press, 1969]). Bale labels the second beast a "figure . . . of all false prophets and ungodly preachers," especially, in his own time, "Mahomet's doctors" and the papacy and other officials of the Church of Rome, although his examples focus primarily upon the latter (*Image*, 436–39). Bale writes that "antichrist's prelates and preachers" (signified by the second beast) have always persuaded "earthly inhabitants, that they should make an image like unto [the first] beast: which is always to choose such an emperor with other worldly governors as shall be for their commodity. He must by the worldly people be compelled to take authority, sceptre, and crown at their hands, so sworn to maintain their fleshly liberties. He must also be fashioned

by their wicked doctrines . . . ; and where such an head ruler is constituted, there is his own image set up. . . . When such an image or idolous prince is thus . . . constituted by authority (his oath once made that he shall always defend them), he may in no wise speak but out of that spirit that their conjurors (confessors I should say) have put into him." Bale cites as examples the emperor Charles V in his own time and Nero, (whom he views as having been manipulated by the flattery and "subtle sleights of that spiritual sorcerer, Simon Magus" (*Image*, 442, 445).

8.   Having rejected the authority of the Church of Rome, Protestant Tudor monarchs aimed to maintain royal "authority over both church and state without the intercession of the pope or any other clerical intermediary" (John N. King, *Tudor Royal Iconography: Literature and Art in an Age of Religious Crisis* [Princeton: Princeton University Press, 1989], 56, 117). On contemporary literary and polemical works and visual images that promoted this position, see especially Chapter 3, "The Crown Versus the Tiara," 116–81, of King's *Tudor Royal Iconography*.

9.   Bale's negative evaluation of King Edgar was shared by at least one extremely influential English Protestant in Sidney's own time, John Foxe, who wrote that " . . . king Edgar, with Edward his base son, being seduced by Dunstan, Oswald, and other monkish clerks, was then a great author and fautor of much superstition, erecting as many monasteries as were Sundays in the year." Nevertheless, Foxe adds, "notwithstanding, this continued not long," for, soon after Edgar's death, King Ethelred and others "displaced the monks again, and restored the married priests to their old possessions and livings. Moreover, after that, . . . the Danes . . . overthrew those monkish foundations, as fast as king Edgar had set them up before" (*Acts and Monuments* [New York: AMS Press, 1965] 1:xxi).

10.   This passage appears in the 1546 (STC No. 1270, J2^v) and 1548 (STC No. 1271, J8^r) editions of *The Actes*.

11.   On Whitlock's career, see Ann J. Kettle, "Whitlocke, William (*c.* 1520–1584)," *Oxford Dictionary of National Biography*, Oxford University Press, 2004 (http://www.oxforddnb.com/view/article29318, accessed 22 April 2005).

12.   See McKisack, 19, and Happé, 18–23. According to McKisack, the allegation appears on "a note now among the Twayne papers in the possession of Corpus Christi College, Oxford" (19). The note's author claims to have been told by Whitlock that "Syr Henry Sidney had all Bales bokes in Ireland" (qtd. in McKisack, 19). According to Kettle, Whitlock reportedly provided "information about the dispersal of John Bale's library" to "his fellow antiquariann John Twyne." McKisack proceeds to observe that, although Sir Henry was an avid "student of antiquities," it would "see[m] strange" that, if Sidney had acquired most of Bale's books, Matthew Parker would not have been aware of the fact, since "he and Sidney were on friendly terms and in the habit of corresponding with one another on antiquarians topics." Thus, McKisack suggests, "Sidney may have had the books for a time only, while he was in Ireland" (19).

13.   I am very grateful to Anne Lake Prescott for suggesting to me in 1999, after " 'Under the Pretty Tales of Wolves and Sheep': Sidney's Ambassadorial Table Talk and Protestant Hunting Dialogues" was accepted by *Spenser Studies,* that I might want to mention in that article that the fact that Sidney's generation would have been familiar with the myth that Romulus was suckled by a she-wolf "lent extra

energy to Protestant cracks about Rome as a whore because one Roman slang term for a prostitute was 'lupa' (shewolf)." Unfortunately, because of a move and change of address, I did not receive these editorial suggestions in time to pursue this line of research before the final version of the earlier article was due; however, I am happy to be able to do so and to acknowledge my indebtedness to Professor Prescott at this time.

14.   Livy, *The Rise of Rome: Books One to Five*, trans. T. J. Luce (Oxford: Oxford University Press, 1998), Book 1, chapter 4, p. 8. Plutarch, in his Life of Romulus, offers a nearly identical explanation. *Plutarch's Lives*, vol. 1, trans. John Dryden, ed. Arthur Hugh Clough (New York: Modern Library, 2001), 27.

15.   St. Augustine explains that Romulus and Remus's supposedly being nursed by a she-wolf was used to help confirm that Rhea Ilia's twins were divinely begotten by Mars, "in that way honouring or excusing her adultery. . . . For they think this kind of beast belongs to Mars, so that the she-wolf is believed to have given her teats to the infants, because she knew they were the sons of Mars her lord. . . ." Augustine also acknowledges that "there are not wanting persons who say that" the twins were suckled by a harlot, explaining that *lupa* could mean both harlot and she-wolf. Yet Augustine himself does not entirely dismiss the more traditional legend, asking "what wonder" it would be if "to rebuke the king [Amulius, who had seized the throne from his brother (and Rhea's father), Numitor] who had cruelly ordered [Romulus and Remus] to be thrown into the water, God was pleased, after divinely delivering them from the water, to succour by means of a wild beast giving milk, these infants by whom so great a city was to be founded?" (*City of God*, trans. Marcus Dods [New York: Modern Library, 1993], Book 18, chapter 21, p. 627).

ANDREW ZURCHER

Spenser's Studied Archaism: The Case of "Mote"

For all the critical consensus that Spenser's poetic diction is archaic, artificial, often studded with dialect forms, orthographically knotty, and above all, difficult, we continue to lack a modern, scholarly reappraisal of this language. In the light of the last century's work in historical lexicography, a huge expansion in the available text base of early modern manuscript and printed materials, and comparable studies of other contemporary poets and playwrights, this gap in Spenser scholarship might be thought severe—especially considering that the only substantial academic accounts of Spenser's language, though now somewhat dated, queried whether his language was originally perceived to be as archaic, or as artificial, as has been supposed. This short, exemplary foray into Spenser's use of the modal auxiliary "mote" pilots, by way of introduction, some of the methods and (here, tentative) directions a more comprehensive study of Spenser's language might take on and take, suggesting that Spenser was studied, deliberate, and consistently engaged throughout his career in the choice of his archaic diction.

"MOTE" (USUALLY MEANING "MAY" or "must" in present and past constructions) is an archaic modal auxiliary much used in *The Faerie Queene*, and important to Spenser's overall attempt to construct a new-old lexis for a new-old kind of chivalric romance. This auxiliary does not occur, for example, in the works of Shakespeare or Jonson, and appears in only its limited, phrasal uses (as part of a conventional periphrastic subjunctive) in, for example, the poems

Spenser Studies: A Renaissance Poetry Annual, Volume XXI, Copyright © 2006 by AMS Press, Inc. All rights reserved.

of Skelton. Spenser exploits modal auxiliaries throughout *The Faerie Queene* to create prosodic flexibility and fluidity, and to achieve certain rhetorical effects (e.g., suspension, division, distribution) in the expression of verbal action. From a purely rhythmic perspective, the liberal use of monosyllabic auxiliaries such as "mote," its preterite "must," "will," "can," "may," "gan," and so on allows a poet to achieve and depart from metrical regularity as necessary, in particular facilitating the use of verbs with an initial weak syllable (*he smote* produces a fine regular iambic foot, but *he conceived* does not; here, as at *FQ* VI.iv.34.4, Spenser opts for *he gan . . . conceive*). The use of modal auxiliaries and other compound verb forms also enables Spenser to imitate rhetorical figures common in classical poetry, where the compound form of the verb, and particularly a compound negative, can be split or distributed across a phrase, line, or sentence. A typical example is the famous negative construction in *FQ* II.Pr.4, where Spenser warns the reader "to yield his sence to bee too blunt and bace / That n'ote without an hound fine footing trace." The heaping up of such monosyllabic auxiliaries also tends to give Spenser's verse a musicality characteristic of classical Greek, which enjoys the same kind of monosyllabic patterning in the fluid use of particles and enclitics.

Spenser's use of this particular auxiliary has usually been thought opportunistic and inconsistent, characteristic of a broadly loose and irregular use of probable-sounding words to "stuff out" his stanzas. As a case study in Spenser's deliberate archaism, though, "mote" provides a fairly representative example of Spenser's fidelity to his sources, as well as the ongoing refinement and standardization of his usage through his career. Careful attention to the spelling of original editions of *The Faerie Queene* also suggests that Spenser himself was probably not as cavalier and inconsistent with his orthography as modern editions might suggest, for variations in the appearance of this word in both positive and negative constructions seem to have more to do with compositorial confusion than with authorial laxity. In addressing the limited, and thus manageable, evidence of Spenser's use (and his compositors' setting) of the word "mote" in its variant spellings and both negative and positive constructions, this brief study offers some reflections both on what we think about Spenser's language, and how we might take a forensically linguistic approach to refining and extending that thought.

In orthographical terms, a first and obvious point is that "mote" hardly appears in *The Shepheardes Calender* or in the earlier, shorter poems, where the preferred form is "mought." "Mought" seems in Spenser's pastorals to embrace both possible and necessary modes in present and past tenses, and to accommodate the optative construction "so mought I [infinitive]." By contrast, the two early usages of "mote" in *The Shepheardes Calender* exclusively insist, judging by context, on the stronger modal sense of necessity and obligation.[1] Diggon pleads with Hobbinol in "September" not to inquire after his lost sheep, for

> Sike question ripeth up cause of newe woe,
> For one opened mote unfolde many moe.
>
> ("September," 13–14)

Similarly, "mote" is paired in a parallel "or . . . or . . . " construction in "October" with "must," in an example so neatly constructed it seems that the poet is advertising, by his own gloss, the modal force of the uncouth auxiliary:[2]

> And if that any buddes of Poesie,
> Yet of the old stocke gan to shoote agayne:
> Or it mens follies mote be forst to fayne,
> And rolle with rest in rymes of rybaudrye:
> Or as it sprong, it wither must agayne:
> Tom Piper makes us better melodie.
>
> ("October," 73–78)

The "old stocke"—words like "gan" and "mote"—are suitable for ribald poetry, where the low, largely dialect diction makes the persistence of old forms permissible, even decorous; such poems, like Skelton's *Elynour Rummynge* (where "mote" appears), are likely to be alliterative and scatalogical. In other generic contexts, as Cuddie laments, the "old stocke" "withers" as soon as it is "sprong." Spenser tailors his outlandish archaism to the subject, introducing and glossing an archaic modal auxiliary precisely in the moment that he apologizes for its presence in a serious complaint. The effects are to undermine the complaint, to illustrate it, and to explain it all at once; but a cognate effect, for us, is that this usage establishes that "mote" seemed a more unfamiliar form than "mought"—used elsewhere and liberally in *The Shepheardes Calender*—and that Spenser considered it worthy of note at this point in his career.

Spenser's position on the proper orthography of this word seems to have shifted over the next ten years. By the time the "Visions of Petrarch," which first appeared in the *Theatre for Worldlings* of 1569, appeared in *Complaints* in 1591, he had altered the fifth line of the first sonnet from "so faire as mought the greatest god delite" to "so faire as mote the greatest god delite"; given the archaic status of both "mought" and "mote" in the 1590s, this does not seem the kind of alteration a compositor would be competent or likely to make. Similarly, the third sonnet of the "Visions of Bellay" had changed from "so hie as mought an Archer reache with sight" (1569) to "so far as Archer might his leuel see." The first instalment of *The Faerie Queene*, printed in 1590, features "mought" in a handful of instances (see below), but "mote" abounds in both possible and necessary modes, in both tenses, and as part of the optative/imprecative formula, as at *FQ* II.xi.17: "Fayre mote he thee [i.e., "thrive"], the prowest and most gent,/That euer brandished bright steele on hye." In all, "mote" appears two hundred and sixty-eight times. Spenser seems to have made a decisive shift, from a preference in *The Shepheardes Calender* and the early *Theatre for Worldlings* for "mought," to a nearly exclusive use of "mote" in all of his works from 1590 onwards.

There are, as noted above, a handful of important exceptions to the abandonment of "mought." Their survival indicates that Spenser's compositors in 1590 were able to distinguish the forms in his manuscript, and that they probably replicated the distinctions they found there; but these few instances, for various reasons, do not suggest that Spenser continued to consider "mought" the equal of "mote." "Mought" appears on only five occasions in the whole of *The Faerie Queene*. The first instance occurs at I.i.42, where the visual play of two adjacent words would have given a poet revising his manuscript, or choosing from two possible forms for the auxiliary, considerable reason to choose the less unusual or deprecated form: "so sound he slept, that nought mought him awake." The other four instances (III.x.18, V.ix.34, VI.vii.50, and VI.viii.32) all supply "mought" at the end of a line, in rhyming position; here Spenser had obvious and pressing reasons, both visual and phonic, to prefer the deprecated form. Again, the single instance of "mought" in *Amoretti*, compared to seven instances of "mote," was clearly motivated by the need to create rhetorical and visual effects within the repeating patterns of the verse:

> Long-while I sought to what I might compare
> those powrefull eies, which lighten my dark spright,
> yet find I nought on earth to which I dare
> resemble th'ymage of their goodly light.
> Not to the Sun: for they doo shine by night;
> nor to the Moone: for they are changed neuer;
> nor to the Starres: for they haue purer sight;

nor to the fire: for they consume not euer;
Nor to the lightning: for they still perseuer;
    nor to the Diamond: for they are more tender;
    nor vnto Christall: for nought may them seuer;
    nor vnto glasse: such basenesse mought offend her;
Then to the Maker selfe they likest be,
whose light doth lighten all that here we see.

(Amoretti, 9)

The patterning and musicality of phonic repetition in this sonnet is, of course, one of its primary structuring elements—working complementarily to the carefully repeated, and occasionally slightly varied, syntax. Within the reflective and self-identifying sound-world of this poem—so much like beams of light bouncing pristinely and instantly off glittering surfaces—the repetition of "sought," "nought," and "mought" plays an important phonic and visual role. The seven instances of "mote" in other sonnets of the sequence (16.5, 33.4, 36.12, 42.11, 51.10, 55.10, 82.6) indicate that Spenser still, in the mid-1590s, considered this the dominant form.

What led the poet to change his mind about the form of this archaic auxiliary is obviously unknowable, but a few observations tending to support Spenser's deliberate, and perhaps almost academic, use of such archaic words and forms should be noted:

1. Of "mote" and "mought," "mote" is the older and purer form of the auxiliary, and is that attested in the standard Tudor editions of the works of Chaucer; "mought" seems to have arisen, through medial forms like "moht" and "moght," through a confusion with the preterite forms of "may" (especially "might"). Whether or not Spenser knew, or discovered, this historical priority of "mote," he certainly ended up preferring the earlier Chaucerian form.

2. The *OED* notes "in the archaistic use of Spenser and later writers ["mote"] was almost always used as a past tense, except in traditional phrases." This is not the case. *The Faerie Queene*, like most narrative prose and poetic works of its time (and ours), is narrated in the past tense, and thus those auxiliary verbs that occur within the narration are, naturally, in the past tense. Dialogue forms a comparatively small part of the total volume of the text, but "mote" occurs in the present tense within such inset speech, and, *pace* the *OED*, in other present contexts—such as the narrator's "asides" to the reader at the openings of cantos. Examples the first two books of the poem alone include *FQ* I.iii.29, I.xix.17, I.ix.32, II.i.29, II.i.30, II.i.33, II.iii.15, II.iii.33,

II.iii.44, II.iv.43, II.viii.25, II.viii.27, II.ix.2, II.ix.3, II.ix.9 (twice), II.ix.42, II.ix.45, II.ix.48, II.xi.17, and II.xii.85. While Spenser does use "mote" in the present tense in the context of traditional phrases, these usages hardly account for the bulk of the examples in the present tense.

3. Spenser's use of "mote," though not inflected (i.e., pl. *moten*) as in Gower, Chaucer, or Langland, seems however to be deployed with studious attention to particular models in his approved authors. The use of the archaic verb "thee" (meaning "to thrive," "to flourish") in the imprecative formula of II.xi.17 cited above, for example, like Spenser's use of the formula at II.i.33, echoes the standard Chaucerian form of the expression; see, for example, *Troilus and Criseyde*, line 341 ("But that is not the worste, as mote I thee"). That Spenser should associate the archaic verbal form with the auxiliary in a well-attested Chaucerian phrase suggests a deliberate and researched deployment of archaic diction. This pattern of the replication of specific models is supported by other celebrated instances of appropriation, both successful and unsuccessful, such as Spenser's famous (and possibly tongue-in-cheek) misprision, "derring do," from a Chaucerian phrase ambiguously deployed in Lydgate's *Troy book*.[3]

4. Nowhere is this studied usage more apparent than in the apparently neologistic contracted form of the negative, "ne mote," as "note" or, in some cases, "n'ote." This contraction occurs once in *The Shepheardes Calender* ("September," line 110), and on eighteen occasions in the whole of *The Faerie Queene*. Herbert Sugden, in *The Grammar of Spenser's* Faerie Queene, has suggested that "note" and "n'ote" are ambiguous forms of a contraction that represents both "ne mote" and "ne wit" (or "ne wote").[4] It may be that Sugden was working on the basis of the misleading *OED* account of "note," which describes it as the "negative form (with prefixed *ne*) of the 1st and 3rd person singular present of "wit" *v.* 1 . . . arising from misunderstanding of that word's meaning."[5] Sugden cites *FQ* I.xii.17 [*corr.* from Sugden's misprinted reference I.xii.7] as an example of Spenser's use of "note" for "ne wote," where Una's father addresses Redcrosse:

> Then sayd that royall Pere in sober wise;
> Deare Sonne, great beene the euils, which ye bore
> From first to last in your late enterprise,
> That I note, whether praise, or pitty more . . .
>
> (*FQ* I.xii.17.1–4)

Hamilton, following editors before him, glosses "note" in this instance as "know not." This replicates the misinterpretation of Oram et al. in their gloss to line 110 in "September" of *The Shepheardes Calender*, where Diggon tells Hobbinoll, "Other sayne, but how truely I note, / All for they holden shame of theyr cote." Here editors have made the same mistake of reading "note" as "ne wote," or "know not." It is important to recognize that, in both cases, it makes better sense to suppose that Spenser is using "note" in the same way that he uses it in seventeen other instances in *The Faerie Queene*, namely as a contraction of "ne mote" (which, in this expanded disyllabic form, occurs four times—at *FQ* VI.x.3 and three times at VI.x.7). In "September," Diggon contrasts what he may or must not say with what others do say—in a rhetorical move typical of Skelton's Collyn Clout, who lurks behind this entire passage—by understanding the infinitive "say," as the elided complement to "note." This is particularly elegant poetry because Diggon deliberately does not say "sayne," whereas "other sayne." Similarly, Una's father distributes the modal lack of possibility across the infinitives "praise" and "pity"; he does not disclaim knowing whether to praise or pity Redcrosse, but rather acknowledges that he praises and pities him in equal measure, unable to do the one more than the other.[6] In contracting "ne mote" to "note," Spenser was following the usage of John Lydgate, as in this passage from the "Septimum Gaudium" of *The Fyfftene Ioyes of Oure Lady*:

> Beseche that Lord my prayer to resceyue,
> And my requeste that he note Refuse,
> My meke complayntes of grace to conceyve . . .
>
> (*Fyfftene Ioyes*, lines 106–08)

It is worthy of note that neither Chaucer nor Lydgate ever contracts "ne wote" to "note." Nor should we set much stock in the minor variations in Spenser's spelling of the contraction ("note," "n'ote," and "no'te" all appear); compositors unfamiliar with this archaic contraction probably handled Spenser's manuscript (which likely read "n'ote" in each case, *pace OED* and the later misconstruals of Francis Quarles and Henry More) in irregular ways, and indeed the consistent patterns of "note," "n'ote," and "no'te" can, in the 1590 instalment of the poem when the contraction was novel, largely be traced to specific compositors.[7]

"Mote" in its positive and negative constructions is a mostly mono-syllabic modal auxiliary with a comparatively small footprint in Spenser's works as a whole, and the observations and arguments presented here may seem conjectural and fairly insignificant. On the other hand, until we have a systematic and exhaustive study of Spenser's diction and grammar, including an analysis of its debts to and departures from his models in Gower, Chaucer, Lydgate, Langland, and Skelton, and a comparative analysis of Spenser's linguistic innovations against, say, those of Shakespeare, we can only continue to advance our understanding of the contemporary effect of his language one small piece at a time. It would be impossible definitively to establish what contribution a given word might have made to the impressions of an average Elizabethan reader of Spenser's poetry; but at the very least we should continue to keep an open mind about the novelty and impact of the language, and the syntax, of *The Shepheardes Calender* and *The Faerie Queene*. Certain scholars have challenged the conventional wisdom of Spenser's pervasive archaism, noting that most of what we tend to think of today as "archaic" was actually fairly common in Spenser's own day,[8] and textual scholars have rightly insisted that much of the archaic-looking orthography so fiercely guarded by Spenser's twentieth-century editors is probably not his own.[9] And yet Spenser's consistent and often apparently studiously researched use of archaic forms of such core grammatical elements as modal auxiliaries suggests that he may have taken more labored care over his language than the new wisdom might suggest; and that in some cases compositorial practice seems to have conserved, rather than to have occluded, Spenser's own spellings. The shift from "mought" to "mote" between 1579 and 1590 seems to signal an intentional and historically accurate revision of an earlier preference, while the deployment of the contraction "note" for "ne mote" seems, despite the here misleading scholarship of *OED*, consistent and historically defensible. Spenser was aware that his language looked both grave and comic—Cuddie's comments on the "old stocke" in "October" of *The Shepheardes Calender* explictly acknowledge this duality—but his language would have seemed neither grave nor comic, but rather grotesque, unless he had got it right. More and more, I suspect, we mote find he did.

Queens' College, Cambridge

NOTES

1. Richard McCabe distinguishes between "mought" and "mote" in the glossary to his recent (1999) Penguin edition of Spenser's shorter poems. The distinction he draws—essentially that "mote" only supports the necessary mode, whereas "mought" accommodates both necessary and possible modes—seems to hold true for *The Shepheardes Calender*, but certainly does not apply to Spenser's writings after 1579—as will be evident from what follows.

2. Such exemplary usages of neologisms—where a new word is introduced and then glossed in an appositive definition or parallel clause—are typical in the humanist English writing of the period, and represent one of the main points of contention in those works of Elyot, Ascham, Wilson, and Cheke to which Spenser (or E.K.) coyly and cantankerously alludes in the "Epistle" to Gabriel Harvey fronting *The Shepheardes Calender*.

3. See *OED*, "derring do," *pseudo-archaism*.

4. See Herbert Sugden, *The Grammar of Spenser's* Faerie Queene (Philadelphia: Linguistic Society of America, 1936), 119, 121.

5. *See OED*, "note," *v.* 4.

6. It is worth noting, in this connection, that in the one other place in *The Faerie Queene* where Spenser uses the construction "ne wote / wote not . . . whether"—*FQ* I.xi.36—the verb in the subordinate phrase appears not in the infinitive, but in the subjunctive: "I wote not whether the revenging steele / Were hardned. . . ."

7. The sixteen instances of "note," "n'ote," and "no'te" in the 1590 edition of *The Faerie Queene* occur in a pattern that suggests the gradual agreement of two of the compositors on a standard, and the consistent (different) practice of a third. Yamashita et al., in *A Textual Companion to* The Faerie Queene *1590* (Tokyo: Kenyusha, 1993) set out a strong case for the collaboration of three compositors—X, Y, and Z—in the setting of the type for the 1590 edition of the poem (see 406–08). Compositor Y always set the word as "note" throughout the printing: at *FQ* III.-viii.23 (Kk4ᵛ), III.ix.24 (Ll4ᵛ), III.iii.50 (Ee5ʳ), and III.xii.26 (Oo5ʳ). Compositor X set the word first as "note" at I.xii.17 (M1ʳ), at the same time that Compositor Z was setting it, correctly, as "n'ote" at II.Pr.4 (M6ᵛ); thereafter Compositor Z set it as "note," following Compositor X's practice, at II.iv.13 (P7ʳ), but then switched at II.iv.4. (P6ʳ) and II.vii.39 (S6ᵛ) to "no'te." Compositor X followed suit, setting it as "no'te" at II.viii.43 (V1ʳ), which Z followed up with another "no'te" at II.xii.57 (Aa6ᵛ). By II.xii.78 (Bb1ʳ) X had reverted to "n'ote," but Z set it once more as "no'te" III.vi.40 (Hh6ʳ) before settling with X on "n'ote" for III.vii.42 (Ii6ᵛ). X then set it twice more as "n'ote" at III.x.6 (Mm1ᵛ) and III.x.15 (Mm3ʳ). (For an explanation of the sequence of printing the gatherings in the 1590 edition of the poem, upon which this analysis depends, see Andrew Zurcher, "Printing *The Faerie Queene* in 1590," *Studies in Bibliography*, forthcoming.) That compositors X and Z should have been confused by what they saw in Spenser's autograph is no surprise; Spenser tended to let his apostrophes drift rightwards across the line in his secretary

hand except when they were to appear before a minuscule "a" or before or after a majuscule (in which cases he needed to lift his pen), apparently because he added such apostrophes after completing the whole word, rather than intermissively during a pen-lift. A typical example of this occurs on the second page of Spenser's very fluent copy of the confession of John Nugent in February 1582 (NA/PRO SP 63/89/18), where "th'end" comes out looking instead like "the'nd." In writing "n'ote" Spenser would of course not have needed to lift the pen between the "n" and the "o," and thus would have added the apostrophe after completing the word.

   8.   See Bruce R. McElderry, Jr., "Archaism and Innovation in Spenser's Poetic Diction," *Publications of the Modern Language Association* 47 (1932): 144–70.

   9.   See, for example, the work of Hiroshi Yamashita et al., *A Textual Companion to* The Faerie Queene *1590*, 405–11.

Index